Careers in Multimedia
Roles and Resources

Hal Josephson

San Francisco State University,
College of Extended Learning

Trisha Gorman

Director, Strategic Relations
IDG/Integrated Media New Ventures

INTEGRATED MEDIA GROUP

I⊤P® An International Thomson Publishing Company

Belmont • Albany • Bonn • Boston • Cincinnati • Detroit • London • Madrid • Melbourne
Mexico City • New York • Paris • San Francisco • Singapore • Tokyo • Toronto • Washington

Multimedia Editor: Kathy Shields
Assistant Editor: Tamara Huggins
Production Editor: Deborah Cogan
Managing Designer: Stephen Rapley
Text and Cover Designer: Cynthia Decker
Cover Photographs: (top) Photo by MetaDesign;
    (bottom) Uniphoto Picture Agency
Print Buyer: Karen Hunt
Copy Editor: Donald Pharr
Compositor: Cynthia Decker
Printer: Malloy Lithographing

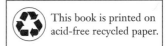 This book is printed on acid-free recycled paper.

Printed in the United States of America

For more information, contact:

Wadsworth Publishing Company
10 Davis Drive
Belmont, California 94002
USA

International Thomson Editores
Campos Eliseos 385, Piso 7
Col. Polanco
11560 México D.F. México

International Thomson Publishing Europe
Berkshire House 168-173
High Holborn
London, WC1V 7AA
England

International Thomson Publishing GmbH
Königswinterer Strasse 418
53227 Bonn
Germany

Thomas Nelson Australia
102 Dodds Street
South Melbourne 3205
Victoria, Australia

International Thomson Publishing Asia
221 Henderson Road
#05-10 Henderson Building
Singapore 0315

Nelson Canada
1120 Birchmount Road
Scarborough, Ontario
Canada M1K 5G4

International Thomson Publishing Japan
Hirakawacho Kyowa Building, 3F
2-2-1 Hirakawacho
Chiyoda-ku, Tokyo 102
Japan

1 2 3 4 5 6 7 8 9 10

Library of Congress Cataloging-in-Publication Data
Josephson, Hal, 1953—
    Careers in multimedia: roles and resources / Hal Josephson, Trisha Gorman.
        p. cm.
    Includes bibliographical references and index.
    ISBN: 0-534-26628-2 (paper)
    1. Multimedia systems—Vocational guidance. I. Gorman, Trisha, 1950– . II. Title.
QA76.575.J68   1995
006.6—dc20   95-30438

CONTENTS

To the Instructor ix

Chapter 1 **Introduction** 1
What Is Multimedia? 2
What Does Multimedia Look Like? 4
Who Are the Players? 6

Chapter 2 **Ten Things to Do to Get Started
in Multimedia** 9

1. Get a Computer with a CD-ROM Drive 10
2. Study the Product 10
3. Go On-Line 10
4. Attend Trade Shows and Join Professional Associations 12
5. Follow What's Happening in Multimedia in the Press 13
6. Find an Internship 13
7. Go Back to School 14
8. Become an Expert in Print 14
9. Put Your Knowledge to Work 14
10. Create a Prototype 15
    Employment Opportunities and Job Resources on the Internet 15

Chapter 3   **CD-ROM Production Roles:**
Interviews with Leading Players in
Multimedia Title Creation 21

Management Roles 22

Executive Producer/Multimedia Visionary:
Marc Canter, Canter Technology 22
Executive Producer:
Steve Linden, Living Books 28
Developer:
Jake Myrick, Big Top Productions 37
    Big Top Productions: The Educational Product Development Process .42
    Career Tips from the Founder of Fathom Pictures 43
Art Director:
Collette Michaud, LucasArts Entertainment 44
Project Manager:
Mark Satterlee, StudioGraphics 52
    The Project Manager Is the Internal Client 58

Production Roles 59
Computer Animator:
Bridget Erdmann, Living Books 59
Graphic Designer/Art Director:
Terry Irwin, MetaDesign 63
Information Designer/Interaction Designer:
Nathan Shedroff, Vivid Publishing 71
Instructional Designer:
Deborah Blank, Electronic Learning Facilitators 79
Picture Editor/Photo Researcher:
Ericka McConnell, Tom Nicholson Associates 93
Programmer:
Britt Peddie, MechADeus 97
Quality Assurance:
Marcia Watson, independent consultant 102
Sound Designer/Composer/Voice Talent:
Dave and Jennifer Evans, Digital Voodoo 106
Video Producer for Multimedia:
Bob Hone, Red Hill Studios 111
Interactive Scriptwriter/Marketing:
Sam McMillan, independent producer/freelance
interactive scriptwriter 117

Chapter 4   **Industry Perspectives** 123

Advertising:
Mike White, DDB Needham 124

Distribution:
Joanna Tamer, S.O.S. 133

Film, Video Games, On-Line:
Michael Backes, screenwriter and computer entrepreneur 139

Multimedia Law:
Mark F. Radcliffe, Gray Cary Ware & Freidenrich 150

     Services of a Multimedia Law Firm 162

Marketing:
Frank Sabella, SABROCO Interactive 163

     Multimedia Marketing Strategies for Multimedia Games:
     A Case Study 168

Publishing:
Randi Benton, Random House New Media 170

     Editor Jane Metcalfe on the Power of Knowing and Not Knowing 173

Recording Industry:
David Blaine, PolyGram Records 175

Recording Industry/Graphic Design:
David Karam, Post Tools 181

     Interactive Art at MOMA 184

     The Mint Museum Goes Digital 186

Executive Recruiter:
Joel Koenig, Russell Reynolds Associates 188

     Tips from Multimedia Recruiters, USA 192

Technology Licensing:
Trip Hawkins, The 3DO Company 194

Training:
Brandon Hall, *Multimedia Training* Newsletter 199

Chapter 5   **Case Study:**
The Judson Rosebush Company 205

A look at the process of CD-ROM production through the eyes, products, and commentary of New York–based developer Judson Rosebush, his staff, and associates.

The Players 207
Staff:
Matthew Schlanger, senior programmer and assistant director;
Michael Smethurst, director of technology and new projects;
Sandy Streim, director of business development

Associates:
Jay Moses, vice president for multimedia, and Dominic Schmitt,
CD-ROM Producer, Times Mirror; Joel Heller, executive
producer, CBS News

Freelancer:
Kathy Konkle, illustrator

The Process 217

Planning, Content 217

Writing 220

Production Heats Up 222

Visuals 223

Programming 225

Product Integration 227

Getting Product from Developer to Market 227

   Sample: Bug Reporting Form 229

Afterword: Writing for Games 231

Game/Story Designers:
Barbara Lanza and Walter Freitag 233

   Computer Games: What Does a Script Look Like? 243

   Titles Developed by the Judson Rosebush Company 246

Epilogue 247

Appendix I   **Glossary** 251

Appendix II   **Works Cited and Selected Bibliography** . . .259

Appendix III   **Conferences** 269

Appendix IV   **Professional Associations** 275

Appendix V   **Multimedia Educational Resources** 279

Index 285

TO THE INSTRUCTOR

Careers in Multimedia: Roles and Resources offers readers a practical breakdown of the kinds of jobs that are available in this amorphous new field we call "multimedia." Rather than dealing in generalities, the book explores a variety of roles in-depth by talking directly to the people who are shaping the interactive media industry, providing their perspectives in their own words. Yet the level of detail is not that of a how-to manual that, for newcomers, can obscure the forest for the trees. The interview approach addresses a potentially dry and arcane subject through anecdote and personal experience, resulting in a text that is extremely readable and accessible regardless of the reader's level of technical expertise. At the same time, because this book is based on the unique personal stories of those currently working in this industry—as opposed to armchair theorists—it is not too basic for those who have already had some specialty training.

This book is framed as a "career" book because of the enormous interest in the burgeoning field among students with a varying range of skills. Yet this should not limit the potential readership of this useful book.

Demand is increasing in the interactive marketplace for players who can hit the ground running. This compilation of diverse experiences is meant to stimulate and provide a basis for determining which new skills to acquire in order to become a part of the interactive multimedia future.

The book is organized into five core areas:

- An overview section comprising the first two chapters. Chapter 1 provides a broad introduction to the implications of multimedia technology and identifies the roles that will be explored in more d etail as the book progresses. For the practical minded, Chapter 2 provides ten straightforward suggestions about how to get started in multimedia.

- An identification of the job roles in multimedia production and interviews with representatives of each of those roles.
- Interviews with people from many of the industries that are already being influenced by multimedia technology—from advertising and film to law and corporate training.
- A case study of a successful multimedia developer illustrating the process by which a title comes into being, from concept to gold master. Interviews with staff members, which echo some of the roles we've already explored elsewhere in the book, are used to show how the various roles fit together into a team effort to create multimedia.
- The book closes with a resource section consisting of five appendices: a glossary and lists of conferences, professional associations, and reference materials recommended by the people interviewed in this book for those seeking a career in multimedia. The final appendix lists a sample of courses being offered around the country and abroad for those wishing to further their education more formally.

Features and Benefits of This Text

The interview approach. Most of the book presents information in the form of interviews with key players in the industry, providing more diverse points of view than would result from a narrative approach. These leading figures from the multimedia marketplace and production studios express their views, insights, and recommendations clearly and in their own words. Anecdotes deliver an experiential context to readers that makes the information more immediate.

Organization by role and industry. The book can be explored in a linear fashion or "dipped into" according to the reader's interest. The case study provided toward the end of the book allows those who have chosen to dip into some but not all of the role areas to tie the entire process together.

Creates a taxonomy of multimedia production. Identifying role names gives readers a concrete handle to help them start describing what kind of work they hope to find. Even if different developers use different terms, by using consistent role names the book gives readers a place to start. They will be primed to match job openings to their own skills and sound savvy in job interviews.

Fills a market need in books about multimedia. In recent years a number of books have appeared about this emerging field, some painting the picture in broad strokes, others providing detailed step-by-step technical instruction. This book falls somewhere in between by providing practical information without being bogged down in too fine a level of detail.

Selective resources. Instead of trying to compile a list of every book or magazine about multimedia that is available, the reader is immediately directed to high-quality resources available in an increasingly confusing field of contenders. We have included only the organizations, conferences, and references personally recommended by those interviewed.

Acknowledgments

Hal Josephson wishes to thank his wife, Cynthia Decker, for her fine design sense and for graciously deferring time together on weekends and evenings to help make this effort possible. I would also like to thank Dana Atchley, Richard Haukom, Eileen Newmark, Keith Metzger, and Richard Heale for their support and assistance throughout the extensive information sourcing, interviewee contact, and overall detail tracking. A special thank-you to Bernard, Shirley, and Louis for their never-ending encouragement to be the best that I can be. A hearty welcome to son Jaime who joined us in March with a big smile bringing me a new lightness of being. A special rememberence to Robert Bell who was a pioneer and inspiration to myself and many others launching careers in the world of multimedia. And, finally, a special round of kudos to my co-author, Trisha, who labored the hardest to pull this book together amidst the multiple interviews and extensive hours of writing and editing.

Trisha Gorman thanks her husband, Laurin Herr, for his steadfast encouragement and support. Appreciation goes to friends Trilby Schreiber and Jeffrey Nemerovski for their behind-the-scenes generosity, and to New York City multimedia consultants Marc Wahrman and Neil Ruggles for their kind assistance. Thanks also to Frederic de Wulf, Microsoft; Yee-Ping Wu, Magic Pen; Michael Pinto, Vanguard; and Robert Gehorsam, Scholastic, for their help in the development of this book.

We also wish to acknowledge the following individuals who gave useful feedback during preparation of our manuscript: Richard Josephson, St. Cloud State University; Thomas C. Richards, University of North Texas; and Rebecca H. Rutherford, Southern College of Technology.

CHAPTER 1

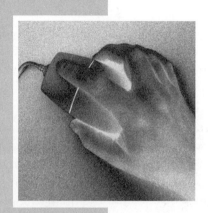

Introduction

More than three decades passed from the time the Lumière brothers pioneered moving pictures at the close of the nineteenth century until sound was added in the late 1920s, creating the "talkies." The path traveled from the personal computer in the early 1980s to the multimedia home computer has taken approximately a single decade. The leap from multimedia on a floppy disk to multimedia on CD-ROM and the Internet in an even shorter span of time has allowed simple text-with-picture click-and-point "slide shows" to increase in sophistication to the point that we are now able to view video and animation, and increasingly elegant navigation schemes.

Still, many observers are disappointed that images in the digital domain have yet to live up to the production values we have come to expect from film and television. They wonder if multimedia is a fad, or if it will ever come to be considered a respectable medium when compared to books, the cinema, or even magazines. Others think they don't want to become involved with multimedia because they are not "computer types." Everyone agrees that there is a lot of hype.

By the end of the decade, people will discover that multimedia has inculcated itself into their lives whether they wanted it to or not, or are even aware that it has. Schoolchildren will learn from it; business people will train on it; products will be marketed and purchased by using it. Students will write term papers based on research in computers located in foreign countries; workers will telecommute using modems to send their work—graphic and text—across town or across the country; grandmothers will receive e-mail photos of baby's first birthday; and kids will play intergalactic war games with friends whom they have never seen.

The argument about whether multimedia is inferior to books or movies is irrelevant. The technical problems associated with multimedia that give it a relatively primitive look today will be solved, and the storage issues will be addressed. The power of unifying media into an interchangeable digital format is an idea as compelling and inevitable as that of bartered goods being replaced by money. Multimedia will have as much, if not more, of an impact on our lives as silent pictures had on that long-ago audience on Boulevard des Capucines, who saw a clip of a train pulling into a station and cried out in utter amazement.

What Is Multimedia?

Multimedia has existed for years in the art and design worlds, as artists and illustrators combined physical objects with their artwork to make collages or assemblages. When combined with sound and light, these art forms were variously called mixed media, constructions, or audiovisual installation art. When linked with theatrics, multimedia events were called happenings or performance art.

In the world of education in the 1960s, teaching foreign language by using audiotapes along with traditional books in a language lab was hailed as an "audiovisual" revolution. In the 1970s and 1980s, the use of laser disks connected to computers gave teachers a valuable "media aid." As arcade and home video games became part of the collective cultural consciousness in recent years, the idea of interacting with media as opposed to having it passively wash over us has come to be seen as normal even before being given the name of "interactive multimedia."

Today, when people use the word *multimedia* they are referring to digital multimedia—the mixture of various media within a computer environment. This mixture involves the combination of picture, video, sound, and text. Picture includes photographs, animations, and illustrations; sound includes music, voice, and sound effects; text is used loosely to imply language and includes on-screen copy, voice-over narration, and spoken dialogue between human or animated characters.

Multimedia is still in its infancy, and much of it is, frankly, disappointing. Shallow multimedia leaves us feeling that we have come up against the edge of the information or game play too quickly. Badly executed multimedia uses few media elements, or uses them superficially, without considering whether the media element is the best one to tell a specific story or illustrate a particular point. A frequent pitfall is creating graphically stunning multimedia that isn't balanced by equally well-designed or well-thought-through content. High production values and a sense of aesthetics are critical to making successful multimedia, but great graphics alone, without being used in the service of something meaningful, can result in a sense of hollowness.

The richest, most satisfying multimedia uses many media elements as creatively possible. These elements are chosen with a guiding intelligence, not simply because the developer happens to have a picture or video on hand. Just as film makers do not include extraneous effects, behaviors, or visual details in their movies without considering the motivation for doing so, the first question to be asked before creating multimedia is *why?* The *raison d'etre* should be that the product results in a worthwhile and substantial experience that could not have been obtained through the use of other media, such as books or video.

Inherent to the concept of multimedia is the nonlinearity of the digital domain, which is the technical and intellectual underpinning of interactivity. Nonlinearity is the ability to jump from place to place within a universe of information, as compared to videotape, whose images can only be accessed in a linear manner, even in fast forward. Nonlinearity permits the user to create a personalized path through data, imparting a sense of control and self-direction that appears to enhance retention in learning situations, or pleasure and satisfaction when entertainment is the goal.

Although using as many media elements as possible enhances multimedia, it reaches even more of its potential to amuse or inform when designed for maximum interactivity. The best interactivity anticipates users' needs without being either confusing or predictable. It is challenging to create intuitive yet imaginative interactivity on a CD-ROM because the finiteness of megabytes on the disk means that no matter how much branching the designers have been able to invent, the user is ultimately restricted to predetermined paths. The seeming limitlessness of multimedia within the on-line world—limited only by one's own computer capacity, modem speed, and bandwidth of connection—holds the promise of media with a higher quotient of interactivity in the future.

Most definitions of multimedia focus simply on the idea of mixing media on a computer screen, leaving the impression that it is primarily a technological phenomenon. Yet multimedia, above all else, is a form of media for communication, art, and expression. Its best practitioners will be technically savvy artists, writers, film- and video-makers, illustrators, and graphic and fine artists. At the same time, technologists and programmers who also happen to be artists or writers will find a new way to engage all their talents more fully. Multimedia is not so much an extension of computer science as it is a new form of media/entertainment, bringing it more into the realm of communications, mass media, education, film, television, games, and popular culture than "MIS" (management information systems).

Multimedia brings new human interface elements—the human eyes and ears—into a world formerly the sole domain of the language-processing part of the brain. At its best, multimedia promises a humanistic breakout from bits and bytes, transforming the computer from its workhorse capacity for number crunching and word processing into a popular tool that individuals can use to extend their minds and spirits.

What Does Multimedia Look Like?

Multimedia comes in many forms, which will continue to evolve over time. There are arcade, hand-held, and home video games. There are computers with floppy disk and CD-ROM drives, and television sets with specially designed, dedicated multimedia boxes and remote controls. And there are the computer networks, such as the Internet, or one of the many commercial on-line services, such as America Online, CompuServe, and Prodigy. Just as music is still music whether it is heard on a cassette tape, an audio compact disk, or over a radio broadcast, so multimedia should not be confused with how it is accessed.

Similar to computer applications such as Microsoft Word or Excel, the content of multimedia has come to be known as software. But multimedia isn't the kind of software that makes your computer perform a certain function; it is the kind you interact with for enjoyment or edification.

There are a variety of genres already developing within multimedia. "Edu-tainment" comprises programs for the home that are entertaining for children while also containing informative content, as compared to "educational multimedia," which is used in schools and is strictly pedagogical. Multimedia games played on the computer by adults or children are considered entertainment software, but when played on Sega or Nintendo machines they are called video games. (The reason for the distinction is partly the difference in platform, and partly due to the fact that video games incorporated video before multimedia did because they were played on machines that connected to television sets.)

In addition to games, there are multimedia products, or titles, that exist in every category found in the book and video worlds: sports, hobbies, science, and art and music appreciation. There are storybooks for children and expanded "books" for adults that may offer the author reading his or her work or provide additional materials to amplify the experience. There are also reference titles and encyclopedias covering every field of human endeavor, including health and medicine, baseball, animals, maps, and musical instruments, to name a very few.

Business uses multimedia for a variety of applications and may be the financial engine to drive the industry in the long run. Companies are already using multimedia to market their services and products. CD-ROMs in the mail may one day be as ubiquitous as the direct mail brochure or catalogue. World Wide Web home pages on the Internet give computer users access to information about companies and their products. Once the security issues related to on-line financial transactions are solved, we will be able to buy products on-line directly from manufacturers, bypassing retail and wholesale distribution channels. The implications of this possibility are staggering.

Business is also using multimedia to train employees. Not only are new employees instructed in corporate culture and taught about health plans and other benefits (saving human resource staff time), regular employees can also be trained as procedures change or new policies are implemented. Because multimedia is nonlinear, employees can learn what they need to know at their own speed and bypass what is irrelevant.

Complex manuals are being put into multimedia form, whether on CD-ROMs or over networks, instructing personnel about maintaining or repairing such complex systems as nuclear power plants and oil refineries. Animations or videos show movable parts and the relationships between them, and digital versions of 1,500-page manuals with intricate charts and diagrams can be easily accessed. CD-ROMs also allow for the material to be available in more than one language on the same disk.

Multimedia is also being used for storing or archiving large amounts of information into visual databases, a practice that is particularly useful for art collections. In addition, many businesses are using collaborative computing—video conferencing on the desktop—to work on information-intensive projects when many of the people involved are separated by great distances.

Who Are the Players?

The main players in multimedia include the makers of the hardware and software tools/systems, the developers of the software or content, and the publishers, distributors, and on-line service providers that bring the products to the marketplace. Hardware refers to the computer (CPU or central processing unit), CD-ROM drive, scanner, external hard drive, video and sound boards, accelerator and compression boards and chips, as well as CD-ROM writable machines and cabling that are all used in the creation and playback of multimedia.

The software used on or with these hardware tools ranges from such programming languages as Macromedia Director and Lingo, Apple's HyperCard, and Asymetrix Multimedia ToolBook to such graphic applications as Adobe's Photoshop, Premiere, and Illustrator, Fractal Design's Painter, or such modeling, rendering, and animation software as Autodesk's 3D Studio and Animator Pro.

Developers of content are people such as Yee-Ping Wu and Philip Liu, whose Magic Pen in New York City has produced children's titles such as *Lenny's Music Toons*, *Wiggins in Storyland* and *Beethoven Lives Upstairs*. On the other hand, there are business-oriented developers such as Design Mirage in Bellefonte, Pennsylvania, a computer graphics and animation studio that produces interactive multimedia company brochures, catalogues, corporate presentations, and training programs.

This book focuses on the makers of content and the vertical markets and application industries that are being impacted by multimedia, such as advertising, marketing, training, distribution, film, museums, and the law. The language used to describe the roles or functions in creating multimedia varies from company to company, but in this book the titles are defined as follows.

Like any other media, multimedia starts with an idea or a concept. Ideas are conceived and implemented into multimedia products by *developers* (as entrepreneurs who create their own companies) or *producers* (if they are part of larger organizations). Ideas also come from material that exists already in another form, such as a book, movie, or piece of music. *Publishers*, or *owners of content*, such as Time-Warner, Viacom, or ABC-TV might take a magazine, a film, or a television program—or a character such as Dr. Spock or Yoda—to which they already own the rights, and either develop multimedia in-house or farm it out to an independent developer.

Sometimes developers take titles they've made based on original ideas to publishers for packaging, marketing, and selling, leaving the developers to concentrate on the creative rather than the business aspect of multimedia development. In such cases, the publishers are often contacted early and invited to become financial partners. Publishers either distribute the final products themselves, as is the case with Comptons New Media and Microsoft Home, or work through dedicated *distributors*, such as Baker and Taylor, Merisel, or Ingram Micro D. The final product is sold in software or computer stores and through mass merchandisers, but it increasingly will be found in book and music stores and may eventually appear in supermarkets, following in the footsteps of videocassettes.

Development or production teams create consumer CD-ROM titles just as film crews come together to make a movie. And just as in the film world, multimedia teams creating entertainment multimedia often work together for one project and then disband. *Project managers* in multimedia are akin to the production coordinators of movies: They are in charge of schedule and budget, and they report directly to the developer, producer, or director, depending on the size of the company. *Art directors* manage the staff members who create or work with visual components—illustrators, graphic designers, typographers, and 2-D and 3-D animators.

Interactive scriptwriters, game designers, information designers, and *instructional designers* organize material, ideas, and concepts. *Content experts* are consulted if the subject matter is technical or specialized. The documents generated during the planning/thinking/writing phase are called design documents, scripts, or storyboards, and they become the blueprint to be executed by the artisans of multimedia productions: the *programmers*, who create the "code" that makes the program run, and the *interface designers*, who figure out how the navigation will work and how it will appear to the user. On-staff or freelance *graphic artists, computer graphic artists*, 2-D and 3-D *animators, typographers*, and *illustrators* create original visuals that aren't gathered from existing sources by *picture editors* or *researchers*, or they visually manipulate images brought in from scanned photographs or digitized video shot by *videographers* and *photographers. Desktop video editors* digitize video from tape so that it can be manipulated on the computer. *Sound editors* and *sound designers* compose, manipulate, and create music or sound effects. Actors contribute their voices or, increasingly, their images as *voice-over* or *on-screen talent*.

These role designations are hard to pin down since they are used differently throughout the industry and across the country. Kirsten Ritchie, a California developer who has made a CD-ROM catalogue of environmental products for the construction industry, says she refers to herself as a "developer" at multimedia industry trade shows but as a "producer" when she meets people outside the business, since they can't understand the designation "developer" without a lengthy explanation. "Producer" can be used in large multimedia publishing companies to refer to the person who oversees the development of several titles, but in small companies it is used to describe someone managing a single product. Senior programmers who manage a stable of junior programmers may in effect be software architects-cum-project managers. And some project managers call themselves production managers, not to be confused with product managers on the sales and marketing side.

What is consistent from company to company is that many people wear more than one hat: programmers who animate, videographers who write scripts, writers who manage projects, instructional designers who produce, and graphic artists who also design interfaces.

This still-developing field will attract and hire the kind of people who have multiple skills, are media-wise, have stories to tell, and have the passion to be part of the invention of a new form of communication.

CHAPTER 2

Ten Things to Do to Get
Started in Multimedia

1. Get a Computer with a CD-ROM Drive

If you don't already have a computer with a CD-ROM drive and a modem, buy one, or any of the parts you're missing. If you can't afford a computer now, try to find one that is available to you at a nearby library, school, or college campus—or barter time on a friend's system.

Multimedia is created on computers. Employers find it hard to take seriously job candidates who don't know how to use the primary tool of the profession. They probably aren't interested in financing you to come up to speed when so many competing candidates are already there.

As for multimedia software applications, it would be helpful to learn one or two of the most popular programs, especially in your area of interest, but don't worry if you aren't already up on the exact programs used by a potential employer. Trying to learn every product in the marketplace could result in a superficial grasp of all and an expertise in none. Employers don't necessarily expect you already to know how to use their software programs, but they are encouraged if you at least have used others in the same category.

2. Study the Product

Examine the marketplace and take note of what multimedia is being sold, how it's being packaged and marketed, and what's popular. Keep track of where multimedia titles are being sold (record stores? bookstores?); the retail arena is going to keep changing, and where multimedia is sold will influence what is funded and what is made.

View as many CD-ROM titles and games as you can, and study them as a professional rather than simply as a consumer. Figure out what you admire about certain products and what you would improve. Ask yourself if the product left you feeling satisfied or not, and why. And don't be afraid to perform this analysis on the products put out by companies with which you are interviewing. At the very least, you'll be knowledgeable about the production and design mentality of the company. At best, you can engage in a well-informed discussion of the product, and if you are brave enough to admit with a degree of diplomacy the product's weaknesses, you might impress somebody enough to hire you.

3. Go On-Line

There are three ways to get on the networks:

• Noncommercial bulletin board services (BBSs) are often run by local computer clubs, hobby clubs, or schools and are free to their members. The way these work is that you post a message, someone responds, you post another message to comment on their response, and so on—hence the name "bulletin boards." Typical "posts" on BBSs are news, questions, problems people are having, items for sale, job openings, and meeting announcements. Bulletin boards are a great place for networking (in the old sense of the word!) because the people posting are often within or near your telephone area code. The BBSs typically supply the communications software necessary to connect to their servers.

- Commercial on-line services such as America Online, Prodigy, and CompuServe are relatively inexpensive and have well-developed bulletin board-like services called conferences, real time conversations on various subjects called on-line chats, as well as electronic mail capabilities and access to selected aspects of the Internet. There are numerous conferences dedicated to careers and job-searching, typically posted by recruiters paid by the companies seeking employees.

- The Internet is noncommercial, but access to it can involve paying a fee to an Internet provider (unless you are a university student or work for certain government agencies). Software to use the Internet, such as Netscape or Mosaic, is free from the provider or can be downloaded from the Internet. Conferences on the Internet are called newsgroups, and they exist on every subject and area of interest imaginable. At last count there were over 6,000 of them. Companies and organizations are putting up World Wide Web sites, which can be most useful for pre-interview research.

Many jobs are also being posted on-line by employers, recruiters, universities, and governmental agencies. Technical skills are heavily represented among the job listings. (See "Employment Opportunities and Job Resources on the Internet," later in this chapter.)

Increasingly, employers in multimedia will prefer to hire people who have electronic mail (e-mail) accounts. Some magazine editors in high-tech fields already prefer to work only with freelance writers and illustrators who can transmit their work digitally. Telecommuting for freelancers who don't live in major metropolitan centers, but who want to work in multimedia on the creative side, will become increasingly common.

Net culture has developed into a sharing culture, by and large, where questions are posted and answers offered freely. Take part in live chats or non-real-time computer conferences focused on specific topics of interest. Ask for help and advice, and give it to others.

Networks have already become a marketing tool to create awareness and word-of-mouth about new services and products. They will become increasingly important as a distribution channel for multimedia, and the model of many-to-many communication that they provide will contribute to the development of interactive television.

4. Attend Trade Shows and Join Professional Associations

The very best way to find work is to know the people who are hiring. The easiest way to meet people in the field is to attend the trade shows and monthly meetings of the professional societies.

Attend conferences in the field and start thinking about what aspect of multimedia you want to focus on. Trade shows—a list of which appears in Appendix III—are great for meeting people who already work in the field. If you can't afford to attend the seminars or workshops, exhibit passes are often free or available at low cost. Talk to as many of the exhibitors as possible, and ask good questions. If you're unsure where to start, attend one of the larger generalist trade shows such as Macworld, *inter*media, or the Consumer Electronics Show. There are also specialty conferences for computer graphic artists (SIGGRAPH), game designers (Game Developers Conference), Director programmers (Macromedia International Users Conference), or those interested in the emerging area of interactive television (Convergence) or networking (NetWorld+Interop).

There are two types of professional associations to consider joining: those devoted to multimedia in general, such as the International Interactive Communications Society (IICS), or those in a specific area of interest, such as ASIFA for animators, or the American Society for Training and Development for corporate trainers. The best way to get to know the people in the multimedia business in your region is to volunteer to work with whichever associations you join. Helping to organize the panels for the monthly meetings is a great way to get to know local luminaries; helping out around the office puts you in contact with the leadership of the group; writing for the newsletter gives you an opportunity to interview the people who are making a name for themselves; and, moreover, your name will start appearing in front of potential employers. If you don't have the time for that level of involvement, at least make the commitment to attend every monthly meeting so people start to recognize you. And be sure to attend the social functions preceding the evening lecture so you'll have a lot of opportunities to meet new people and exchange business cards.

5. Follow What's Happening in Multimedia in the Press

The more informed you are about the trends—and gossip—in the industry, the more impressive you will be in a job interview. To know which companies are merging, going into bankruptcy, or putting out new products, read newspapers such as *The New York Times*, *The Wall Street Journal*, or *The Los Angeles Times*, and such trade publications as *NewMedia*, *Wired*, *CD-ROM Producer*, and *Multimedia Producer*. (For a list of recommended publications, see Appendix II.)

The general newspapers cover the big picture—the convergence of the computer, entertainment, telephone, telecommunications, and publishing industries. In some ways newspapers are the best source for the beginner because they reveal trends that help place multimedia in context. The trade publications provide tips on how to use software applications, review new hardware and software product releases and CD-ROM titles, and offer interviews with industry leaders. In addition to the multimedia press, there are also the general computer magazines, depending on which platform you're working on and your level of expertise: *MacUser*, *PC World*, *Byte*, and *Iris Universe* (for users of Silicon Graphics machines).

6. Find an Internship

Most production companies have entry-level positions for interns, which is a great way to become exposed to multimedia and to create opportunities that lead to future employment. Insiders tend to hear about jobs within a company first, and their work is the proof of their competence.

Internships run the gamut from being an exchange of service for access to equipment or training, to working for a reduced wage. Look for companies that make products you admire, and make sure your internship has elements of rewarding work and is not dominated by tasks centering on brewing coffee (though that may well be part of it).

Set up a specific term for the internship—a summer, Saturdays for a semester—and meet with your supervisor after that time to assess the mutual benefits. Also, keep in mind that internships are a great entry portal, but can be abused for the purposes of acquiring slave labor. When you start assuming responsibility for professional work, talk to the powers-that-be about moving the internship into a part-time or full-time job.

Good internship positions include quality assurance, researcher, video digitizer, rights clearance, and assistant to a producer, developer, or project manager. Approach developers at conferences, contact speakers on panels, or think of any relationships you have that could lead to personal introductions.

The student graduating from college with a degree and a couple of internships under his or her belt will be leagues ahead of those who have only academic credits.

7. Go Back to School

There are two approaches to continuing education. The first is to take courses in your area of specialty as they apply to multimedia—for example, if you already know video, you might take courses in digital video editing, or if you are already an illustrator, you might take a course in a graphics software application. The other approach is to take courses in areas of multimedia you know nothing about but want to expose yourself to in order to understand other aspects of the field. For example, if you are a project manager for an animation studio and want to learn more about multimedia, you might take courses in a high-level programming language such as Macromedia Director or HyperCard. Round yourself out so you can talk to as many people on the production team in their own language as possible.

8. Become an Expert in Print

If you write well, approach a magazine or newsletter about contributing an article. Research the topic, interview key people, compile information, and write an article that—once printed—becomes your calling card to a potential employer about how knowledgeable you are.

9. Put Your Knowledge to Work

You are probably a content expert now without being aware of it. You've been skiing since the age of five, or you're an audiophile and know everything there is to know about jazz—or wine, chess, or dog training. If you have a hobby or passion about something that might make a good CD-ROM title, let it be known that you are available as a subject-matter expert (SME) within the multimedia community in your area. Finding yourself a role on a team as the SME will give you a credit that could catapult you into the next job, and it will expose you to the process of how a CD-ROM is put together and help you determine what other skills you have.

10. Create a Prototype

Taking your expertise in content one step further, create a piece of multimedia by using the skills that you have. Or take a multimedia course (see Appendix V) that results in your having created something by the time the class is over.

Suggestions: Make an interactive Christmas or Hanukkah card, develop an interactive résumé, or use photographs you have taken or artwork you have created to tell a simple story. The process of making the prototype will force you to ask the questions and learn the skills that will be relevant to a job in multimedia.

If you are already employed, don't quit your job to "get into multimedia." Take a concept for a CD-ROM about your field to your boss, and try to produce the title with an outside developer who can teach you the ropes as you go along. Research and come up with a viable idea to market your company's products or promote the company's name recognition. Spearhead a new media division within your company, with you in charge. (Knowledge is relative.)

Employment Opportunities and Job Resources on the Internet

The numerous job-hunting resources on the Internet have been reduced to a digestible, comprehensive guide by Margaret Riley, circulation and computer resources librarian at Worcester Polytechnic Institute in Massachusetts. Riley initially created the guide to help her students make their way through the wilds of the Internet jungle, and she has continued to update it and to make it available over the Internet to users. Employment opportunities are posted by every conceivable entity: federal and state governments, large corporations and small companies, universities and colleges, and professional societies.

Riley, who served as a consultant to Joyce Lain Kennedy's book, *Hook Up, Get Hired: The Internet Job Search Revolution*, can be reached through electronic mail at mfriley@wpi.edu. To locate the complete "Employment Opportunities and Job Resources on the Internet," which is known informally as "The Riley Guide" and was at 60K at last count, access the World Wide Web at this URL (uniform resource location):

http:\\www.wpi.edu\~mfriley\jobguide.html

Check your word processing program to see how to create the tilde (~). Also, remember when using the World Wide Web that addresses are specific and case-sensitive. (Capital letters must be capitalized; lowercase letters must be lowercase. The Web is unforgiving about typos, number of forward slashes, extraneous spaces, or misplaced "dots.")

The following is a summary of the places where career information is being posted on the Internet, with samples of organizations and their electronic addresses provided for each category. Consider it dipping a toe into the pool. (Note that Internet addresses may have changed or no longer be in operation, and they are given as a sample of what the guide looks like.)

MARGARET RILEY'S EMPLOYMENT OPPORTUNITIES AND JOB RESOURCES ON THE INTERNET

1. Usenet Job Listings
2. Services via Telnet
3. Services via Gopher
4. Listservs, Mailing Lists, Academic Discussion Groups, and Electronic Newsletters
5. World Wide Web Resources

1. Usenet Job Listings

Access the following lists through the Usenet newsgroup network. The Usenet is a network of bulletin boards—essentially formal and informal discussion groups—each one dedicated to discussing a specific topic. Some are scientific and highly technical, and some are for hobbyists (for example, beer brewers). Usenet groups are not real-time chat rooms such as found on commercial on-line services; rather, messages are posted and then called up by others at their convenience. Responses are formulated and then added to other postings.

a. *Worldwide Newsgroups*
   misc.jobs.misc ....discussions about jobs/job hunting
   misc.jobs.offered............general positions available
   misc.jobs.offered.entry ..entry-level positions available
   misc.jobs.contracts ....contract positions, usually short term
   misc.jobs.résumés ....post your résumé here, ASCII format only
   misc.jobs.wanted............people looking for jobs

b. *Regional Hierarchy Newsgroups—United States*
   ba.jobs.contract..............contract jobs, San Francisco Bay Area
   balt.jobs..........................Baltimore/Washington area
   git.ohr.jobs.digest ....Georgia Institute of Technology
   triangle.jobs ....Triangle Park area (Raleigh/Chapel Hill), N.C.

c. *Regional Hierarchy Newsgroups—International*
    aus.ads.jobs ....jobs available/wanted in Australia
    bln.jobs ....Berlin, Germany

d. *Alternative Hierarchy Newsgroups*
    bionet.jobs.....................job openings in the biological sciences
    msen.jobs.résumés.occ ..résumés from the Online Career Center
                              (Gopher)
      pdaxs.jobs.computers
      pdasx.jobs.construction
      pdasx.jobs.retail

2. Services via Telnet

One of the basic features of the Internet, Telnet is a software program that lets you connect to a remote computer and use it as if you were sitting in front of it. Telnet creates an interactive link, like a telephone. You can issue commands to computers directly and get responses such as library catalogues and databases. The federal government database—Fedworld—can be accessed for government documents at no cost.

- H.E.A.R.T.—Career Connection's On-Line Information System, a human resources electronic advertising and recruiting tool. This is a menu-driven system with presentations of career opportunities, at no charge to the job seeker. The system is supported by the member companies so they can reach the most qualified candidates for their advertised positions.
  [telnet career.com   By modem: 415/903-5815 (14.4 bps); 415/903-5840 (2.4 bps)]

- FJOB—Federal Job Opportunity Board: Information regarding jobs available in the federal government.
  [telnet fjob.mail.opm.gov   By modem: 912/757-3100]

- ALIX—Automated Library Information Exchange: A service of the Federal Library and Information Center Committee, Federal Library Network—federal and non-federal library positions.
  [telnet alix.loc.gov]

3. Services via Gopher
Gopher is a menu-driven international network of universities, community organizations, and others.

    seymour.med.gov login: gopher
    cat.ohio.link.edu login: gopher
    consultant.micro.umn.edu

a. *Great Job Listing Gopher Sites*
   • Academe This Week (*The Chronicle of Higher Education*) — the best source for academic and research positions in colleges and universities in the United States along with many international institutions and research companies.
   [gopher chronicle.merit.edu]

   •Online Career Center (Msen. Inc.) — OCC operates exclusively for not-for-profit purposes for institutional, health care, government, and educational organizations, including the help wanted database on America Online.
   [gopher gopher.iquest.net]

b. *Other Gopher Sites with Employment Listings*
   Check the various colleges, research labs, professional organizations, and companies with gophers in geographical locations or research areas/products you are interested in.
   American Mathematical Society — professional information and opportunities for mathematicians.
   [gopher e-math.ams.com]

c. *Gophers with Pointers to Many More Gopher Listings*
   AMI—a friendly public interface/employment opportunities and résumé postings.
   [gopher gopher.mountain.net]

d. *Job-Hunting Resources Documents to Examine via Gopher*
   All State Employment Offices by State (Maintained by Dartmouth College).
   [gopher gopher.dartmouth.edu]

4. Listservs, Mailing Lists, Academic Discussion Groups, and Electronic Newsletters

These are lists and newsletters you can subscribe to through the Internet and receive messages from in the form of electronic mail. Listserv is a software program, but the term has come to mean an electronic mailing list of some type.

- Directory of Electronic Journals, Newsletters, and Academic Discussion Groups.
  [gopher art.cni.org]

- Association of Research Libraries.
  [arl.cni.org]

5. World Wide Web Resources

WWW is a network of interlinked hypertext documents that permit users to move from one to another to expand upon information found in each.

a. *Commercial Job Advertising Services*
- Career Mosaic—a guide containing not only new job opportunities but also information supplied by potential employers about their companies and what they think they have to offer. Nationwide listings updated by Bernard Hodes, a large recruitment agency.
  [http://www.careermosaic.com/cm/]

- E-Span, The Interactive Employment Network—"A searchable data base of high-tech job openings as well as a wide variety of resources for the job seeker. . . . Job seekers are invited to e-mail their résumés to resume@epan3.espan.com."
  [http://www.espan.com/]

- The Monster Board, Adion, Inc.—operated by a large recruitment /advertising agency in New England.
  [http://www.monster.com/]

b. *Professional Societies/Academic Job Listings*
- American Astronomical Society Job Register
  [http://blackhole.aas.org/Job Register/aasjobs.html
  (indexpage http://blackhole.aas.org)]
  Positions available in the field of astronomy.

•YSN Archive (Young Scientists Network)
[http://snorri.chem.washington.edu/ysnarchive/joblist.html]
Positions posted to the USN joblist Usenet Group.

c. *Corporations/Recruiters/Research Labs Listing Their Own Positions*
•Martin Marietta Energy Systems
[http:///www.ORNL.gov/mmes-www/MMESemployment.html]

•NCSA—The National Center for Supercomputer Applications,
Champaign/Urbana, Ill. "Work for the guys who gave us Mosaic!"
[http:///www.ncsa.uiuc.edu/general/jobs/00Jobs.html]

d. *Collections of Pointers to More Collections of Job Information*
•Virtual Library of Employment Opportunities
[http://galaxy.EINET.net/GJ/employment.html]

•Online Job Services
[http://rescomp.stanford.edu/jobs.html]

e. *Other Job Resource Documents on the Web*
•Job Listings Available via Dial-Up BBS—contains several BBSs
(bulletin boards) and some Internet resources with job listings.
[http://rescomp.stanford.edu/jobs-bbs.html]

CHAPTER 3

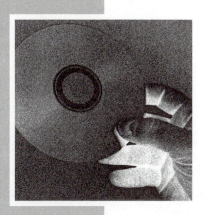

CD-ROM Production Roles

*Interviews with Leading
Players in Multimedia
Title Creation*

Management Roles

Executive Producer/Multimedia Visionary

Marc Canter
Chairman, Canter Technology
San Francisco, California

Multimedia as we know it today would not exist without Marc Canter. He developed what has become one of the premier "authoring" programs, Macromedia Director, and has continued to be an industry innovator, pundit, and provocateur. His vision of new media/new technology is grounded in a love of music. He studied guitar, cello, and voice and then went to Oberlin Conservatory of Music in 1975, but ultimately felt limited within the traditional music world by not being able to incorporate the exciting developments that were happening in the realms of computers and electronic music. "The computer to me was a new instrument that combined the worlds of music and art, and offered whole new possibilities," he says. "I saw the computer as a paintbrush that made music." He left Oberlin in 1978 to attend the School of the Art Institute of Chicago, where he studied computer graphics, video synthesis, holograms, and kinetic sculpture. His limited access to video equipment at that time is still a driving motivation: "With an off-the-shelf desktop micro-based system I have tried to enable creative access to the sort of power and functionality of a high-end audio or video studio. . . . My life-long crusade has been to get high-end equipment into the hands of artists and musicians." After working at the world's largest video-game company, Bally/Midway, in the early 1980s, Marc and others ("We were a software rock 'n roll band") founded Macromind—eventually Macromedia—in 1984. With the goal of "developing tools to create video games," the company became the first true multimedia company in the computer industry. Using Director (originally called VideoWorks), they created the first interactive business presentations, training pieces, and marketing tools—all on a black-and-white Macintosh. Marc has since moved on to running his own company, which, reflecting his musical roots, aims to develop the technology to create interactive opera as well as interactive television content. Along the way he is developing CD-ROMs that will eventually tie in to location-based entertainment theme restaurants that he calls "cyberclubs" or "MediaBars." As the first step to actualize his belief that "inter-

active music videos will become the Lotus 1-2-3 of the info highway," he has developed a CD-ROM called Meet the MediaBand. *It is one part hyperfiction (an interactive love story in which the user chooses what happens) and one part free-form "house jam" where the music and images change randomly according to the user's interaction. Marc's vision is to move beyond point-and-click interactivity, in which audio is a secondary concern, to a new genre—the interactive music video—that will "defy the term song, movie, or game" and will be truly original, rather than a repackaging of existing musical and visual content. As Marc says of* Meet the MediaBand, *"the more you click, the weirder it gets."*

How did you get into multimedia?

I hate to say it, but I was in it before it was called multimedia. In fact, my degree in college was called "intermedia" because in 1979 "multimedia" meant a slide show with pointer. So I started back in 1970 with a Moog synthesizer, which evolved into computer music. I built my own analog music synthesizer, connected that to a video synthesizer at the Art Institute of Chicago, learned about computer graphics, from there got into laser disks, and so forth. I've been doing this stuff for over twenty years.

How did you learn to program?

We were shoving numbers on a DAC in 1975. The only way you could do that was by moving your fingers on a keyboard. Programming to me was one of the ways to make music. We were controlling little boxes with microprocessors, like an Apple I. It was all exclusively for doing music and video. I've never done programming for "business purposes"; it's always only been within the realm of multimedia art. That work evolved into my making these little tools that enabled others to do animation and sound effects and music, and suddenly I thought, "There's got to be a better way. There's got to be something to help the creative people do this stuff. Thus was the birth of the concept of authoring!"

What was your original vision when you created VideoWorks?

It was that the computer offered the opportunity of authoring music and video at the same time. We created something called SoundVision, but the publishers wanted us to break it apart. So we came up with two products: MusicWorks and VideoWorks.

How did things change?

We discovered that there was a lot more money on the animation/video side than the music side. There was an inordinate amount of programming for musicians—there's a ton of MIDI software out there—so we stayed over on the graphics and animation side. What became evident was that adding interactivity as a quotient into a complex animation program was a really interesting combination, so the vision grew. We were developing an animation program in those days—what we came up with was an authoring program, Director.

Why do you think multimedia took off, and what role did Director play in it?

Clearly, multimedia couldn't take off until we had an authoring tool "for the rest of us," shall we say—something that was as dynamic as a video game and didn't require you to be a programmer. I think that was a key element.

The main thing about multimedia, though, is that it's not a single market. Multimedia raises the ante of technology in general, so suddenly the presentation market is better, suddenly the training market is better. Anything that benefits from visualization becomes enabled because of what we call multimedia technology. It's really a hodgepodge of a lot of different things all thrown into a big Cuisinart and made into a nice paté.

What became possible with Director?

For those of us who keep track, we were there before HyperCard. Anyway, HyperCard is a static-base metaphor: You go to a card and everything's still; you go to another card and everything is still. In Director the emphasis is on these looping ranges of fields, so things are dynamic and changing. That's probably the key feature: Menus and screens can have animation and things glittering, whereas most HyperCard stacks are static and flat.

Have times changed, and how have they changed? Is it still fun?

When you have an industry with so many hucksters and snake-oil salesmen and "schmucks" all jumping on the bandwagon, it's very hard to differentiate the true believers, the people who understand it, from everyone else. That's really endemic of any new industry in which everyone wants to get in on the gold rush and make money. The trickle-down effect is interesting to me. Mr. Telco says, "I'm going to spend seven billion," and you watch that money go down through the system as everyone gets their bit. Right now there is no such thing as a director/animator who's unemployed, because there's just so much work for them to do. So there's a feeding frenzy, and as a result, there's a wide variety of quality.

What advice would you give someone who's trying to jump-start a career in multimedia?

The most important thing is to do it. You can get these machines for a couple thousand dollars. There are a certain base set of techniques you could learn, but in fact since everything is starting to look the same, we are looking for unique techniques and different looks. People just need to get their hands wet, to get in there and create something.

What should developers be aware of when authoring for multi-platform delivery?

First of all, they have to realize that the Mac is always going to be better than Microsoft Windows, by definition, both in the sense of performance and in terms of ease of use. For a Macintosh person to turn off extensions when you need memory is a no-brainer. How are you going to do that in Windows? How are you going to say "Go to "config.bat" and change a couple of drivers"—and don't forget about "auto.exec." It's a nightmare. Unfortunately, we're stuck in a world where Apple shot themselves in the foot. But just because Apple is relegated to ten percent of the marketplace doesn't necessarily make Windows better.

I'm assuming that these poor schmuck Windows users have accepted that they will never have something as good as Mac. So, consequently, they're willing to do more work and more effort to try to get their things running, even just to get the thing to play. So that's a key thing. The particulars of multimedia authoring issues—like the eight-dot-three naming convention, the limited sound capabilities, or low graphic card resolutions—all those issues are real stumbling blocks, to the point where I basically ignore Windows and author for the Mac.

What do you think are some of the creative possibilities when programming multimedia for interactivity?

I think that's a real challenge. Right now, most interactivity is browsing and navigating—scrolling through these 3-D hallways, clicking on a button to move here or there. But once you get there, what do you do? With my CD-ROM, *Meet the Media Band*, I try to focus on how the music, graphics, and animation change as you click the mouse. These are areas that very few people have really investigated, and I really think they're the areas that people should focus on.

Should programmers be included in the design of titles?

I believe that technology should not dictate content. We shouldn't look at a CD-ROM project and think only about eight-bit graphics, eight-bit audio, a limited access rate, and so on. We've got a lot of really bad content today because it was dictated by the technology. What I think should happen is that the content should dictate what technology is used. Do you want stampeding elephants? Do you want a hundred video monitors flying around? You want laser beams? Fine, go design it. Once you've implemented your dream, then you can scale down the content. So since there is no precedent here, don't let others or their business reasons drive the project. Let your imagination go for it, and nine times out of ten you're going to come up with something unique and creative. And being unique and creative are the keys to success.

Do you see CD-ROMs as a limiting factor?

We call this a CD-ROM industry. We didn't call it the floppy disk industry before, so how come we're so focused on this delivery mechanism? We should be focused on the fact that we have a cheap way to distribute it today, but tomorrow it's going to be something completely different, and the day after tomorrow the technology's going to be upgraded again. So I think the proper thing is to focus on where we're going and then work our way back and figure out what steps to take to get there.

How would you characterize what's required to create interactive programming for TV?

It's an understanding that the production values of Hollywood and television are much higher than those in multimedia. Also it's already out there and available—it's called Nintendo! What's required is compelling interactivity and great production values.

What about set-top boxes and interactive TV?

First of all, there are all the classic NTSC issues: colors, single-pixel thin lines, safety zones, etc. The next thing to consider is the difference between a random mouse and tabbing between settings. But the key issue is really understanding the users and what they want. It's very unclear today if users want to browse information, look at twelve-point text, or in general use multimedia on a TV set. We know they want to play games, we know they want to look at movies and so on, but it's unclear if they want to do anything else. So I don't know if we're going to have this content that's going to play back across this wide range of platforms. You probably want your video mail to find you wherever you are, but I'm not sure if I want to go browse encyclopedias on my TV set.

What is your opinion of the so-called Information Superhighway?

As I see it, there are three different infobahns: There is the Internet that's naturally evolving from a text-based world (maybe with graphics). There are the phone companies, which are going to continue to want to do communications. And then there are the cable guys who are stuck with coaxial cable; they've got to figure out some way to position themselves. These three different groups hold a virtual monopoly. None of them really understand what else to do with the technology besides video-on-demand and shopping. That is not all there is to interactivity. There's going to be a rude awakening when these guys realize they can't control every single thing.

In general, multimedia will be everywhere, but how it gets personified in the Internet is completely different than how it gets personified with television. Is video teleconferencing multimedia? It starts to be a matter of semantics.

What is your definition of multimedia?

Aside from being the press's latest buzzword, technically you can say it's a combination of many different data types. But multimedia is not just one thing. It's whatever you want it to be to do whatever you want to do. It raises the ante of technology, using visual, sound, and interactive features to make communication better—or training, presentations, or visualization.

What would you think should be required reading for people starting careers in multimedia?

In general, let me say that by definition, anything that gets printed up is already stale news. In the old days, the only way we'd ever get any information was from *InfoWorld*, from *MacWeek*, from the periodicals. But today, information is changing so quickly, I'd have to emphasize more of an oral tradition. Even if you go buy an Adobe Photoshop guide, there are going to be things that aren't mentioned. The reason we've got such a stale industry now is that everyone's really from the same box and doing the same stuff! I'd rather have somebody read *Zen and the Art of Motorcycle Maintenance*. Just get into it on your own. Don't go copy everybody else.

Executive Producer

Steve Linden

Executive Producer, Living Books
Random House/Brøderbund
Novato, California

After getting a degree in industrial design from the Rhode Island School of Design, Steve started his career working as an art director at television stations across the country. Then he worked for eleven years at (Colossal)Pictures in San Francisco in a number of positions, including creative director, executive director, and head of the animation division. After running his own production company, where he created animated films and logos for such clients as General Magic and AT&T, he joined Brøderbund in 1994.

What does an executive producer do in a large multimedia publishing company such as Living Books?

I don't know what the universal experience is, but an executive producer here is principally in charge of day-to-day production, as well as foreseeing the long-range production plans of the company. I'm helping to shape the three- and five-year plans of what storybooks we are going to be publishing. More and more, I hope to focus on acquisitions and finding the right authors and titles. I'm working closely with a creative director to establish additional lines of Living Books, to capture as many niches in this new market as we can.

Basically, I'm a tie-breaker in any creative disputes that arise between directors and animators, sound directors, or producers. My focus is all on the production side, not the marketing side. I sign off on a product when the "gold master" meets our expectations and goes out for duplication.

I'm looking hard at production efficiency, both schedule and budget considerations. My direct reports are the producers and their coordinators; the senior project director, as well as other project directors; the head of the sound department; and head of the technical department. And they all have their own reports, the people who actually do the work.

Who are "the people doing the work," and what does managing them on a day-to-day basis look like?

We've got a certain number of in-house teams run by project directors who control animators, computer graphic technicians, production coordinators, and sound designers. These production teams run from five to fifteen people, some of which are in-house and some of which are out-of-house. Above the project directors are producers, who are coordinating many books at a time.

In terms of day-to-day production, we have five to eight Living Books being produced at any one time. I'm playing the part of the person who is watching all these projects, putting out fires, seeing where our production is lagging and where we can increase efficiency. My goal is faster, higher quality, less expensive production.

Distinguish between a project director and a production coordinator.

A project director has full creative control over how we've translated an existing book into a Living Book in terms of what's on each screen, what the action is on each screen, what the characters look like, and the quality of the animation, backgrounds, and sound. The production coordinator is the hands-on person who walks around with a basket collecting fruit from every workstation. They're actually talking to each animator about how many frames of animation they have; they're keeping the scripts up-to-date. They're in charge of getting the actual animation drawings from the animators to the people who scan them (getting pencil animations into a computer) and from them to the people who colorize them. This sounds more like a factory than it really is, but there are certain operations that go from station to station, and the material gets passed back and forth either physically or over the network. And the production coordinator oversees this process.

What does a producer do?

The producers are the gatherers and the compilers of day-to-day production lags and setbacks. In other words, they're taking the temperature of every person working on these productions in terms of whether they're meeting their quota of animation drawings, or how many gags they're writing in a day, and if they're going to finish the script in the two weeks they're supposed to. With around 50 in-house people, and a couple of other companies outside doing these storybooks, no one person is capable of visiting every one of them every day to find out the status of their work. Moreover, what we produce here is a bit opaque in terms of taking a quick glance and understanding what's going on. You can't look out on the factory floor and see how many carburetors are piled up next to somebody's workstation! So the producers talk to each animator and sound designer and find out what they're working on, what the schedule says they should be working on, and whether they're ahead of or (usually!) behind schedule.

How does being a executive producer in multimedia compare to the same job in an animation production environment?

The biggest difference is the pressure in a production studio at a place like (Colossal)Pictures, where the executive producer's biggest responsibility is bringing the work in. I had to talk to clients—both new and existing—and represent the company and its ability to deliver the next film, commercial, or series. Once we had the job, I'd turn it over to a producer for budgeting and putting a team together and basically launching the production process.

Around here, we've got a mandate from the board of directors to produce a certain number of titles a year, so I have to figure out what titles we'll produce, in what order, and with which team. So here as executive producer I'm managing production rather than fostering it. We've got a ready-made supply of work to be done. So I can totally forget about selling our services and doing a competitive bid for a job, and instead concentrate on who is the best project director for a certain book, who are the best animators to work with that director, etc.

The questions I ask myself are, "When do we want to bring in an outside director? Do we want to bring that director in or send him or her off to an outside animation company to do the work?" It's all keeping the production rolling rather than generating the excuse for the production in the first place. It's very different pressure.

How is pressure in a multimedia environment different from other production work?

Usually with multimedia, there are a lot of scheduling issues—figuring out how to deliver things on time. Primarily it's a matter of balancing quality and speed. We could tweak these products forever. Our biggest concern is keeping the quality as high as it's been in the past, all the while doubling our production. We're bringing in a lot more outside production services; we're going to be working longer hours.

Hopefully, we'll be bringing more efficiency to the process because we'll be doing series, like Berenstain Bears. In cases like this, we can benefit from the experience because we're using the same cast of characters drawn in a similar way from book to book. The inkers and animators will be used to drawing them. Our crew will get better and faster as the series progresses, understanding the characters better and how they react. We won't have to search for new voices for each book, and so forth.

What are the most important skills for a producer?

Focus and attention to detail, and an ability to work well with creative egos. Getting good work out of people. The organizational skills to deliver a really complicated product with a lot of moving parts. To be able to spot trouble before it starts.

You need to be a good manager of people because there are always personality conflicts and differences of opinion when you're putting creative products together. You need good communication skills because you're pulling a tremendous amount of information together among a variety of people.

Describe the degree of organizational skills you're talking about.

It's hard to look at one of these projects and imagine that all these bits and pieces of paper and drawings are going to come together at some point. And that the drawings will comprise animated sequences, and the animated sequences will become part of what goes into any one screen. And to make sure that a series of these screens will have the correspondingly correct sound, music, and sound effects—all this complexity for a product that a three-year-old can run!

The degree of perspective that's needed not to lose sight of all these details has been an interesting challenge to master. It's easy to get lost in the details, and at the same time it's easy to get caught in the glamour and the big picture, and miss the details. You have to balance both of those and keep one eye on each one. You have to keep in your mind what this whole thing is going to look like when it's done. It's easy enough to re-do and tweak every little aspect, but there are so many small parts that before you know it you've got a late schedule and extra expenses.

How or why did you get into the business of multimedia?

After leaving Colossal, I was on my own for two years trying to do a less expensive version of commercial or animation production. But I couldn't help feeling that technology was slipping by me and would leave me in the dark. I felt like I was missing what was happening. I couldn't bring in enough hardware and software to start doing my own video/animation production. I hadn't a clue how to get into multimedia. I'd taken a couple of courses and seen

Living Books and other CD-ROM products. Getting into multimedia seemed to tap into everything I'd learned over thirty years of film, TV, and video production. Plus, what I love about music, kids, art, and books . . . before I realized it, I saw that I really wanted to work in this industry.

How much technical knowledge does one need of CD-ROM production to manage it? Do you have to have created a program yourself?

I sure wish I had before I came here. The industry is still too new to expect to find people who will already have had experience. It's pretty important to us that producers have a good visual sense. We are drawing from all of the related fields and skills: audio, video, film, syndicated TV production, writing, animating, and producing.

Sound designers need to have worked on computers, and more and more we're wishing the animators who walk in here have done some computer work. We find conventionally trained paper animators are the ones who come in with the best sense of timing and styles and ability with the pencil. But if we've got to start from scratch explaining how that stuff gets on the computer, it slows us down quite a bit.

What backgrounds do you find to be the best fit if they haven't actually produced multimedia?

Video production, commercials production—producers who have managed the creative process and can balance that against budget and schedule constraints. We brought a CEO in from animated TV series production, which is a field that is an amazingly good fit because they're always juggling many kinds of people and a lot of production. In our case, since we're an animation-based product at the moment, producers who have done animation are good. They can speak to artists and animators and know what the terminology is. I have a feeling that producers who have only worked in a computer environment, like commercial computer graphics houses, are used to working with only one or two programmers and a designer. And I'm willing to bet that they don't know a whole lot about what that designer does. So they don't have the experience working the larger teams, nor with the hands-on way that we do things around here.

Knowing about high-end conventional video post-production will increasingly become a good thing to understand as we use more and more video, whether it's live-action components within the storybook or "meet the author" segments.

What in your background or career has most directly helped you in what you're doing now?

I worked with artists, designers, and animators for a long time at (Colossal)Pictures. Before that, I worked at a variety of TV stations as an art director back in the days when everything was done by hand—working in those stations helped me learn to work with people.

Another thing that's helped me is reading to my kids—just the one-on-one experience of snuggling up and reading books to kids, and watching the way their eyes drill into an illustration on that page. I can almost see their imaginations at work. It reminds me of how engaging and satisfying a book can be.

What do you like best about your job? The worst?

Being the father of a couple of small kids, the best thing is that they know what I do for a living and I can be proud of it. I love bringing this stuff home, testing it on the kids. There's something about a complex process that delivers a simple product that is perversely satisfying. These products are so elegant and clean, unlike a lot of multimedia products that strike me as ugly, overly complicated, hard to operate, and not intuitive.

I'm proud that I'm working with a product that seems so natural. And also the fact that we're working with writing, illustrations, and animation: they're all satisfying art forms. I love talking to authors and arranging projects, offering them the opportunity to be a part of this new medium. I don't feel we're doing anything to hurt the future of books or reading. In fact, my experience is that multimedia storybooks have promoted reading and gotten kids aware of books, illustrations, and animation—things they can take back to the world of print books.

We received a letter from the mother of an eleven-year-old autistic girl in Oregon who said that since her daughter had started playing with *Just Grandma and Me* she had talked for the first time. Apparently, it's spreading—some schools for other autistic kids are now using these products. There's a very natural, non-preachy intuitive way that these multimedia books give something to kids if they want it. It doesn't shove it down their throats like drill-and-practice types of products.

I'm having trouble coming up with the worst parts. The hardest part right now is how slow the production time is, given the current state of technology. It takes a long time; these products are hard to create. If you want to fix something, it takes too long. It's frustrating to wait for the technology to catch up to what we want to do.

Since it's so competitive, what special thing would set someone apart?

We see a lot of people who seem to have related, but not precisely on-target, skills. We're going to have to take a chance on almost everybody we end up hiring. There are a few people who come in with products they've created, and then we can at least decide whether we like their products. When it comes down to a draw between a couple of candidates, what we're basing our "guess" on is whether they are intuitive, personable, and enthusiastic. We do work on top of each other in a rather unique working environment here, and so we need to select people who will fit with the rest of the team.

Does age play a part?

A person's age doesn't matter as long as they have shown the inquisitiveness to take on new technology. I like seeing people with some experience and mellowness; age doesn't work against you. Storytelling, illustration, and animation are timeless.

Are there any positions that are different in multimedia than the commercial production world?

I was shocked by how many skills sound designers in multimedia combine in one person. In this business, they often are composers, performers, engineers, sound effects editors, directors of voice talent, designers of the musical content of the entire product, and sometimes singers, all in one. They go from role to role, playing all the parts themselves. In commercial production, I used to hire one person for each of these roles. You'd hire a composer, who sometimes did the performing. You'd go to another studio to record and mix it. You'd go to another service bureau for the sound effects.

Project directors, as we define them here, are unique to this business. Basically, they're their own producers, their own designers, and their own editors. They take a book that's in one format and figure out how it works in this other format. They become writers: writing the events, the dialogue, and the gags. They're managers of the other people who work on the team. They have a lot to do with the schedule, in terms of managing the people resources. They're animation supervisors. They do an amazing amount of things all in one.

What does the word multimedia signify for you?

For me, it's control, the ability of the user to control all these elements of sight and sound coming at them. Their ability to choose their own experience.

What, in your estimation, are the hallmarks of a good interactive CD-ROM?

Ease-of-use is at the top of the list. Nobody likes reading manuals, and they won't anyway, so you might as well make something that you can just turn on. Our test of a good CD, if we get one in we haven't seen before, is to try to run it and see if it responds in a pleasing, interesting, rewarding way. We're into "clickability" around here, so we try to see if clicking on things makes something happen or whether it stalls the program.

We want it to talk back to us and give us what we think it should give us. Or increase the mystery of what it's not supposed to give us, if that's the intention. I like programs that allow kids (or adults, for that matter) to figure out what's going on and learn with no negative reinforcement. The best ones praise you when you've done it right and wait for you to figure it out when you've done it wrong. They give you gentle little hints that don't allow you to know you're being taught.

What do you see for the future of this medium?

Better video. Higher resolution. Faster operation. Sooner or later there will be voice recognition that's good enough for kids to talk to the computer directly and not have to figure out how to operate buttons. Our future wish list is dominated by wanting to see these products run better, easier, smoother, and faster.

Speaking more broadly, I would love it if computers and the software weren't so very expensive. I want it all to be accessible to a broader range of the public in terms of cost. There are too many millions of people who don't even use computers. I'd also love to see the day when on-line will give us access to all the CDs published, or fiber-optic cable delivery, so people can pay a subscription fee or go to their local library and try out these products. There's no real reason you have to buy the disk— someday CD-ROMs will seem bulky, huge, and old-fashioned as a delivery medium.

What advice would you give someone who wants to get into producing multimedia?

Before I came, I took some courses to understand the terminology and some of the different applications, such as Macromedia's Director and SoundEdit Pro, and Adobe's Photoshop, Illustrator, and Premiere products. I didn't walk in here with any product, but in the interviews when they started talking about how CD-ROMs were made, at least I knew what the tools were. Having experience in any aspect of one of the components of this field gives you an edge—whether it's live action video, animation, writing, editing, or managing people to do these functions.

Don't wait to get the knowledge. Learn as much as you can about this business and what the products are doing. Go to MacWorld and other trade shows, try things out, and figure out what you can bring to it. Don't let the mysteriousness of the technology, if it seems mysterious, stand in the way of the creative contribution you can make. There's much more happening than just the technology. They're just tools; they're just a means. What's really happening is communication, stories, pictures, art, design, and music.

What magazines do you read?

Wired is the most fun. *New Media* gives me a lot of information. I read the required Mac magazines. *Publishers Weekly*, to keep up with books and what's happening in the publishing field. I don't read any of the computer game magazines. I still keep up with the conventional graphics design/production magazines, such as *Communication Arts, Print,* and *Graphis* [a Swiss magazine], which I read because the look of CD-ROMs still hasn't reached the elegance and the beauty of conventional TV and print design. I look at these to know what's going on in media that have been designing themselves for many more years than the computer business has been in existence. I look at them partly for typography, partly for photography, and partly for illustrations.

Which professional societies would you recommend for someone interested in learning more about multimedia?

I attend the Software Publishers Association meetings sometimes, to keep up with the business. The Computer Game Developers Conference I shunned at first because I thought it would only be about the hand-held and arcade games. But, like SIGGRAPH, they present excellent academic papers. For example, they discuss issues such as what kinds of software girls like, or how to get away from violence, and what's new. They are going beyond Nintendo and Sega-style games to CD-ROM development for computers.

Developer

Jake Myrick

President, Big Top Productions
San Francisco

Brothers Jim and Jake Myrick founded Big Top Productions in 1994 after having created "Peanuts" titles for a company called Image Smith. Jim is the external face of the company, handling marketing and sales, while Jake is the internal manager, handling the day-to-day operations, making sure in his own words that "the product gets out the door and budgets are realistic." Growing up in Rochester, New York, they worked at their father's data processing company: "We grew up with computers." Mom was an art director. Fresh out of high school, they started their own video production company, making commercials and programming. Jake had a Hallmark Card scholarship to study art at the Rochester Museum of Art, and after graduating from Buffalo State in 1985 in broadcast journalism and speech, he worked for various companies as a graphic designer, project manager, and technical consultant. He also lived in Osaka, Japan, for more than a year, studying Japanese language and business, as well as computer graphics. "Getting into multimedia was an evolution," says Jake. "I never had a specific career goal in mind. This just seems where I should be. I love art, teaching, and computers; it's a natural fit."

There are many words used to describe the companies that create multimedia titles: developers, publishers, or in the Hollywood model, producers . . .
We use "developers," which to me means that we come up with original concepts and use them with multimedia elements, such as sound, text, and graphics, to express a new idea—and have a shrink-wrapped product at the end. Using our licenses for Hello Kitty, Keroppi, and Felix the Cat, we have created edutainment games. We've also come up with products such as *The Groove Thing*, a create-your-own-music title for ages ten to thirty, and a game to teach adults how to develop psychic ability. Yet we are also publishers, because we publish titles for other developers, such as Bird Tree Associates.

In the credits on the titles we produce, my brother and I have the title of "executive producer." Here at Big Top we have people called producers who oversee software projects in terms of budget, time lines, hiring freelancers, and managing certain aspects of the creative process. But in our company at least, the producer shares the role of determining the "look and feel" of a title with the product manager (along with the graphics person and the programmer), so the Hollywood model of the all-powerful producer doesn't really hold. We have a lot of people here from the print graphics industry who are used to the team approach of the advertising world. We use the terms *developer, publisher,* or *producer* for internal functions, depending on the circumstance.

What are the steps in producing a title from "idea" to "shrink-wrap"?

Because we're developing children's edutainment titles, there seems to be a couple more steps for us. First, we need to come up with a target audience we're trying to reach, which in our case is often determined by the types of characters we license. With the characters in mind, product managers have games they've been thinking about, which they then propose, and do some prototypes. Internally, we'll look at those and see which ones are worth pursuing. And at that point, we'll send them out to teachers.

Our sister, Lucinda Karstedt (this is a real family operation!), is a teacher in Boston, and she takes the prototypes into the classroom. She's very familiar with computers—she's been a computer graphics teacher for years—and she's also an elementary school teacher. So she understands technology and what it is we're giving her. She walks the kids through it and writes up their responses. Or she'll call us and tell us about something that needs to be tweaked.

At that point we'll do a few more rounds until we actually have a "working prototype," and then she'll do more research, come out here and spend some time with us to figure out exactly how to put more of the learning steps into it. The ideal is for the game to become more difficult as the kids play it.

Then the bulk of the work starts: finishing all the graphics up, which takes the most amount of time. Once the programming is 90% finished, we take it out to the alpha stage to be tested. We test the functionality of the programming to make sure all the levels are working, to make sure the "way-finding" path is intuitive. Children don't read manuals, especially the two- to eight-year-old age group we're going after.

Then we send it out to beta testers in the area, a lot of whom are adults who have children. We conduct focus groups. Meanwhile, Lucinda is still giving her input. At this point, it's just a matter of getting it to work, and that's the hard part: the last 20% is always the hardest.

Once that's done, it goes through another set of testing, for bug/fixes; it goes to the Apple and Microsoft labs. By this point, all the graphics have been done for the packaging, sales sheets, and hopefully all the approvals have been signed off on. Each step of the way, the license needs to be approved. (The license holder approves the original concept; then we show them a working prototype and try to keep them involved as much as possible all through, because they need to feel the graphics are true to the character.)

Meanwhile, the marketing has been going on all along. We make a working demo version early on so the marketing people can go out there and start showing it to buyers, rep firms selling it, the press. What we see and what they see are not always the same!

The next step is the manufacturing—printing up the boxes, manufacturing the disks, and doing the fulfillment, which is putting it all together. We create all the art and gold disks here, and then we send it out to a print shop. The fulfillment depends on whether the product is floppy- or CD-ROM-based, though we're evolving towards only having CD-ROMs. Then we have a product!

How long does it take to make a title?

It takes from three to six months, usually, though ones with a lot of animation or graphics may take nine months. We work on two to three projects at a time. We made seven titles in the first year we were in business.

There are twenty-eight people on staff, and at any given time, we use four to six regular freelance programmers and graphic designers. The latter include "clean-up" graphics people for the software, and others for the packaging and printing of materials, the collateral.

What, in your estimation, makes a good consumer title?

Roll of the dice! I always look for good graphics and sound, and repeat playability. Graphics don't necessarily have to be 3-D; they can be simple, but the key is that they be done tastefully.

We have a little bit of a different focus than the Learning Company or Davidson, who concentrate more on the educational side. Our philosophy is that because it's a children's product, we want it be immediately entertaining, and if there is some educational value at the same time, that's a good thing. We try to create titles that a child could play for 20 to 40 minutes while the adult is making dinner, so the child is entertained but the adult feels there is some value there, too.

What makes a hit?

It's difficult to say. That's why we're going after licensed characters, because of the immediate brand-name recognition. I'm always amazed at the low quality of some of the products that make it to the Top 10. One of the most popular encyclopedias has a lot of text: Why would anyone want to read text on the screen?

What are the best and worst things about being a developer?

It's the magic of seeing your ideas out on a shelf, walking into a software store and seeing something you've put together there. It's hard to beat that sensation. And now that we have our own company, it's also having control over what is put out. That's always nice.

The legal aspect is probably the biggest nightmare. This industry is plagued with legal problems such as dealing with independent contractors (their legal rights and what they can and can't do); the licensing aspect; the software piracy aspect; employee contracts. I'm on the phone with my lawyer a minimum of three times a week and will probably be hiring a full-time lawyer. Anyone getting into this industry better bone up on the law and find themselves a good multimedia lawyer, not a regular lawyer. It makes a big difference if you have somebody who understands this industry. That's my best tip.

What are the best personal characteristics for being a developer?

You have to know when to stop tinkering. The problem is that technology keeps changing every few months, and then you want to update all your programs. Until you get it shrink-wrapped, you always have the tendency to add one more feature, or change this graphic. You have to have determination to cut it off and say, "This is the best I can do at this point—I'm going to finish it off today."

What is the best kind of background to be a developer?

To be a creative person who has some art or writing background, and has started something and taken it all the way to completion . . . from nothing to something. In the early days of multimedia it was good to be well-rounded, with a specialty in one area, but that might change to where people will need to be more and more specialized.

What would be your advice to people who wanted to open their own shop, as you and your brother have?

Get your feet wet working for other companies before you jump into it by yourself. You have to understand business and finance. And to double whatever they think it takes to capitalize a company, and then add another 20–40% more. Also, a lot of people underestimate how long it's going to take, and how much time they're going to spend on the business aspect of it. You're no longer doing it at the kitchen table; you're managing, you're checking budgets, you're talking to your lawyer: all those things add into the time factor that you didn't have before.

Oh, and hiring secretaries, that's something developers forget to do when they're first starting up. You've got to get the support people. Too many try to do it alone, thinking they can answer all the phones, and take all the orders, and call all the channel distributors—there just isn't enough time in the day.

When hiring, do you look at résumés? What kinds of people do you look for?

We get ten to fifty résumés a week, and our vice president of operations does look at them. He'll pass ones that catch his eye to the producers, who will keep them on file for future projects. But it's pretty hard to get in the door just by sending a résumé. The reason we're in San Francisco, the reason we located ourselves in Multimedia Gulch [a part of town where many of the multimedia companies are located], is because of all the referrals. Mostly we hire based on recommendations from someone we know. It's a big risk to take an unknown quantity. When we do hire, they are on a one-to-three-month trial period. We look for people who are really driven; I think everyone here could probably start their own company, or has. Because they've been freelancers, they know what it's like, so they're willing to pitch in.

What's a good entry-level job in a production company?

Beta testing is a good way to get in, because the only experience you need is to understand something about computers, be a good note taker and be well-organized. We have two people here from that background—one is now in graphics, and the other in technical support. Another good way to come into our company—for men or women—is as a receptionist, because you get a good idea of how the whole company works. Former receptionists are now working in administration, sales, and another is developing sales strategies for the education market.

What advice would you give to people getting into the business?

They should be open to possibilities. They should get in any way possible, even if it's "beneath them," and then move around once they're in. Also, they might get more experience working for a smaller company than a big, famous one.

What magazines do you read to keep up?

Child, because we advertise in it. *Time* and *USA Today*, to see what the public is reading and how the layouts change. And the industry rags: *Digital Imaging, Computer Weekly, Computer Retail Week, Electronic Publishing*.

BIG TOP PRODUCTIONS: THE EDUCATIONAL PRODUCT DEVELOPMENT PROCESS

1. Market research.
2. Input from teachers.
3. Multidiscipline module prototypes.
4. Direct testing in schools.
5. Modules enhanced for playtime and educational content.
6. Improved modules retested in schools.
7. Feedback process continues.
8. Approved modules moved into production.
9. Final sound, graphics, and interface completed.
10. Final field test on control group of children in target age.
11. Final production.
12. Beta test, fix, test, etc.
13. Compatibility testing on Apple platform.
14. Gold disk Apple (CD-ROM version).
15. Slim down Apple (floppy version).
16. Gold disk Apple (floppy version).
17. IBM PC conversion.
18. Gold disk PC CD-ROM and floppy.
19. Disk duplication and package assembly.
20. Ship initial load in.
21. Monitor first two thousand (v. 1.0).
22. Update, bug fix (v. 1.1).

CAREER TIPS FROM THE FOUNDER OF
FATHOM PICTURES

Interactive entertainment is the only business around today that is still a "garage industry," says Garry Hare, president of Fathom Pictures of Sausalito, California, which has produced such interactive titles as *ABC Sports Presents the Palm Springs Open* and *Escape from CyberCity.* "It's the only business in which you still can have reasonable control over the creative process. You can decide what you want to do and, basically, execute it. In that regard, it's a lot of fun."

He says it's harder for those on the creative side of the business to enter the field than it was in the early 1990s, so he recommends that would-be developers do whatever it takes to get a title, or part of a title, on the screen. "If you're really serious about it, sell your car, do anything," he says. He took out a second, then a third mortgage on his house in order to start his company and says he wasn't alone: "You have to prove that you're able to do something that turns into a product."

Although he suggests that entry-level applicants "bug" people to get work, he notes that it doesn't do any good to talk to somebody who doesn't have job openings: "I can't hire you if I don't have any jobs, even if I really like you."

He recommends spending time to find out about companies you're applying to. He relates a story about a graphic designer who came to him showing "adult-oriented" designs. "It's just not the kind of stuff we do, or would do. Why this guy thought I'd be fascinated by looking at the product is beyond me," he says. "I wasn't."

One fellow who did impress him was a software engineer who offered to sleep on the floor and work for free. Hare ended up hiring the engineer (and paying him) because he was struck by the applicant's sincerity about wanting to be involved in multimedia and not "just wanting another job."

Garry often asks job candidates to evaluate an existing Fathom Pictures title, but he isn't looking for blind praise: "I know the problems with our titles. I like to hear what they think they would do differently to make it a better product." He says people looking for work should play it straight in situations like this.

As for the future, he believes that in the next few years half of U.S. households and a third of homes outside this country will be linked with personal computers. The personal computer he envisions people turning to for interactive entertainment will be a hybrid television/telephone, with the content designed by the users themselves: "There's almost no way to stop it now. The platform, the network, or the roadbed will be there. How people choose to use it will surprise the daylights out of me."

Art Director

Collette Michaud
....

Art Director, LucasArts Entertainment
San Rafael, California

Collette majored in commercial art and advertising at the University of North Texas, graduating in 1985. She worked for graphic design firms doing corporate identification, program logos, brochures, and T-shirt design before moving to California to help start the art department for the Learning Company. She was the first full-time artist the company hired, working on the Super Solver animated learning game series. After three years, she was asked to become an art department supervisor at LucasArts, and now in her early thirties, she is the art director.

How did you find work at LucasArts, and what is the process for those you hire?

When I went through the job process here, I sent in floppy disks and flat artwork—drawings, sketches, figure drawings, even projects I'd worked on in my own free time that had nothing to do with graphic design or computer graphics—like Christmas cards, that sort of thing. Of course, I included work from the Learning Company that was applicable to what I thought I'd be doing here: digital backgrounds, animations on the computer.

The portfolio is all important; you've got to show what you've done. I really insist on people sending me work on VHS videotape and, in addition, flat artwork (never any originals!). I do not accept disks or CD-ROMs any longer, because it takes too much time for me to dump the files onto a hard drive and make sure I have the right program to play them with.

I have someone who receives the résumés and screens them for me. We send back a card when the packet arrives. I'll review the ones that look like they are specifically applicable to jobs we're hiring for. Then I will call them back for an interview. I will not see people who show up at my door without an interview. It's very annoying. I recommend people wait two weeks before calling after sending their work, and maybe only call one more time afer that. They shouldn't call too much. Some of them get irate, and don't understand that in two weeks' time I can get between fifty to sixty portfolios. We will always call people back if we're interested, but we cannot call everybody back to tell them we're not interested. It's just too time-consuming. Some people seem to think that being annoying is how to get a job.

How much multimedia background do you like to see?

On the art side, I'd say "zero." But they have to have some experience with computers. It would be nice if they worked with some of the software that's used a lot in the industry, whether it's the graphics industry or the computer game industry. In general, that would be Adobe Photoshop and Premiere, AutoDesk's 3-D Studio, and Electronic Art's Deluxe Paint on the Mac or the PC, and on the Silicon Graphics (SGI) platform, Alias Upfront from Alias Research or SoftImage.

It's almost better to bring in people with little experience who we "grow" here. Because when they come in with a lot of outside experience, especially in the traditional commercial art industry, they tend to be really jaded. They get into these ruts where they say "I don't do that. That's below me." It's really hard to get productive people that way. I feel bad saying that, but I haven't had tremendously good luck, and other art directors in other companies have told me the same thing. You can learn a lot from these people—don't get me wrong—they're very smart, and they're very specialized. But they don't tend to last. They're frustrated because the quality of the graphics is not yet up to the level of TV.

Those who come in without that background are much more open-minded about the content we get to put into games here. People from the traditional industry want you to tell them exactly what to do. And I like to have people who are much more self-motivated, who tend to think three steps ahead, not just one step ahead—people who don't need someone to hold their hands the whole way.

In this industry it seems that people need to have more than one primary skill.

Budgets for computer games are not as big as movie budgets. You can't have one person doing just one job and another person doing another job; you have to have one person doing both those jobs. Until recently, for example, we hired programmers who also had backgrounds in creative writing, to create the stories and write the dialogue. In the world of TV commercials, each artist does a specific job, whereas here we have two or three artists on a project and they do everything: their own modeling, animation, and texture mapping. That gives them a lot more control over what they're doing. I really look for people who like to have a lot of input into what they're doing. I don't like to hire people who say "I'm only this" or "I only animate" or "I only do special effects." That drives me crazy. To me, that's when people start to feel like machines. You don't get the commitment. You get people who come to work 9-to-5, do their little piece of it, and hand it off.

Do you develop here on Mac or PC? Do new hires need to know one platform over the other?

We develop on PCs, Macs, and SGI machines, but it really doesn't matter which computer platform you're familiar with. Artwork is artwork. It's funny how we've come full circle. When this business first started, artists were using keys on the keyboard or, later, drawing directly into the computer using a mouse. By the early 1990s, scanners had gotten better and more cost effective. Now, we're back to drawing on paper again. These days, when hiring animators or background illustrators, I look for people who have really strong drawing skills on paper. They have to be able to know how to use a pencil.

And drawing skills help for anybody doing 3-D art as well, although I have 3-D artists who don't necessarily have them. A lot of time, industrial designers, or people who have a really good sense of objects in 3-D space, can't draw on paper but can actually create things in 3-D that are amazing. I've found you don't have to be an incredible craftsman on paper to be a great 3-D artist.

What other kinds of artists do you manage?

We have digital media artists, or video specialists. Our games now involve live actors, and video technicians take the data and process into a form that can be used by the programmers and the artists. The video technicians work with the project leaders to get the right look. They are very much a part of the creative process and becoming much more so.

For these positions, you look for people with traditional video backgrounds?

Yes, but they also have to be very technical with computers, which in video production means Macintosh. They have to know the hardware and software; it's very computer-intensive.

And they have to know games?

When they come into this industry, it helps if they've played games and like them. They don't necessarily have to know the mechanics of making a game.

Tell me about some of the roles or jobs in your department.

The project leader is the person who conceives the core kernel of the design. On each team we also have a lead artist or artists—that's usually broken down into a background artist and an animator, though it can be one person, depending on the type of game we're doing. If it's a 3-D game, the lead artist will be a 3-D artist. After that, each team has assistant artists, animators, video technicians, and art technicians.

What do art technicians do?

They get the art from the animators and background artists and put it through software. They process the art and get it into a form that is usable by the programmers. Often when an artist creates an animation and gets it into the computer, he or she can't just hand it over to the programmers. They give it to an art technician to put it through some of our in-house software to get it down to the right number of colors, to compress it.

It's not absolutely necessary for art technicians to have formal art training. I've had people in this job who can't draw. However, they do need to have an artistic sense. This position is a good one for people who want to get their foot in the door. And they don't have to be completely computer literate. I've come across people who I feel are bright and motivated, so they can learn the process. I've brought them on, and they've worked out splendidly. They just have to have a real open mind to learning. My senior 3-D artist started in the testing department, moved over into being an art tech, and within three weeks was doing graphics for me on games.

I suppose a lot of people call you up wanting to be an intern?

I don't like bringing people on for free. If I feel like they have some skills and can learn and be productive, I'll start them as an art tech. I don't feel right about people doing work for a company and not getting paid for it.

What would be your advice to someone trying to get into this business?

My advice to someone right out of school is to get a job any way you can. If you've got a great portfolio, you won't have any problems. If it isn't so great, find any job, for example, in a testing department, and then work your way into the art department.

For those coming with experience in other fields, I would say to get the job in your field—for example, marketing—and keep working on your portfolio! Once you're on the inside, go over to the art department and show them that you're interested.

If I see someone's résumé who has no actual work experience that is art-related, I don't consider them—unless their portfolio is absolutely incredible! You've got to have the work to back it up if you want to cross over or get into the industry. We can't afford to train people how to be animators or illustrators any more.

On résumés, I like to see what art-related software they know or have a familiarity with. Borrow someone's computer or rent time on a computer: get experience using some of the software that is used in the industry. Do research about what's being used. Call up the human resources department in these companies, and then buy the software, take out a loan—something! You've got to find some way of getting that experience. If you don't, you'd better make sure you've got a great portfolio!

Finally, look at the kinds of games that are out there, and give examples in your cover letter of games you like. I read cover letters more than I read résumés. I skim résumés; I read cover letters. I like to see cover letters (which shouldn't be long) reference products they've seen and liked, and what they liked about them. It tells me that they have an interest in the industry. They've actually played games.

Tell me about the job of the art director. What does it entail?

Good psychiatry skills! Basically, I work with the project leaders (who come up with game designs) to select the artists and staff the projects. Sometimes we use freelancers, but we prefer to use in-house artists because we invest a ton of money to train them in how we make games here. It's very costly to let artists go and then have to hire new ones again.

After I staff the project, I work with the lead artist to estimate out the project in terms of the art needed. We go through the game and pick out every single piece of animation or background. And then they go through and estimate the amount of time it will take for someone to create each of those pieces. That feeds into a final number, which I review. A lot of times the estimates are too low.

After that is done, we move into pre-production, which entails doing the art list, character design, the background concepts, fleshing out the design. During this phase, I basically try to be there to assist the artists.

Tell me about the "day in the life" of an art director.

Lots of phone calls—calling software houses, returning calls to recruiters, calls to set up meetings. Being an art director means lots of meetings—scheduled staff meetings, impromptu meetings with people coming into my office wanting to ask me a quick question that ends up being 30 or 40 minutes of discussion. Once a week we have an art meeting where the entire group gets together and talks about issues on the table: what products are doing well or not, products that are coming up. I try to fill them in on what's happening from a business perspective.

Being an art director means looking out for the entire group. For instance, artists will call me up or E-mail me to tell me that they don't have the right machine; they need a certain type of software or the right kind of chair. So I'm the one a lot of times who makes sure that those kinds of things are put into place.

A big part of my job is interviewing artists. From January to October of 1994, I hired about fifteen artists—and that includes art techs, video technicians, 3-D, animation, and background illustrators.

Oftentimes, project leaders will come in and tell me that an artist is not working out well. We'll have a discussion, and I will go back to the artist, get their side of the story, and sometimes we'll all talk about it. I put out fires a lot of times because project leaders often don't feel comfortable going directly to the artist.

Do you have time to do your own art anymore?

I try to. Whenever possible, I work on general art department issues in the morning and then work in the afternoon on my projects. I do storyboards, game design, and character animation.

What is the best thing about being an art director?

Seeing people grow, seeing them produce something really amazing. In 1992 I was responsible for hiring all the artists for *Rebel Assault*, which was our first 3-D graphic game. It was scary hiring the artists because there were no examples of games with 3-D graphics. They had no format to work from. I tried to nurture them and give them all the support I could, and it was really exciting and fulfilling for me. They blew me away with what they came up with. They were mostly "green"—at that time, we couldn't get professional 3-D artists who wanted to work in the games industry. It was the same reason animators didn't want to work in it: the resolution was too low, there weren't enough colors, and the animation wasn't fast enough. Now they're knocking the door down to get in.

What are the worst aspects about being an art director?

The most frustrating thing is artists not getting credit for the work that they do. The amount of design work the artists do for these games is enormous. The way artists draw and animate characters, the backgrounds that they come up with, totally affect the design of the game. Too often artists are still thought of "wrists": their brain is not being used. In actuality, they're using their brains a lot on these games. This attitude is changing, though.

What is frustrating is when project leaders think that artists should be there just to fulfill the project leaders' vision. I believe in getting artists involved, getting their input. They want to give it you, and when they are given that opportunity, their commitment to the project is deeper. The products are better. The projects in which the artists have had a lot of input, a lot of control over their art in terms of how it's produced—those are the ones that have been the best projects, the ones that come out relatively on time and on budget. The ones where the project leader or designer of the project has been a dictator who has not wanted any input, has kept the design close to the vest, have failed or have never come out. And you burn out artists that way. They don't want to work anymore after that. They want to leave the industry because it's been such a frustrating experience for them.

Do you wish you'd done anything differently in preparing for your career?

I wish I'd studied animation. I thought in school I wanted to be the most famous graphic designer there ever was. When I started at the Learning Company, I thought it would be temporary. In fact, at one point I quit, but I found that the minute I left to go to a graphic design job that I missed working on the computer; I missed this industry. So, personally, I wish I had studied animation; I wish I'd known when I was a kid that this was where I was wanting to go. When I started out in the late eighties, it was OK that I was a graphic designer, because things were much more stylistic. Now, with better technology, we can do much more full animation, and it can be anything we want it to be.

Nowadays, I look for people who have animation training. It used to be that I hired people just on their drawing skills alone. Now I look for people that do have the video experience, animation or illustration training. They just can't walk through the door and have great drawing skills. I take chances still, but it's not the way it used to be.

Where do you see multimedia games going in the future?

I can only speak about educational and entertainment games. I see the industry going in the direction where games are much easier to play, where the interfaces are very simple. I see production values continuing to improve to the point where they rival what you see on TV. From the artists' standpoint, production values are going to be everything. People aren't going to want to play games that don't look good. That's why I'm going to have to find animators who have a familiarity with video, because there's going to be more combination in future products. Games are going to continue to get more cinematic. People need to know how to story-board out a game so it's cinematic; it's not just from a doll-house view anymore. In the past, art games had small characters, and you could see the walls and ceiling and floors. Now we're seeing more close-ups and screen direction.

My prediction is that we will go through a period where almost all games will contain video, because it will be the hot new thing. And then we'll come back around again, where some things will use video and other things will be animated, depending on what fits the game design.

It's going to get more competitive in terms of finding jobs in the industry. The skill level is much higher. The thing about multimedia games is that they're getting more expensive. You can't take as many chances as you used to. That's why we have to hire people who can get down and do the work.

What kinds of magazines do you read to keep up?

For this industry, *Computer Gaming World* has been around forever, though I prefer the magazines with a broader perspective that talk about all types of products, not just games—*CD-ROM World, CD Today, Multimedia, Wired, NewMedia.*

Are there any books you would recommend?

Game Over: How Nintendo Conquered the World, which gives a great back story on how the game industry came to be.

Project Manager

Mark Satterlee
Production Manager, StudioGraphics
San Mateo, California

Mark received a B.A. from the University of California, San Diego, in 1982, majoring in visual arts and communications, and minoring in economics and history. He also took classes in video and film, and after graduation started freelancing as a P.A. (production assistant) with the intention of becoming a video editor. Soon he was working at a cable company in San Jose, first switching commercials, and next as a tape operator, but then he decided to go into sales. In time, he moved to a video production house and started selling the company's services. His first exposure to interactive multimedia was in 1987, when he had an opportunity to work for a company making videodisk-based merchandising kiosks for clients such as Florsheim Shoes. He became a project manager through connections in the IICS (International Interactive Communications Society), of which he was president in 1989. It was through the IICS in 1994 that he met the president of StudioGraphics, Richard Bennion, a meeting that led to his being hired. StudioGraphics is a developer of interactive multimedia marketing and computer-based training programs for corporations.

About the nomenclature—I see your title is production manager. Some people use the term "project manager."

Every company is different, and some people even use "producer." My idea is that the title of "production manager" can exist on any project, referring to the person responsible for pulling together all the resources required, anything from human beings to digital assets (audio files, graphic, video files) to tangible gear (computers, videotape, laser playback).

To me, the title "project manager" is used when there is either a lengthy development time (two to three months or more) or where there are a lot of different phases to coordinate and manage. Project managers are responsible for managing budget and schedule, and communicating to the various disciplines—programmers, graphic artists, video and audio production—about the deadlines, requirements, and technical specifications for delivering a certain product. The project manager is responsible for making sure things are on track. It's a job that isn't noticed until it's not being done properly!

How much creative input do production or project managers have?

That's where this role veers into that of being a producer. With experience, as project managers attend more client and creative meetings, they definitely can work with the creative people to formulate ideas. Whether they have any creative input would depend on their role in a particular business.

Tell me about some of the projects you've done.

We did an interactive marketing piece for a small technical company that had new graphic accelerator chips that supported digital video. They wanted a program to play at trade shows and to give to OEM [original equipment manufacturers] to show the next generation of the technology. It was a sales/marketing CD-ROM of 30 megabytes and included music, narration, and digital video. My role was that of a project manager/producer. I went to the initial client meetings, then worked with the writer to define the content based on what the client had told us. I was also responsible for generating and maintaining the creative approach to the project—for example, communicating what graphic "look and feel" the client was after, who the intended audience was, what the objectives were. Once we went into production, I managed schedule and budgets. Budget items included the outside cost for video footage, video editing and digitizing, and narrative recording. I evaluated the final work (matching the images against specific script marketing messages) and, based on that approval, showed it to the creative director/president of our company, and then delivered it to the client.

Another project was a linear presentation—a loop as opposed to an interactive piece—for the same high-tech chip company, but in this case they were introducing a real-time 3-D rendering engine at Comdex. On this project, I was responsible for making sure the creative person—the project lead in this case—had all the assets from the client: all the logos, animation, outlines. In this project, the client provided the images and sound, and there was no script, so my role was purely logistical.

In both these examples, my participation was extreme, whereas I sometimes jump in and out of a project, rather than being involved throughout. An example was a management training project for a local 50-store restaurant chain. The 10–15 minute program teaches managers how to forecast and schedule bulk food orders—how much lettuce to buy, and so forth. We wanted to make the program fun, so instead of testing the managers, we created simulation experiences based on information they had just been presented with. I worked with the writer but was also involved with other projects at the same time. Then, towards the end of the project, I came back to work with the programmer to make sure his results were meeting the specifications we had defined in documents in the beginning.

Speaking of documents, please review the kinds of documents the project manager either creates or deals with.

The first document on a project is the one-to-two-page project overview, which briefly defines the objectives, the people involved, and the time frame and schedule. It is usually written by the project manager unless the producer has already written something up. Other documents include:

- Functional Specification: A step-by-step detailed outline of what we're delivering. Is it an executable file, to be integrated into the client's program, or is it a turnkey program that is self-installing? The functional spec needs to specify what's included—video, audio, narration, etc.

- Content Outline: An outline detailing the specific points of content that the client wants included in the program. For example, if they have a new chip, how fast is it, what video does it support, is there key marketing jargon that needs to be included? The content outline is usually not my responsibility; it is written by the creative director or the project lead, depending on how complex it is. On occasions, I serve as the project lead and in those instances generate this document.

- Flow Chart: Defines how the program will flow depending on responses of the user. It is a creative document that you've "spec'd" with the client's input. We use any number of tools to create the flow chart, from paper and pencil, to draw programs, to a flow-charting program for Mac or Windows called Inspiration. The nice thing about it is that it will give you a flow chart from an outline.

- Script: Written by the writer. A script includes narration, if there is any, as well as on-screen text and a precise description of what happens. If I were the outline generator, I'll be involved in answering the content and creative questions a writer may have. If I'm not the one who delivered the outline, I'd just deal with the deadlines and payments.

- Storyboard: Where pictures and graphic images are applied to the content. Still paper-based, it's done in-house with the art director and animation director, with help if needed from other graphic artists. My input ranges from proofreading—to make sure the text and graphics match (that the narration in the frame matches the visual)—to evaluating the pacing. My function regarding the storyboard is to act as "quality assurance." Once we have a storyboard approved, we have a solid, well-defined project and can give a firm internal estimate of what our time commitments will be for each task. Ideally, we haven't done any production work before getting client approval. (Part of the project manager's job is to make sure we don't waste resources in producing things that aren't approved.)

Also delivered to the client is the complete design, and if warranted, a "color comp" (a color printout of the screen design to give the client an idea of what the project looks like).

What is your typical day like—what is the process?

I evaluate our schedule and determine what needs to be accomplished that particular day. I check to see if anything has changed since the previous morning or afternoon. Are there any new issues, or have any new priorities arisen? I'm constantly checking to see if we're on schedule. There is also a lot of administrative work. I check the lists of things I need to provide for the production processes: graphics needed, audio filenames to send to a post house, etc.

Since I have a film and video production background, sometimes I'll digitize video or audio, and edit. On occasion, I'll lay those things into programs.

What are the best and worst things about being a project manager?

It allows you the opportunity to play an integral role in producing multimedia. My skills are more people-oriented and organizational, and project managing allows me to participate in multimedia without being a graphic artist, C programmer, or writer.

The downside is that the production world in general is deadline-driven. Many times with multiple and sometimes conflicting deadlines and priorities, it's a somewhat stressful existence.

What are the best kinds of traits or characteristics to have to do this kind of work?

You need to have clear and precise communication skills. You are communicating with so many different types of people: the client, video people, graphic artists, programmers. And you need to have a knowledge base over multiple disciplines: graphics, animation, video, audio, etc. None can be learned at once, so it's a skill set that's built up over a period of time.

What is the best kind of education or training for this job?

There is no specific degree, but any discipline that challenged someone to be organized and to be exposed to technical issues would be useful. You can't be a technophobe. What we produce is visual communication, so you also need some love, appreciation, or conception of what visual communication is all about.

Is the job of project manager ever a freelance career?

Project management is almost always an internal task, mostly because companies like to maintain control. However, multimedia is populated by a lot of small shops where several projects can come in at once and inundate their resources. They might need help but not necessarily hire someone full time. Freelancing would give you the chance to explore a lot of different companies.

What would be your advice to someone trying to get into this kind of work?

You've got to be flexible and learn as much as you can about the outlets for multimedia. Learn the marketplace and who's doing business, and then take a hard look at your skills and see where you're going to fit. Get active in professional organizations, which gives you an opportunity to work with people at a professional level but in a more informal environment. People don't know you until you work with them.

What can someone do to stand out from the pack?

Have a breadth and depth of knowledge and experience. The more you know about the technical and artistic aspects, about organization, the process and flow of the process, the better chance you will have.

How did you get your current job?

I had a project binder of real projects from past work, including all the correspondence and definition of what the project was. For a project manager, that's a portfolio piece. I also had a floppy showing projects I'd worked on for kiosks.

What does your kind of job evolve into over time? Where does it lead?

Ultimately, into being more of an executive producer. As the organization grows, you end up managing other project managers.

Regarding your own background, what kinds of things were you involved in as a hobby or pastime that ended up contributing to what you do now?

Growing up, I was enamored with media in general; as a teenager, I used to make audiotapes of radio songs and programs. I would edit them and make my own satires. Subsequently, I worked for the local college radio station in high school, doing news and sports announcing. It was fun. I was also interested in documentary film and classic cinema as a kid. Multimedia seems to be an extension of these interests.

Do you wish you had done anything differently to have prepared you better for the work you ended up doing?

I should have listened to my father and taken my math and science classes more seriously. You can't ever know too much technical information.

What computer programs do you use?

For administration, I use Filmmaker Pro and Microsoft Word, Excel, and Access. I also know Corel Draw, Inspiration, Adobe Photoshop, a little of Macromedia's Authorware and Director.

What magazines do you read to keep up?

NewMedia, *Multimedia Producer*, and the IICS's national [*The Reporter*] and local [*Chapter Notes*] newsletters. Because of my video production background, I also read *Videography*, *Post* [video/film magazine], and *SMPTE*.

THE PROJECT MANAGER IS THE INTERNAL CLIENT

Much of the responsibility of the project manager is understanding the project as a whole from the client's perspective, notes Deb Nathan, executive producer at Them Productions in San Francisco. "That entails understanding what the client wants and what the platform can deliver, and educating the client as to what really works. If they want something that's all-text, perhaps instead they should think of doing a book, because people don't like to read text on computer screens. Full-screen animation doesn't work across all platforms necessarily, either. The project manager has to know how to explain this to clients."

Much of her day is spent "handling" the client—changes made and sent, regular reviews, making sure everything is documented: "There's a lot of writing of confirmation letters to the client, repeating to them what you think they said."

She says that while Fortune 500 companies are starting to use multimedia for advertising, many of them still think it's not good for much beyond catalogues. "It's a big education," says Nathan, who worked for SoftAd and Iconic before founding Them Productions with her partner, David Mandala, in 1993. "You need to know your stuff so that you can educate others. Managing the client is a big responsibility. They have to respect you. In corporate pieces it might be the first time they've used multimedia, so that can be difficult."

A project manager, she says, is a jack of all trades. The hard part of the job is not having "your own little piece" to turn in at the end of a project. "You don't get patted on the back for finishing five art screens. Your work is ongoing. You have to believe in yourself and be proud of what you're doing. It doesn't matter how long you worked; the client could care less." She has taken to creating weekly worksheets in order to enjoy the satisfaction of crossing off completed tasks.

"You have to know that without you it doesn't happen. You're making the whole thing come together."

Production Roles

Computer Animator

Bridget Erdmann
Senior Project Director, Living Books
Novato, California

Bridget received an associate degree in advertising design in 1982 from the Colorado Institute of Art in Denver and later took animation courses with Marcy Page and Martin McNamara at San Francisco State University. She then interned and later was employed as a production coordinator, model maker, and animator at Boyington Films, creating 2-D animation and special effects. She had always expected to be a traditional animator; it wasn't until her late twenties, when she created animation for coin-operated video games at Atari, that she began working with computers. Later she worked as a freelance animator for (Colossal)Pictures and McVey and Vogt, doing commercials and feature film work. At Living Books, she started as an associate art director and was responsible for the Mercer Mayer title Little Monster at School *(for CD-I and Mac) and* Arthur's Birthday, *by Marc Brown. Bridget, who is in her mid-thirties, feels Living Books gets her closer to "real" animation. "I'm not just making little lightning bolts but getting to create characters and give them personality."*

How does being a computer animator differ from being a traditional animator?
Basically, the skill set is the same. But to use a computer, the animator has a whole new set of hoops to jump through. Where the traditional animator has a light table and flips through pieces of papers, computer animators can cut and paste as they create a moving character. Also, in traditional animation you have to shoot your image on video or film and screen it on a projector before you can see how it looks. With the computer, the feedback is instant.

One of the big problems I see today is that there are a lot of people who are calling themselves computer animators who don't have a traditional animator's background. The computer makes it easy, and it allows them to enter the field quickly. Then the public complains that animations in CD-ROM titles don't have life and things look choppy.

There is a myth that computer animation is faster than traditional, but it's not true. All the colorings of traditional animation still have to be done before they're inserted into the computer.

What is the process of animating on the computer in multimedia?

The process starts out as traditional animation on paper. Then the images are scanned into the computer using either a flatbed scanner, a video camera, or a digital camera. Then we color and clean up the image, drop it into a scene, and time it. An animator might do all these steps or parts of it, depending on the person and the project.

At Living Books, a typical animator has a light table and a computer with three screens. One screen is for the exposure sheet (a chart that directly relates to what the viewer will see on the screen, having to do with issues of timing), another window is for painting or drawing, and the third has the video camera output, so you are constantly playing things you've shot, re-drawing and moving things around.

What programs do you run here?

We use Adobe Photoshop, Macromind Director, and sometimes Fractal Design's Painter. To manage platform issues, we use De-Babelizer, from Equilibrium.

How does working in a multimedia environment differ from more traditional companies?

There is less pressure here for me than when I worked as a freelancer creating animations for commercials or feature films. With commercials, a company purchases a slot on television ahead of time, so if we didn't have the animation ready by a certain date, they'd lose money. In feature films, special effects are done at the very end of the production process. By the time we had to do our work, there was no money or time left. Working here allows more time for brainstorming.

What are the best things about being a computer animator?

There's a lot of job security, because there is such a need for us out there. And for the first time in decades, animators are paid well. Because we're in such demand now, we're allowed a lot of freedom to conceptualize. When I was freelancing, they told me what to do when I was working on commercials: "Here's the Trix rabbit. Make him jump up and down." I never even thought about changing that. It never occurred to me that I would be allowed to write a script or change a character. I was just the animator. Now I'm in the position—and this is true of anybody in this company—where I can end up directing a whole piece. The field is wide open. There are lots more possibilities for animation now than ever before.

What are the worst aspects about being a computer animator?

The hardest part is that we're designing for so many kinds of computer platforms, with who knows what speeds or ability to put out good colors. We have problems with lip-synching, marrying the picture and the sound. Traditional animators output to film, so they can be as elaborate as they want to. In multimedia we have to fake it: we just try to make it look as good as we can and hope for the best.

What traits does an animator interested in multimedia need to have?

You've got to be an animator who is interested in technology and what computers can do. I've hired people from Disney who were great animators, but they had no interest in computers. Some people take to computers, see doors opening to them, see ways it is useful. Others don't get it.

The best thing you can have is a real desire for being an animator. It's such a highly skilled art form that it requires a lot of dedication, like ballet or piano. Since it takes so much practice, it better be fun.

What advice would you give someone trying to get work?

I want to see a reel—your artwork on a videotape or on a floppy. It doesn't matter where you went to school or who you know, but what you've done.

They should do their homework. Get hold of products you like and find out which company made them.

People are getting pickier about who they are hiring than they were a few years ago, so if you're a beginner, go to one of the conferences like MacWorld and seek out the startups. They're the ones with only a few titles out. Or if you want to go with a more established company, look for one with several different lines—kids, adults, games—because that's an indication they're constantly coming up with new ideas and there is more room for a newcomer to enter on the ground floor.

Finally, you need to find what inspires you and focus on that. You can't approach it as "I am a computer animator. I'll do whatever."

How does the job of computer animator change over time?

Compared to traditional animation, computer animation is a great place to grow because there are so many directions to go in. You could end up writing your own project if you want to. Traditional animation doesn't offer a lot of room to grow. With multimedia, you don't have to wait for someone to die to be the art director. There are never enough good ideas.

How did you get your job here, and where do you find candidates?

I got my first job at Living Books because I went to school with someone who works here. I recruit out of some of the best schools for traditional animation: Sheridan, near Toronto; the California School for the Arts, in Valencia; and the Rhode Island School of Design. At the same time, you don't have to necessarily go to the best schools. If you learn the programs and read the manuals, you'll give yourself a good education.

Often, I screen applicants by giving them a test. I'll send them some art we have here and ask them to clean it up or animate it and send it back.

What do you do as a senior project director?

I direct the entire project, or "book," which is an interactive children's storybook on CD-ROM. The largest part is directing animation, but it also includes directing voice talent, writing visual and verbal gags, painting backgrounds, and animating some of the characters. As the director, I try to see the vision of the author and create a cohesiveness in the product based on that author's ideas and expression.

How would this be different from a creative director?

The creative director attempts to create a cohesive vision for the department, for all the products we produce and call Living Books. As a project director I'm running a particular project, or several projects in the case of a senior project director. I'm also in charge of keeping in touch with external animation companies.

What kinds of magazines do you read to keep up?

Animation Magazine. We use Macs as development tools here, so I read *MacWorld* and *MacWeek*. I also read *Wired*, *NewMedia*, and *Computer Gaming World* to stay up on what's going on.

What professional societies do you belong to?

ASIFA, an international animation association.

Graphic Designer / Art Director

Terry Irwin
....
Partner and Creative Director, MetaDesign
San Francisco, California

Terry received her master's degree in design from the Basel School of Design, Switzerland, and then remained in Europe working for Anspach, Grossman in Portugal on projects for Hewlett-Packard, Ampex, and Diamond Shamrock Oil. Upon returning to the United States, she joined Landor Associates in San Francisco, where she was a project director working with various companies, including AT&T, Pacific Bell, and Bell Atlantic. While at Landor she was involved in developing a revised identity (both in terms of design and strategy) for IBM's former printer division, Lexmark, which connected the existing logo with a corporate tagline. She has since founded her own design firm, MetaDesign, with Erik Spiekermann. (They also have offices in Berlin.) The firm designs all matter of printed and electronic materials (including on-line), "particularly ones that require a high level of typographic expertise, such as schedules, timetables, forms, and books." MetaDesign's first CD-ROM project, which was for Boston-based PSW, was VizAbility: Experiences in Visual Thinking. *Aimed at students from kindergarten to college, it shows nondesigners how to look at things differently and translate what they see to paper. In addition to interactive lessons and games, the CD-ROM also contains video interviews, some of which use Apple's QuickTime Virtual Reality that allows the user to scan around a 360-degree space.*

What is the role of the graphic designer on the multimedia team?
The role of the graphic designer on a multimedia team is primarily to help develop a "look and feel" for the piece. It involves working with authors and developers to define what the objective is in terms of the tone of the piece, and how the interface will look and work. This would extend to all areas. For example, it seems essential to me that we bring our views on how the sound is going to interact with the visuals on-screen and in the interface. I see us as being the entity with the broadest view in terms of what the user's experience is going to be and how the entire thing is going to "look and feel."

How does the designer create the "look and feel"?

First, we and all the primary members of the team sit down and discuss what the project is with the authors of the book that's being turned into a CD-ROM: What are the objectives? What should the tone be? What should the user's experience be? What kind of personality should the product project? Based upon that, we try to find the levels of complexity. It feels to me very much like a typical graphic design problem, in which you look at the overall content and at how complex it is. Once you have that, you can begin to develop a hierarchy, so naturally the look of the screen is going to be defined pretty much by its worst-case scenario and its best-case scenario. Out of that evolves a lot of the physical design elements.

Could you clarify what you mean by "worst- and best-case scenarios"?

When starting a new project in multimedia, designers will often approach the screens at random. We prefer looking at the worst and best cases, from the point of view of complexity, when we design the prototypical screens. On the one hand, we ask: Which will be the easiest to design? Which screens will have the least amount of information? What is the optimum design? Then we'll look at the other end of the spectrum—the worst case. Which screen has to have the most elements on it? Which screen has the most buttons on the interface, or the most text, or has to have video on the same screen as a static image? What is the most complex situation we'll find ourselves in with this product?

First, we try to see if we can change any aspect of the worst-case scenarios—can we redistribute the message or change the pace? After that, we go ahead and design for those extreme cases, the easiest and the worst. We try to get the lay of the land right up front. Otherwise, if you design for the norm, you may design yourself into a corner.

How is graphic design different in multimedia than other media?

It's not as linear. As graphic designers, most of our experience has usually been in the area of book design and brochure design, and multimedia seems to be a lot more holistic. You have to think about the fact that users are not going to have a linear experience like they do in a book. They're not going to be turning pages, they may be choosing paths. All of the types of considerations—like pacing, tension between sections, and trying to define different environments that they might be in—are somewhat similar to magazine design.

But I find that multimedia is ultimately very different, because you always need to provide the user with clear navigational or way-finding tools—a trail of bread crumbs back to the place they're familiar with. That means designing an interface that's pretty clear and almost invisible, if you do it well—an interface with a comfort zone where it's easy to tell where you've been and where you're at. If I get lost in a CD-ROM within two or three moves, I get irritated and throw it away.

Because it's so easy to get lost along the way, the design in a multimedia title needs to be much clearer than it would be in a book design. You can get so much more information on a book page than you can on a screen, so we're constantly having to function practically as editors. We find that the authors we're working with want to get so much information on the screen—they're always asking if we can put three paragraphs of text on. We're constantly having to remind them that it's harder to read text on a screen.

I think your attention span is just inherently different. I don't know whether that's the psychology of looking at a screen or the psychology of looking at a book or a brochure, where you're more prepared to focus deeper. We're still experimenting ourselves about the psychology of viewing a screen and the attention span, but in general I'd say we're having to function as editors a lot more than we ever did before.

How do you tell the difference between good and bad design in multimedia?

If I get lost or I get bored, it's not working. The design is certainly all tied up with the content, but I've looked at many products in recent months where I just get confused. I get lost in the paths. There's too much text; I don't want to read it. In my aesthetic, I would say that it's over-designed. That means that I'm looking at the design of the thing, instead of the information itself. I find that a lot of the products we review in our office tend to be over-designed. It's almost as if what you can do on screen is still so seductive in terms of the colors and the slickness that it often gets in the way of getting the information across itself.

Can you give a concise description of the role of good graphic design in the creation of the user interface?

I think of myself as being a communications designer more when I'm working in the realm of multimedia. There's something about the term *graphic design* that feels like we're talking about surface design or cosmetics, and I think if there's one place that you need to abandon that concept, it's certainly in multimedia. If you're throwing anything extra into the soup in terms of just decoration or design, I think you're going to obscure the information you're trying to get across.

As I said before, in terms of communication design it's important to sit down with the authors and really talk about the objectives of the product, what kind of experience the user should have. For instance, for the CD-ROM *VizAbility: Experiences in Visual Thinking*, we decided that the product shouldn't get down so deep that the user would be apt to lose his way. That said to us we had a little more leeway in the kind of interface we could design. We could come up with some conventions that weren't in the typical computer vocabulary, which is always a fine line I think you're walking as a designer.

We've been using computers long enough that there's developed a certain vocabulary that regular computer users are very comfortable with. You can't do things, for instance, like "gray back" a lot of type on the screen, or people are going to think that something is inactive. But because this product doesn't have such deep vertical paths, we were able to try some new things in terms of the interface, because people are very unlikely to get lost.

What's the role of an art director on a multimedia team?

That's an excellent question; it's one we're still grappling with. For every project I've been on, the roles are a little different. But, in general, I think the art director would be the person who's trying to keep an overview regarding visual consistency throughout the product. That includes interface and the general on-screen design. This entails keeping a special eye on typography, which in my opinion is one of the single biggest problematic areas I see in multimedia. It's also making sure you haven't lost the original vision, that the product isn't being splintered into different modules that feel like they've been produced at different times. We see that a lot.

How do you manage designers?

We have a structure that is pretty flat in terms of hierarchy. All the designers work very collaboratively. I think that we may differ a little bit from other offices in that everyone tends to work together on a project. The designers aren't taking their own little project and going off in their corner and doing something and then looking to me to give them feedback on it. Usually, my partner or I will bring a project into the studio and brief everyone on it collectively, and then usually a designer will be designated as the point person—the primary liaison between the client and me. We want the designers to be interacting with our client on an ongoing basis.

In terms of managing them, I'm usually the one with the advantage of having the overview. When they're working on a project day after day, they can't help but lose a little bit of the overall perspective. I can help them pull their focus back. But I also advocate a lot of group critiques within the office. There's a constant check and balance: Are we still fulfilling the objectives? Are we still on track with this? Are we not going down any blind alleys in our exploration?

What is the best way for a client to get the most out of a design firm?

To be very careful in their selection, to talk—really talk—with the potential designers at length beforehand to make sure that there's a good chemistry. To make sure they understand the designer's approach and philosophy, to make sure that they're qualified. Graphic design is a profession in which there's no accreditation. You need to make sure that you're dealing with someone who has the capability to complete your project with good design on time and for the budget.

Once you've hired them, step back and let them do it. It's a visual world that we live in—everybody can see; everybody has opinions on what looks good and what doesn't look good. Every time you buy a piece of clothing or get dressed in the morning, you are making aesthetic decisions. So it's very hard for nonexperts to pull themselves out of that arena and understand what's the difference between making a subjective aesthetic decision and letting our consultant make decisions that are meeting the objectives of the project. We tend to have a lot of dialogues with clients where they say "I just don't like blue." And, hopefully, if you've hired a qualified consultant, they're going to be able to take a large amount of that subjectivity out of the design process, and it's going to be grounded in some very sound decisions based on meeting those objectives. That's a very difficult thing.

Much of what we talk about with our clients in the very beginning is explaining what we can do for them and what we won't be able to do. We must be able to design something that they're comfortable with. We don't want to ask them to put on a suit of clothes that doesn't feel good, but on the other hand, we do have a certain amount of expertise that you're paying us for. That dynamic of overcorrecting designers is very tempting and, I think, just a natural aspect of being a human being with eyes.

What schools of design have influenced you personally?

The modernist schools—I'm sort of a die-hard modernist. I did my graduate studies at a school in Switzerland that was founded by some of the Swiss typographers of the fifties, so my training and my background come from that direction. It's the classic "form follows function" as opposed to the postmodern movement or decorative movements. I think you could divide designers into two schools of thought. There are those who tend to want to be more expressive with their work; they like to bring something personal to it. They see themselves perhaps more as artists. And then there are people who see themselves more as communicators or problem solvers, and I fall into the latter group, definitely.

Are there any specific design principles that are unique to the multimedia environment?

A general design principle that is emerging is the need to be absolutely clear. I would say "form follows function" definitely applies here. If you bring anything extra to the design, the potential for a user to become confused or lost in the environment is extremely great. I think people aren't yet completely comfortable navigating in the multimedia environment. Way-finding is a huge issue, and therefore principles of being clear and concise are essential.

I would absolutely bring the principles of typography to the area of multimedia. We still haven't found ways to solve the dilemma of the resolution of type on screen. And so certainly one of the principles to apply is "less information is better."

What do you think is the state of multimedia today?

It's still in its infancy. It's a very young medium. You have that feeling of excitement and energy that is characteristic of any new media or movement. I remember when personal computers first started to play a major role in our field, there was this sense of potential and energy and excitement. Along with that came frustrations, because no one knew quite how to do anything. There weren't some defined methodologies that would ultimately save you money and allow you to get your things in on time, on budget. I think that's still the wild card in this area, but there's also a lot of excitement that comes with it.

What do you think is the greatest strength of multimedia?

That its potential is still undefined. I haven't really seen anything from a design point of view that knocks my socks off—but I'm very critical!

What's happening from a communications point of view is that multimedia is disseminating information in an entirely new way. It can be brought instantaneously to people who need to learn things.

What do you think is the greatest limitation?

It's still very costly, and it takes a lot of time to produce. I think you have to be extremely well-organized; you need to have a reason for doing the project in multimedia. What we see still are a lot of products that look like they've been brought to the multimedia arena just to have something that's new. If you can't bring something more to the equation, then why not do a book or a printed piece? That's something we keep asking: Why is it being produced in this media if there isn't a reason for it?

What are some of the good reasons to do a project as multimedia?

I think it has to offer the potential to, for instance, hear someone speak about what they do or hear an expert talk about his area of expertise. That's always much more compelling than reading words on a page. Typography can only be just so expressive. You know, pictures are worth a thousand words.

We're working on a project right now for a major corporation to help educate employees on paradox and change in the workplace. What they've been doing so far is just producing pages and pages and pages of written text which outlines their mission statement and their aspiration statement, and most employees are not going to be willing to sit down and plow through all that text. But the minute you can click a picture on a screen and hear your CEO talking about how he plans to help the employees through this time of transition and how they plan to get more on target with their marketing strategies, it's extremely compelling and it's quicker. It's an instantaneous way to get the information.

Where do you think multimedia will be in two, five, ten years? What's the future?

It's exciting to think about that! In two years, maybe, what we'll have to look forward to is the rules being a little more defined. There'll be some procedures and tools in place that will make our jobs even easier, which always means more time for creativity.

In five years—once any media matures, you start doing things by rote and it becomes more and more difficult to bring that fresh spark of creativity to the product. Thinking in the long term, ten years from now, we haven't even begun to discover the possibilities for education. I'm not so interested in the whole entertainment sector, so I don't spend as much time thinking about it. But in education we're going to see things happen that we can't even conceive of. We'll take learning to a higher level.

What advice would you give a traditional designer who wants to become a multimedia designer?

The best advice would be not to think about that distinction so much. I think what we can offer the multimedia world as designers is a certain amount of naiveté in what the technology can and can't do. I think that naiveté often fosters lots of creativity, lots of new ideas. But the minute you start letting a medium define what you do as a designer, you limit yourself.

The generation of designers now coming up that has only ever used the computer as its primary tool, that generation's vocabulary is driven by what the computer can and cannot easily do. I think there's a huge danger for that to happen in multimedia. If you become a designer who is driven by what the computer can and can't do and by what has already been done in a relatively new media, you limit your vocabulary.

So I would say this: Become a well-rounded designer. Learn about the principles of good typography. Mix color—color is an issue in multimedia because you're so limited with what you can do now, but if you don't understand the basic principles of how to create hierarchies in dimensional color, you will be even more limited with what you can do on the screen. It's like trying to be a designer without learning how to draw. I can't conceive of that.

How do you approach the balance of form and function in the design of multimedia?

To me that means: How do I bring the principle of "form follows function" into design media or multimedia? I think the answer is constantly evaluating what design elements you're using. Are you using things that are only here for decoration? That tends to be my compass in whatever I do. If I'm using elements that aren't essential to the message and aren't essential to the interface or the on-screen design, then I get rid of them. There's enough to deal with as it is. If you cannot come up with a design based on the information itself, you're really just styling hair. That's a really strong opinion, but that's the way I look at it. You're talking about cosmetics as opposed to communicating.

What book would you recommend to a graphic designer wanting to enter multimedia?

I haven't seen a book I'd recommend specifically about multimedia; I'd refer them back to Paul Rand's books, which try to distinguish between design as a problem-solving activity versus a stylistic function. Most of the books about design treat it like an issue of visual form, which I don't think it is. If people would get their thinking processes honed down, I think they'd do a better job.

Information Designer / Interaction Designer

Nathan Shedroff
....
Cofounder and Creative Director, Vivid Publishing
San Francisco, California

Alvin Toffler's The Third Wave *was a revelation to a kid in the ninth grade who had "always been interested in communication and information." Nathan went on to earn a B.S. in 1989 in industrial design from the Art Center College of Design in Pasadena, California, where he specialized in transportation design: "I'm basically a car designer by training." He took additional courses in graphic design, environmental design, and architecture at the University of California at Berkeley. While still in school, he interned with industrial design companies and immediately upon graduation started working full-time for Richard Saul Wurman's San Francisco-based The Understanding Business. There, Nathan helped develop ideas for Pacific Bell's* Smart Yellow Pages *and also worked on directories for the American Association for Retired People, the steel-case company Vecta, and the seed producer Pioneer Hi-Bred. He also worked on the books* Office Access *and* Information Access *before starting (with others) his own book publishing company in his late twenties. After developing* Understanding Computers *and the highly-regarded* Demystifying Multimedia, *Vivid Publishing started getting assignments to do interface design, interactive production, and CD-ROM consulting. Nathan created the interface design for the CD-ROM title* Voices of the Thirties *for WINGS for learning, Inc., of New York, as well as the information design, interface design, and some visual design for Hands On Technology's business and marketing title* Crush.

What do you do at Vivid?

My official title is creative director, although at typical multimedia firms of our size, which is about 25 people, everyone wears a lot of different hats. So I end up doing many things, most of them in the area of design—interface design, information design, interaction design, and a lot of visual design.

As creative director, I'm responsible for the quality of all creative aspects here. That includes writing, visuals—whether photographs, illustrations, charts, or typography—and to some extent, animations, video quality, and sound quality. By "quality" I mean design quality, not fidelity.

An example of something I might do would be helping to choose which sound, video, or image bites to use, and how they are manipulated.

I'm also responsible in a corporate sense for making sure that everyone is "getting their creative growth in." In order to keep good people, you have to make sure they're happy, and that usually means them feeling like they're growing. So I have creative reviews with people that aren't necessarily job performance reviews, but more along the lines of "What are you learning?" "What do you want to be learning?" "What do you want to be working on?" And then we figure out how to help people meet those goals.

One of the things that we're doing here at Vivid is offering a school, using our own employees as the teachers. Vivid School meets one night a week and on some Saturdays, and has a process track and a tools track. The process track covers information design, interaction design, and writing or text issues. Then we look into all the graphic issues: graphic illustration, photography, typography, color theory. We also consider animation, sound, video, and programming.

It's important to us to make sure that people are growing and as well-rounded as possible. Because sometimes we'll get an emergency—maybe someone is sick—and we've got to get the work done anyway.

You also function as an information designer?

Yes, and also interaction designer. They are my specialties, but those are usually on a project basis as opposed to a Vivid-wide basis.

What does an information designer do?

It's the person responsible for clear communications. Information design is all about the purposeful organization and presentation of messages so that communication is effective.

How does that differ from what the writer is doing?

Anyone who communicates is doing information design to some extent, except most people don't have the background for dealing with the information itself. Writers communicate, graphic designers communicate, photographers communicate, everyone communicates, and to that extent, everyone has a potential for being an information designer. But an information designer is someone who has specifically been taught or at least understands certain principles about data and information, which allows them to create better communications.

What kind of principles?

The first is that data and information are two different things. Our culture treats them as the same thing. We use the words interchangeably, but they're not interchangeable. Information is something that is more useful than data. Data are all those little bits out there, and as such they have no meaning to your life. Especially as a consumer, we get bombarded with too much data as it is. And the reason we feel bombarded is because it is not useful to us. Information is data set into context and therefore made more meaningful.

The next distinction is knowledge. Knowledge is information that is enabling. It's something you gain through a richer experience. This is where interaction design comes in. You use interaction design principles when you're trying to create an experience. What we gain from an experience is usually knowledge. You're gaining information as well, but it's a different kind of information.

The next step up from that is wisdom. You can only really build products that give experiences and help build knowledge, but people have to build wisdom for themselves. You can help them by teaching them how to build wisdom and giving them meta-information and meta-concepts.

Are there people working solely as information designers?

Probably not, because there is no academic courseware or few if any degree programs in information design. So people migrate here from somewhere else. You can't narrowly define someone as an information designer out of context from their background. They might come from a writing, graphic, or industrial design background. They could be a photographer or an animator.

Once they come from these backgrounds, is there actually a job title called information designer?

In our company there is, but in most companies there isn't. You have to realize that most people have never heard of the term "information design." Most people don't even realize that these issues need to be broached. Information design is part of the process of developing multimedia.

What is the process in your company?

Usually, the information designer is involved at the very beginning. They are there to help determine who the audience is and what skills and needs it might have. What is the message to be conveyed? What are the goals of the product? And then, of course, the information designer looks at the content and the mission statement, and tries to juggle all these questions to find a solution. They're responsible specifically through the prototype and the design, and somewhat through the production, for making sure that the communication is clear, whether regarding content or organization. For example, rather than just having a chart somewhere, it should be a well-designed, informative chart. Maybe there is a pie chart when there should be a bar chart. Or maybe there shouldn't be a chart at all. Or maybe some other interaction would be better. So information designers are there always to check on things and make sure things are "kosher."

An information designer is the user's advocate, always checking to see that whatever a user is experiencing at any time is exactly what they should be experiencing. The information designer focuses on the communications, the messages, and the features of navigation. Are the messages and navigation clear? Or not—if that's the desired effect, as is the case in some games.

How does one get trained in information design?

There are no good courses that I know for information design, and very few books that even broach the subject. This is always a problem every time you have a new need, such as that multimedia has highlighted regarding information design. That need always precedes schools fulfilling the teaching of it.

And interaction design? Could you expand on the meaning of this skill?

It's even less known. It's the designing of an experience. There are a lot of issues that need to broached, such as whether you need to create a narrative or not. What should the features and interactions of a product be, meaning what kind of navigation, control, and user feedback are you using? That's a real multimedia product issue.

Point of view needs to be considered: How are you presenting this information? Are you just presenting it from one point of view? If it's an educational piece, you may want to present several points of view so that someone gets a richer understanding of what you're communicating.

So point of view, narrative, storytelling—anything to do with creating experience is what interaction designers are all about. Should the product contain any guides or helpful agents that will help the user? Are there any co-creative elements to the product—is there anything that lets them participate, build, and create things for themselves, either with their own content or with content that's shipped on the product?

All of those things need to be shaped purposefully and consciously. That's what interaction design is all about.

Both of these areas—information design and interaction design—apply to everything about communication, not just interactive multimedia. They apply to lectures and seminars and classes and books and films and conversations and performances—everything.

Perhaps it's just more noticeable when information design is lacking in multimedia . . .

Oh, you do notice it much more. And multimedia is new. People have been around school plays, so they know about creating performance presentation in that format. People have conversations, so they've learned *ad hoc* how to communicate. But if you consider improv comedy, some people are naturals at it, some need to take classes, and some people are just never going to get it. There are all these forms for the more established genres of experiences.

If someone wants to work in this area, should they present themselves as something else that happens to contain this skill set?

It's time information design was recognized as a separate discipline instead of just shuffling it into something else. I've seen people packaging themselves as information designers. And every time they go for job interviews, they've got to explain what the hell that means! But that can be good, because otherwise those hiring might just say, "We don't need a creative director," if that's what you were calling yourself.

It seems like information designers have a long, hard haul just trying to get a job. How else can they present themselves so that people understand?

You can package yourself as an interface designer. Interface design is a three-part process: information design, interaction design, and then what I call the "sensorial," which is the design of all the media—media such as the visual, auditory, time-based media (like video or film), lighting, illustration, sound design, engineering, and music. The production of music, the writing of music, the performance of music, voice talent, sound effects—that's all in the auditory area. All these sensorial media have entire historical traditions.

But to be a designer in all these fields seems overwhelming!

Oh, no one person is. But that's why everyone from one of these backgrounds touches interactive media. You need interaction and information design to be constantly guiding the way and structuring the experience.

Most people think interface designers are coming solely from a graphical point of view.

That's the problem. It's grown into being visual and graphical screen design, but the issues are much farther reaching than that. They are all the issues of information design, plus all the issues of interaction design, as well as any kind of media design for computers.

Are you saying information designers need to have some visual design background?

The only way to express the information and interaction design is through the sensorial media. Graphic design was just my particular way into information design. But for writers, that's their way in. But you can't sit down with someone and say "This is how we structured the product. You're going to go here, and then you'll see these things." It's like seeing the backstage behind the curtain: you're destroying the experience. You have to show them.

But wouldn't that person, then, just be a writer?

No, you're not "just" a writer. Nor would an information designer with a sound background simply be a "sound person." Anyone who's an information or interface designer needs to understand all these issues. They don't need to understand all the tradition of film design or all the issues of graphic design. That's why you hire experts in those areas. But the person in charge of the interface needs to be dealing with all these issues and communicating to all the "sensorial artists" and making sure those issues are addressed and completed through whatever media are part of the product.

Let's say you're designing an interactive piece for children—perhaps it's a diskette, so you can't rely on a lot of audio or video. We may have very little audio or no audio, and very simple black-and-white graphics. We need to pick a style of graphics and possibly some animation. We may want to use text on the screen to show the speech of characters. All the issues involved with designing that experience and presenting that information in the end get expressed visually, and possibly graphically and through sound and music. So those artists and experts need to be in sync all the time. The information/interaction designers—the interface designers—don't necessarily have to be producing those screens or writing that text. But they're in charge of making sure that the text that is written and the screens that are designed, when integrated, work the way they're supposed to work. They may not have any idea of what illustration style to use, but they'll go to an illustrator or a graphic designer and say "These are the issues. This is the audience. This is what we're trying to communicate. What do you think would be a good style? Why don't we explore some styles and see what works best?"

Which multimedia products have you seen that were well-conceived from an information design standpoint?

This is another problem with information design: when it's done really well, you don't notice it. Most of the time, the aim is not to have problems navigating or finding things or understanding things. So when everything is in A-OK condition, you don't notice the hand of the information designer.

There are certainly books I think are wonderful, from an information design standpoint. *Powers of Ten* by Ray and Charles Eames is a great book, though I think it's out of print. It's organized like no other book is organized, but it's perfect for their messages (which is about their unconventional design approaches). Some other books are the *US Atlas*, by Richard Saul Wurman. Just about anything Richard has done is really wonderful, like the Access guides. They are a totally different way of doing a travel guide and wonderful to use because of it. Unlike most travel guides that put all the hotels in one chapter, restaurants in another chapter, and so forth, these books orient you at any given moment to surrounding geography. Richard's approach is exactly what information design is all about.

How would you describe Wurman's approach to information design?

That approach is purposefully organizing and presenting information and data. It is building information in a way that communicates the messages you're trying to communicate, achieves the goals you're trying to achieve.

Let's take a travel CD-ROM. Why not figure out what you're trying to communicate? Let's say I want to communicate what Prague is, what it's like to go to Prague. How do you help people orient themselves so they can build a cognitive model of Prague? That's what you build over time as you live in a city, whether you have a guidebook or not. I would ask: What are all the different ways I can organize this information? Let's do some exploration. And then let's pick the ones that seem to work the best for making the messages clear. That's what information design is all about.

What are the best traits or characteristics to succeed in this kind of work?

Good organizational skills! People who are overall good communicators. There's no accepted tradition of information design, no programs you can come out of with a portfolio of information design pieces. Employers have to look between the lines when hiring for a position like this. For example, a lot of graphic design is oriented towards making things pretty. Not that there's anything wrong with that, but sometimes you want more. The pieces should look good *and* be really organized, well-presented. And innovative, too. So when I interview people, I look for information design skills; I listen to how they converse. It's not easy to find good information designers. The best ones are all coming from performance traditions: theater, dance, music, comedy.

Why?

Because these are the only places where you get trained in how to build an experience for someone else—a live 3-D space, a real-time experience. Improv comedy is the best. In multimedia, all the issues are usually the same: You're building an experience. What are the components of an experience? There might be sound—foreground sound content versus background. Then there's the time-based experiences, which brings in storytelling and narrative—the whole start-to-finish process of what you're trying to communicate over time.

We're talking about people interacting. To make that a coherent experience, you need to know a lot about what it's like for people to watch things and still keep them interested. And you need to know a lot about thinking on your feet and being creative so you're ready for whatever happens. That's what improv is all about. The audience yells something, and bang, the performer has got to go!

The creative process for dealing with that and still building something that is interesting to watch—a rich and wonderful experience—is exactly what interaction design is all about. Most people aren't trained in those issues, and they're certainly not put through rigorous tests like improv training. I think the best thing for anyone who wants to be an interaction designer is to go take some improv comedy classes.

Are there any books you'd like to recommend besides Richard Saul Wurman's excellent Information Anxiety?

There's also a *Design Quarterly* issue Richard created called "Hats," from the MIT Press, that distills the ideas from *Information Anxiety* into 32 pages. It introduces the metaphor of "information hat racks" as a way of explaining the importance of organization as a tool for understanding. Edward Tufte's books are good: *Envisioning Information* is one of the premier books on information design, and *The Visual Display of Quantitative Information* is an important source of ideas and contains guidelines on making charts and graphs that communicate effectively. There's a good book called *A Primer of Visual Literacy* by Donis A. Dondis. It's really more of a graphic design basics book, but it's a good foundation for understanding those issues as they relate to information design. And there's a good section on it in *Multimedia Demystified*.

The Art of Human-Computer Interface Design, edited by Brenda Laurel, has some fairly advanced papers on many aspects of interface design, as well as great articles on multimedia, hypertext/hypermedia, color, and narrative. It is one of the best sources of current developments and thoughts on these topics.

Instructional Designer

Deborah Blank

Principal, Electronic Learning Facilitators
Director, Interactive Systems Division
Bethesda, Maryland

After getting her Ph.D. in curriculum and instruction from the University of Maryland in 1985, Deborah worked as a consultant to the National Geographic Society in Washington, D.C., developing teacher's guides and learning activity books for children. At the same time she was an instructor at Trinity College, developing and directing the Computers in Education and Training Master of Arts program. She is widely published and a frequent presenter at conferences on computer-based training and interactive video.

Tell me about your company.

ELF is a technology-training company that was founded in 1991. We started off teaching children and adults how to use computers, then began training businesspeople to use business applications. In other words, I became intrigued by the computer as a teaching tool. So we got involved in some limited computer-based training (CBT) development, gradually evolving into multimedia in the late 1980s, which has become approximately a third of our business.

We develop multimedia courses for the educational sector and the training sector, so we work with a lot of publishers, corporations, and governmental agencies that require performance-based training. To differentiate ourselves from other companies, we're very experienced in dealing with large amounts of information. A lot of multimedia companies do presentations or public access kiosks that have touch screens. We focus more on applications that have large, large content. For example, we're doing a project for the National Head Injury Foundation that is a three gigabit application of stills and text—anything you want to know about head injury. It will be a resource available in major hospitals for patients, their families, nurses, and doctors. Doctors have very little time to converse with families in trauma centers, and even though it is a kiosk, so to speak, it contains much more information than most multimedia I've seen.

What is instructional design as it relates to multimedia?

I don't think of the multimedia aspect first; I think of the instruction aspect first. I define "instruction" as engaging the learner in whatever he or she needs to do to achieve the objectives of the course. Those might be taking on board new information, new skills, new processes, or a combination of all these. Where the media comes in is that it provides that wonderful blend of the sensory elements, which you don't get sitting in a classroom. Also, you have the benefit of the interaction. Having been a standup instructor for many years, I believe there's nothing like an instructor in person, but students, on the other hand, don't get the one-on-one feedback that you get with multimedia. So the combination of the media plus the one-on-one feedback provides a very rich environment.

However, you don't get the same quality of feedback as you do in a live class. When I did my Ph.D., I looked at the kinds of decisions and activities real teachers engage in to see how we could build some of that into software. Indeed, it's very, very hard, because a live instructor is processing information herself at a rapid rate: Who's getting it? Who's not getting it? What else can I say? How can I rephrase that? How can I paint a picture for them? Unfortunately, when we create multimedia, we are bound by a computer program that can branch in just so many ways. So we have to think as far ahead as we can and anticipate students' needs, all the while knowing that we can't really respond the way a good human teacher can. So it's a trade-off between that kind of on-the-fly feedback versus all this wonderful media that we can bring to bear, plus the students' control over the environment.

Could you elaborate about the sensory elements of multimedia?

In the best of all possible worlds, a live class would use lots of video, graphics, and animation, but unfortunately we don't tend to develop courses that way. We tend to have an instructor blabbing with overheads and some charts, maybe. When you use multimedia, you can engage the learner in controlling the media. We did a program for Roadway Express, an Akron-based long- and short-haul trucking company, that teaches hazard recognition to truck drivers. Basically, we're teaching defensive driving. We let the user control what happens on the road. There's no other way you could teach that—you couldn't do that in a class. It does provide opportunities for allowing the media to actually do the teaching.

Because what people control is where they need to learn?

That's part of it; that's control of the environment. But in this program, the screen becomes the road, and they're sitting at the keyboard and watching a road and cars and a series of interactions among the cars. And they have to decide whether a hazardous situation is developing, and if it is, then they have to intervene. So that's control over the media itself.

Depending on what they choose to do and the timing of their decision, the video changes and they see the natural outcome of their choices. So if they notice the hazardous situation too late—say, it's a child chasing a ball—if they don't respond until the child's halfway out into the street, they'll hit the child on the video, because you can't stop the truck that fast. But if they notice beforehand that a child was playing with a ball and they interacted with the program to slow the truck down, then when the ball runs out in the street, they can stop the truck in time. So that ability to simulate the real world with multimedia, the whole cause-and-effect environment that you can create, is incredibly powerful and, to me, beyond anything that you could do in the traditional classroom.

Where some instructional designers might be hired to help in the creation of a CD-ROM title, in your company they function as producers and hire the rest of the team—the programmers, graphic designers, writers, video directors, producers, as well as other instructional designers.

That's correct, because instruction is the main object of the kinds of programs that we do. Our project managers are instructional designers. I believe with the kinds of projects we do, which are so information-heavy and skill-heavy, that a good instructional designer can really picture the program as it will exist in its final form and therefore can direct the technical and production personnel in a way that one of them could not direct the rest of the team. In strictly entertainment projects, instructional design might not be as critical.

Your résumé indicates you've been involved in "the design, development, and evaluation of multimedia training materials since 1980"—what did "multimedia" refer to before digital multimedia?

In the really old days it referred to slides, audiotapes, and videotapes, sometimes used together. Then in around 1981, when computers were first used for instruction, we used them to make CBT—computer-based training. Later, the term changed to CBI—computer-based instruction, because that was a more encompassing term for the world of education. Then it became CBE—computer-based education—there were all these variations on a theme.

What they had in common was that they were pretty boring, mainly because we were so limited by what we could put on the screen. I think when multimedia was born, people were very keen to have a new term that didn't sound anything like CBT. However, what I've noticed lately is that in the profession we are going back to using "CBT" again, and what we really mean is what is called multimedia. CBT now has nice graphics, and motion video, and so forth . . . everybody's just a little confused about the terms! I think if there is any distinction to be made regarding CBT, it's on the "T" for training, because if you just talk about multimedia, it is a collection of media. So maybe CBT is the better term in our field.

Given this history, I would be interested to hear your definition of multimedia.

Obviously, there's the technical one, which is the use of sound, graphics, and video to convey some sort of message. For our purposes here, it is the use of those media to provide a learning environment. So multimedia by itself is an environment that can be used for anything; in our world, it's an environment that's used for instruction.

Taking one of your multimedia products on CD-ROM or laser disk, can you explain to me what the role of the instructional designer was in creating the project?

I referred earlier to a program for Roadway Express called *The Million Mile Challenge* that teaches hazard recognition. It's essentially a simulation of the driving experience. It contains seventeen different scenarios that are presented to the user in a game format, and the objective is to earn a million accident-free miles. They accumulate points, or miles, by handling these scenarios in a safe way.

In this particular project, the role of the instructional designer was to work with a team of subject matter experts, or SMEs, who were actual drivers who had earned awards for accident-free miles. They suggested ways for the users to interact with the program. The instructional designers knew they wanted a series of scenarios, so the SMEs helped us plan what those should be. They based the scenarios on accident records to find out what seemed to create the most problems. Then they helped us work those out for the purpose of filming them, in terms of how to recreate the hazards, how to position the vehicles.

The instructional designers basically do a brain dump from the subject matter experts. Very often we find that subject matter experts know material backwards and forwards, but they don't know how to break it down for the novice. So one major skill that designers must have is the ability to put themselves in the role of a total novice while at the same time being able to organize the information as it's being reeled off by the subject matter expert. And ask the right questions, and fill in the many, many gaps there are bound to be. Because the experts make a lot of assumptions.

These interviews with SMEs are absolutely critical to the instructional design process. That's part of the fun of instructional design, because you're essentially taking somebody else's data base of information and restructuring it. At the front end, that's one thing the instructional designer does.

The other thing they do is to elicit the course objectives, hopefully in behavioral terms, so the user will be able to do something specified when they're finished with the course, We break the objectives down into two types: "enabling objectives," which are the ones that they must master as they progress through the course and "terminal objectives," which is what we want them to be able to do at the very end of the course (what they'll walk away with). The enabling objectives result in the terminal objectives.

Describe the process of creating a title, as it relates to the instructional designer.

Getting the objective set and getting the content defined and organized are the critical front-end pieces. Then comes the really fun part: figuring out how we're going to facilitate the mastery of those objectives using the multimedia environment. What kinds of activities, what kinds of media, what kinds of interaction with the media can we provide to make sure that people learn? That's what we call the "preliminary design phase." Once that's worked out and agreed to by the client, then the instructional designer oversees or participates in—depending on how senior they are—what we call the "detailed design process." That's where we do all the scripting, all of the specifications for all the visual material—graphics, video stills.

At that point, we do this tedious process called "storyboarding," which is where we create either a screen-based or paper-based place holder for every single interaction: what will happen in the program. We specify at each interaction what the visual is, what the audio is, text, and the branching (where it goes). A lot of people these days are skipping storyboarding, because they're using authoring systems and building screens as they go. But we haven't done it so far, because the courses we develop are so big. We feel we need it all thought through before we begin any kind of coding. But for tiny courses, you can do it on the fly, as long as you can keep track of everything.

From storyboarding, we go into actual production. There the instructional designer is in a review mode, looking at what the production staff is doing: looking at what the artists are creating, supervising the video production. This is not from a producer/director standpoint, but just making sure that whatever needs to be captured in that video for instructional purposes is really there. And they also work with the programming team to answer any questions about what should be appearing or happening. So the role of the designer is reduced as you get into the production phase. It becomes more of a resource person role.

Eventually, the course is actually finished. If the project calls for it, the designer will be involved in the implementation and the evaluation. Very often we do pilot testing where we go out and watch the users and make sure the program is communicating what it needs to communicate. We do any fine-tuning that we need to.

If there is an evaluation component to the project, then we can actually look at data collected by the program, analyze it, and get the students' reaction to the learning environment. It's an evaluation of the program from students' perspective: How much did they learn, and what did they think of it? Most of the training courses we develop have an instructional management system built into them, which records individual student data and spits it out into a data base or some other readable format. Sometimes clients ask us to look at that data to analyze it from a particular perspective. For example, how much did a student learn? If the program tracks exactly where a student went through the course, we can evaluate that to see if one route seems to be superior to another route. We can look at the validity of the questions we asked. We can, if necessary, do a two- or four-week follow-up to see how much students retained. So we can do just about anything that anybody would want to know.

But lots of time the evaluation component isn't there—the client takes the effectiveness at face value. If it seems to work and if students pass the end-of-course test (if there is one), the client is happy. So we don't get to do as much evaluation as we would like.

What is the relationship between interface design and instructional design?

That's one of my favorite topics! To me, it's always been of vital importance to make sure that the design of the interface doesn't get in the way of learning the material. Most instructional designers are aware that they are going to have to choose between teaching the interface directly at the beginning of a program—these are the buttons you're going to encounter; this is what happens when you press each one of them; if you want to try them out now, go ahead—or allowing the user to discover the interface. That means the first time you click each button there may be an instruction that says "We now suggest you click here to find out X." So it's a progressive revealing of the interface. We've done a lot of discussion internally, and we think the first method is probably superior for adults, because they don't like discovery learning that much. They're a little timid, and when they use these programs they're already in somewhat of a compromised situation. They know they're being taught and evaluated. If they have to learn how to operate the machine, it can be difficult. Because CBT, or multimedia, is software, there's bound to be some degree of a learning curve. And any relatively complex training course will have an interface that takes a little getting used to.

So what we've been doing lately is explicitly, at the front end of the program, making the interface available and giving students the option of reviewing it (i.e., being taught it) before getting into the content. If they choose to bypass it, that's fine—then they can go into discovery mode—but at least it's their choice.

With kids it's different—they love discovery. They're not intimidated by the environment, and they're not interested in your telling them how to learn the program. This is true up to about the teen years. It's different with boys and girls. In general, boys are more adventuresome when it comes to exploring the computing environment. Girls start to get a little shy around twelve or thirteen years old. It's sad, actually. Girls are adventuresome while they're children; they're much more open then to making mistakes or having the computer not respond the way they want it to. But once they're in the middle school years, the girls have a more tentative approach to the environment. We're not sure whether it's because boys play more video games or exactly what is accounting for this—math phobia, fear of mechanical things?

Do instructional designers at your company create interfaces?

Our instructional designers do the interface design. We have a couple people on staff who are particularly good at it. This is separate from our graphic designers, who create the interface screen from a visual standpoint but who aren't really the interface designers.

Let's say there are a series of buttons on the screen that lead to different options. The instructional designer working as an interface designer will define the functionality of each button and will know whence it came and where it's going. Because that's directly tied to the instruction. The graphic artist will be shown a simple sketch done by the instructional designer and then will create the buttons so they look very professional. But that graphic designer doesn't have a whole lot of say over the functionality of the buttons. That's the way we do it here. That's not to say that the graphic artist shouldn't have input, but they're not necessarily privy to how the particular buttons on the screen at a given time relate to the whole program. That's the instructional designer's area.

Does it help for instructional designers to have graphic design skills? Do they have to draw their interfaces?

They don't have to be artists, but they have to understand how people interpret what they see on a computer screen. At the end of the preliminary design, we always do a prototype, which is a quick-and-dirty version of the program from an interface standpoint. We mock up all of the basic screens with their buttons, and we try them out with real users—on computers, not on paper. They don't look pretty. But we watch the users interact with the program and quiz them on each and every button. We'll ask them what they think particular buttons stand for, particularly if it has an icon. But more importantly, we ask them what they think will happen when they press a button. If they can't predict what's going to happen, then we've done something wrong. Adults in particular are terrified of getting lost in a program, so they want to be sure when they click on something that they know where they're going. We test the predictability of each button. And that ensures we don't have an interface that's going to cause anybody any problems.

Obviously, instructional designers are used in developing multimedia for training purposes. How could instructional design be useful in the development of other categories of multimedia?

That's where you get into the ability to organize information. One of the things that instructional designers are good at is being able to define hierarchies of information. A public information kiosk of any sort needs to have the information organized so that people can find it quickly. So you need to do some surveying of how people think about certain subjects.

A number of years ago, I was involved in one of the early shopping programs trying to set up a way to order food off an interactive system. And the question was How do people shop? When they go to the supermarket, what do they do? We researched it, and it was fascinating because essentially people have an idea in their heads of what they're going into the store to buy. They want to buy a can of soup. So what do they do? They find the row with the cans, and then their eyes go through this interesting scanning process, looking for visual cues to the product. It all happens quickly until they zero in on the product.

When you're providing a computer environment for something that isn't a traditional function for a computer—e.g., shopping—you want to come as close to the natural way of dealing with the information as you can. So one of the early designs for this project was to show the conveyor belt and let people stop it when they saw something they wanted. But that was insanity, because it was so unnatural compared to the way people actually shopped. They had to sit there waiting for all this stuff to pass by! So once we made this discovery about how people actually shopped, it became clear that the computer screen was the wrong mode of presentation. What we really needed was paper with lists and lists of items in alphabetical order that people could page through very quickly, put a bar code next to it, and scan it in. Up on the computer screen would come a visual representation of the item; they were asked if this was what they wanted; and then if they said "yes," a shopping list was generated to the left of the screen. This was far faster than anything we could come up with, and much more satisfactory.

This brings up an important point about multimedia: We shouldn't forget about paper. It can be a very quick supplement. Despite the reputation of a computer, it is still not as much of a random access environment as paper is. If you have a booklet with a table of contents, or everything is in alphabetical order inside it, you can flip to what you want very quickly. And particularly if the computer is offering one set of information and the paper is offering another, the two can work very well in combination, rather than scrolling on the computer screen. So you can keep the book open in your lap as you refer to the screen. Very often, we find that the addition of paper as a support material is really useful. Students actually prefer it to a window, where they have to scroll up and down, or worse yet, to those situations in which the original screen goes away completely! We're not seeing much of that anymore, but there was a time! So I don't think paper should be completely discounted. At the front end of a project we always look to make sure that we're using the right mix of media. We try not to be too blinded by the technology.

What do the studies show about the effectiveness of multimedia in learning, training, and retention?

Students seem to learn up to 50% faster, and the retention is better. On the retention side, it's very clear that the interaction plays a major role in helping them remember what they learn. In an instructor-led class, or if it is a matter of just watching a video, students can just sit and not pay attention. With the computer, it's going to sit there until you do something.

What are the hallmark elements of a multimedia title with superior instructional design?

One is that the user feels comfortable using it. By comfortable, I mean the user is not intimidated by the program; they understand all the instructions. They feel like they're getting a fair shake and that nothing is happening in the program to make them think that the designer didn't know what they were talking about. If they know the answers are right and the computer is telling them they're wrong, it's poor design. That happens more than it should.

It's not a technical problem; it's more that there are fine points to the material that maybe the designer didn't uncover—another way of thinking about the material. Or it could be that the user is very sophisticated and interprets the material in a different way. It is incumbent on the designers, working with subject-matter experts, to make sure that every accommodation is made for multiple viewpoints when you're saying a response is "right" or "wrong." That's true with any kind of instruction. But when learning with an instructor, the difference is that students can raise their hands and say "I politely disagree" and you can have a discussion. With the computer, you can't, so people feel wronged. Good material doesn't let that happen.

Another hallmark of good instructional design is that the feedback is useful. It's not just a matter of "Sorry, that's not the right answer; try again." It needs to be as explicit as it possibly can be with hints and helpful examples. This becomes a budget issue, so sometimes you can't fault the designer. If the client wants a very inexpensive product, sometimes you have to resort to less explicit feedback. One technique we like to use is a hint. It might be "You're thinking along the right track, but you might also want to consider X." We give them a piece of the answer.

We did a program for children where they can date fossils by looking under a microscope. The program would ask "What period do you think the fossil comes from?" and the periods were listed as options. After the child chose a period, the program might say "No, you're a little too early." Or even a better hint would be "Note that this animal actually was an amphibian, and we know that amphibians came after reptiles." So it hones in on the information.

Another approach is to provide multiple hints. So there might be the first hint, and then there could be a button that's called Another Hint. When pressed, it tells you something more, just as a human teacher would try to elicit an answer. We can build that into programs, but it's more expensive. The closer we come to replicating what a human teacher does, the more expensive the program gets.

Is the job of the instructional designer in multimedia typically a freelance position, or are there many staff jobs?

It's both. It's nice for us to have a staff of instructional designers—we have six people who are full-timers—but we also hire consultants for smaller projects or if we need a particular expertise. There are lots of very good consultants. Lots of companies use a combination of staff and freelancers.

The newest thing is the virtual multimedia company, where there's just a single individual who hires a team for each project, and the team may never work again together.

Tell me about the education of an instructional designer. Which undergraduate majors best prepare one for this field? Is information or library science helpful?

Most of our designers come from either a psychology background or an education background. These are the best ones for understanding how people think and how they learn. Most of our people go on to get a master's degree in ISD—instructional systems development—where they actually study how to design instructional systems. It's a two-year program, and we find it gives people a real good background. Now, those programs don't necessarily focus on multimedia; they have it as a component. It's a nice curriculum because it addresses adult-learning theory and different media, how to organize information. And then if the program has multimedia built in, that's ideal.

One reason ISD is popular in the Washington, D.C. area is that a lot of the government contracts require an ISD approach. It's been a good model for many years, way before computer-based training, because it teaches people how to deal with large amounts of information, and very often the government contracts require tons of instructional objectives.

Is it necessary, in your opinion, to get an advanced degree before practicing this profession?

No. There are natural-born teachers, and a lot of them gravitate to this field, particularly if they like instruction more than they like kids.

Your background expertise is also in cognitive psychology. How does that relate to instructional design?

Cognitive psychology looks at the thinking side of psychology. So much of what we do in multimedia design is controlling people's brains. That sounds crude, but everything we put on the screen has some sort of impact and makes people think something. As we move from screen to screen, we are directing their attention and their focus. So we need as much insight as possible into how we're doing that.

Aside from organization skills, what intellectual, technical, and personal skills does the instructional designer need?

They need to be really good listeners so that when they work with subject matter experts they're open minded and can take information on board quickly. They need to be gregarious because they're working with a team of people; they need good interpersonal skills. They need to be smart.

Again, that sounds crude, but some of the topics one encounters as an instructional designer are very technical in some way. So people need to have basic knowledge of how the world works and then be a "quick study" about information they know absolutely nothing about.

They also need to be very flexible, because at least in areas we work in, the courses metamorphose as we go through the design process. The client may reveal a whole body of information they failed to let us know was part of the course early on. They'll say "We really should cover topic X." And we'll ask if they have any existing materials, and they'll answer "I have few videotapes and two dozen books," and soon the course is twice as big as you expected, which causes all kinds of contractual problems. For the designer it means taking a deep breath and finishing what they were doing. Flexibility is very important.

How did you get drawn to instructional design?

I taught high school for a number of years, then went on to teach college—I was training teachers and supervised student teachers. I found what I really loved the most was planning for the instruction as opposed to delivering the instruction. I enjoyed organizing the information. The planning was what was fun, so it naturally evolved into these "teachers in a box." It's a little embarrassing: Aren't teachers supposed to love getting in front of their classes?

In general, instructional designers have to love information and really get excited about putting it into order for maximum effectiveness, maximum transfer. That's really an important value they have to hold: it does matter how you organize information.

Why did you decide to work in the area of multimedia?

I've often wondered about that. I know precisely when it happened: it was when the Apple II was born, in the early 1980s. A company called SRA put out a little math program to teach long division. It was just a simple little thing. I saw it at a conference, and I was blown away. I thought: this is unbelievable that someone could sit here and have the computer teach them. The whole concept of one-on-one instruction made a lot of sense to me, because I had done enough teaching to know how powerful it could be. And here was a way to get it at much less cost than human tutoring.

I was a reading specialist at Trinity College at the time and went to my department chair, who told me to find out everything I could. Within a year, we were offering the first computers-in-education-and-training course. I was 15 minutes ahead of my students in terms of what I knew. We cobbled together whatever software we would get at the point, which wasn't a whole lot, and started designing our own programs. It was fun.

What advice would you give to someone who wanted to enter instructional design of multimedia?

They should look at lots and lots of computer programs and decide what their own philosophy is. They should find out what types of programs appeal to them and try to make a match between what they're seeing and their own learning styles. And maybe watch other people use programs so they can get insight. That's something I generally find is lacking when people come to us straight out of school. They may be technically up to speed, but they haven't seen a lot of programs, and they haven't watched many people use them.

If you're going to be a really good multimedia designer, you need to have a whole repertoire of techniques. And you need to know how people respond to these different techniques. Here in Washington, D.C., the National Geographic Society has a whole room of interactive systems. And it's really fun to go down there and watch people use them: watch kids, watch adults. You can learn a lot about how well the program is communicating to them. And people are even good about letting you interview them.

So there's formal training, the courses at the schools, and then there's this informal self-exploratory mode.

Is there anything students of instructional designers need to be aware of that they sometimes overlook?

We're in the business of multimedia for profit. One thing that's not taught in schools and that people should be aware of if they are producing material for sale—either custom products or off-the-shelf products—is that unlike the school environment where you can take your time and re-do things and obsess, once you're in the commercial world it's different. You have to be aware that very often you're working with a budget and to a schedule set by the clients, which may impose constraints on you that you're not used to. So sometimes the fun side of this business—the creative and artistic side—can be stifled by the situation. That's why I mentioned flexibility before. If someone wants to play with multimedia, play with creating it, they shouldn't be in a business environment; they should be in an academic environment or in R&D. In the average multimedia production environment, people who are primarily intrigued by the new technology, who care more about the process than the products, or who want to achieve something new and different with every project may be disappointed. People need to know themselves well enough to know if they can adjust to a bit of compromise sometimes.

The other thing people need to remember is that multimedia is software. In the end, what you're producing is extremely complex and will be used without you being there. So you need to anticipate the user's requirements at every turn. And to be constantly humbled that you won't be able to think of everything that the user might want to do, see, or think. You need to make yourself as open to new ideas as you can and at the same time not be frustrated by the fact that you can't be all things to all people through this medium.

What are the best and worst things about being an instructional designer?

The best thing is just falling into pits of information you knew nothing about. So all of a sudden you're learning about something not only that you didn't know anything about, but you didn't even know existed. That's lots of fun, particularly when it's a job skills program, where you get to learn somebody else's job. The worst? The limitations of the medium itself to do what you want to do, as well as the contractual limitations. We sometimes have fabulous ideas, but it's not in the budget or the schedule, or the medium won't support it. That can be a little bit frustrating.

Which books or magazines can you recommend for people interested in entering this field?

Most are pretty pedantic, but one I think is wonderful: *Managing Interactive Video/Multimedia Projects* by Bergman and Moore. A good general training magazine, though somewhat academic, is the *Journal of Interactive Instruction Development*, which contains studies of what research people have done. *NewMedia* is good because instructional designers need to be technically literate, and this magazine is a good way to keep up with what's going on. *Multimedia Producer* is good because it gives you summaries of new products, so, again, you can get ideas about how people are designing.

Which professional societies do you suggest that people join?

The American Society for Training and Development and the Association for Educational Communications and Technology, whose conferences are good. The IICS is probably the best one, because it has a lot of local chapters. It's the most focused organization in terms of multimedia, with a lot of good networking and workshops.

Picture Editor / Photo Researcher

Ericka McConnell
....

Production Researcher, Tom Nicholson Associates, Inc.
New York

Ericka received a liberal arts education at Lewis and Clark College, where she majored in fine art and graduated in 1992. She studied art history, painting, and photography, but she took few computer courses. Her only exposure to technology during those years was a summer course in Adobe Photoshop that she found less than enticing. In college she had the opportunity to spend six months in New York City with ten other classmates, interning at the 20x24 Polaroid Studio (a commercial studio where an enormous Polaroid camera is rented out to famous photographers such as William Wegman, Joyce Tenneson, and Lorna Simpson).

After graduating, she returned to New York to start her career as a portrait photographer, initially working at a photo gallery editing pictures and helping the photographers they represented organize shows. She got the job through someone she had met during her internship the year before. A turning point came the summer after she arrived, when she went to the Center of Creative Imaging in Camden, Maine, for a three-week course in Adobe Premiere and Photoshop. For the first time she became excited about the idea of manipulating images with computers, especially because so many of the instructors were "creative types," not just "computer types": "I saw that there were people interested in technology who were people like me."

Soon afterwards, she got a job as an assistant at Magnum Photo, the photo agency. For a corporate executive, she updated portfolios and helped create a CD-ROM showcasing the work of their photographers. On this project, she edited pictures and scanned them, and also spent a lot of time trying to explain the technology to the photographers, who were suspicious that the digital age was making their work too easily accessible.

She went on to Voyager, the multimedia publisher, starting out as a production assistant working on five CD-ROMs, scanning photographs, toning, cropping, and getting images into the right format and size so they could be put into the CD. Now at Tom Nicholson Associates, she is working with a team on a museum kiosk project.

What CD-ROM titles did you work on at Voyager?

Maus, Art Spiegelman's Holocaust story told through illustrated characters; *Comic Book Confidential*, based on a documentary about comic books by Ron Mann; Marvin Minsky's *Society of the Mind*, a philosophical treatise about technology and culture by the Harvard professor; and a CD-ROM about Stephen J. Gould and his thoughts about evolution and Darwin.

What is the work of a picture editor in a multimedia company?

You go to meetings when new projects are announced and work with the production coordinator on the scheduling, and also with the designer, to see which images will be needed to be included in the CD-ROM. Sometimes you're looking for images that will go into the interface; other times you're trying to find images that will appear in the packaging. One time at Voyager, I had to look for fabrics from the 1960s for the interface of Ephemeral Films, but usually it's a matter of finding pictures, drawings, or historical maps.

Once you get the assignment of what to look for, you have to figure out how to get it. I've often worked with the Library of Congress tracking down historical images or old books. Once I was working on a project that involved classical composers, and I went to record stores to look at old album covers. I'd see what they had done, look at the credits, and try to find those designers to see if we could make something for the CD-ROM that matched the style of that period.

The kind of research varies depending on what's being adapted. If the CD-ROM is being adapted from a book, then I work with the book publisher to see what images they might already have. Sometimes the job entails dealing with legal rights and usage fees, too.

Many companies don't even have the role of picture editor as a separate job; the producer or designer might perform this function. But at Voyager and at Tom Nicholson, they came to the point where they saw they needed someone on this full-time.

What kinds of software programs have you used working as picture editor?

I've used Photoshop, HyperCard, Filemaker Pro, and Retrospect, a storing and retrieval program. Mostly I had to pick up my knowledge of the programs on the job. In one job I started learning Quark and was hoping to do some design work.

What kind of company do you work for?

Tom Nicholson develops multimedia titles for the consumer and education markets, and for public audiences, such as in museums. Some of the titles this company has produced in the past include *The League Leaders* (for a kiosk at the National Baseball Hall of Fame), *A Visual History of Sailing* (for IBM), and a number of interactive projects used internally by Apple Computer, IBM Corporation, Citibank, and other companies.

What are you working on now?

We're now working on two projects: the interface design for the Delphi Internet Services and the Mashantucket Pequot Nation project. A museum is being built on the reservation of the Pequot Indians in Connecticut, using money from their successful casinos. They're trying to tell something about their history. It's a challenging assignment to create images because there is not a lot of existing material and very little in the way of written records. I'm working on a content team to help determine from a visual perspective how to handle this limitation; we're hiring designers to draw pictures. I'm also doing factual research, working with historians and going to libraries. I create a series of questions called a content outline and then read books to try to answer these questions. After I've turned in the content outline, it gets presented with other material we've collected to a board of Pequot Indians and historians to review if what we've uncovered is correct.

The mockup/prototype/final product process should be finished in the beginning of 1996, when the museum opens in Ledyard, Connecticut, near Mystic. Our work will appear in 32 kiosks on 32 different subjects.

What are the best traits or characteristics for this kind of work?

Definitely you have to be an active person, someone who is excited at the prospect of going out into a city and tracking things down. You have to enjoy looking for things, because things don't just come to you. You also have to be able to work well with people. Picture editors work very closely with designers.

I think it helps having a visual background; it has helped me determine what is visually pleasing or beautiful, what will look good in a program.

Have you had any interesting experiences tracking something down?

Once at Voyager I had trouble finding a map to be used for the Gould CD-ROM. It had to be a map of the world from the time of Darwin's *Voyage of the Beagle*. I couldn't find it at any of the normal research sources in New York or at the Library of Congress. Then one day I happened to be walking on the Upper East Side and came across an antique map in a funky map store. And the map only cost $20, whereas most of what they were selling was in the $300–$400 range. That was pretty exciting.

Here at Tom Nicholson I've been researching caribou, since Pequot used to hunt them with spears for their food source. I've had to call Canadian and Alaskan radio and TV stations, as well as government offices, to collect documentaries done on a famous herd of caribou which lives in the tundra and which is studied a lot. Eventually, I collected about twenty documentaries, reviewed them, edited them, and made a three-minute QuickTime movie of the best clips (that may or may not be incorporated in the final project). I'm learning about subjects I knew nothing about for which there is a wealth of information. It's a learning process for everyone. For example, the two producers came up with a certain image—a caribou being speared—but then we discovered that since European contact the Indians have used guns to kill caribou! So images before the time of Columbus of caribous being speared will have to be drawn, not depicted in photos or video. We're always having to adapt our expectations.

What attracted you to work as a picture editor in multimedia?

I saw that the arts were merging with the world of computers, that there was a lot of change happening and that it was very exciting. Multimedia is affecting the way we view the arts and how we look at things. It makes information more accessible. For example, the Maus CD-ROM not only shows the artist's work; it shows his artistic process. CD-ROMs provide a similar kind of excitement as movies; they're a nice environment to learn things in.

What are the most interesting aspects of working as a picture editor?

When you find an image and it works. It's exciting when you've been able to get hold of something really fast. It's great when the designers are thrilled by what you've been able to track down.

What is the least interesting part of your job?

When you're not excited about what you're looking for. Then it becomes rote, and you feel like you're a machine, not contributing to the creative process.

What advice would you give someone interested in this field?

Take a few classes in different software programs. Research the different companies you're interested in, and try to see their products. Try to make something creative and original in Premiere, Photoshop, or some other program so you can show them that you can control the technology and can make something really thoughtful.

It's also important to remember that because multimedia is such a new field, there are people coming in from many backgrounds. There is no one approach. I see people with film backgrounds who come in without computer skills, but any experience you have can't hurt. What's fascinating about the industry is that because it is so new, there is a broad mix of people coming together to create something that any one of us would have a hard time doing on our own.

Programmer

Britt Peddie
....

Programmer and video guy, MechADeus
San Francisco, California

Originally from the Pacific Northwest, Britt started out as a musician playing drums professionally in a new wave/electronic-dance-music band. Eventually, he was introduced to people using computers to write music and moved to where much of the early work was being done, San Francisco. During this period he repaired computers and sold them through retail stores. While setting up Novell networks, he started meeting people using multimedia in kiosks at trade shows and began solving problems for them as part of his own apprenticeship. Now in his mid-thirties, Britt has worked on corporate products in programming, project design, and implementation, including kiosks for Trigem, a Korean computer manufacturer; a demo disk for Aldus Freehand; and a laser disk kiosk for Bandag, a truck/tire retreading franchiser. He quit school in his senior year of high school and is self-taught as a programmer.

You started out as a musician and ended up a programmer.

My constant analogy is that multimedia production is like playing in a band. CD-ROM developers are the rock bands of the nineties—small groups of people with varying skills who all need to work together to create a product. The guys who put together *7th Guest* or *Myst* are the type who will be the rock stars in the year 2000.

Describe the role of programmer.

There are different levels of programmers. Lead programmers, or program designers, design the program for implementation, which involves creating the feature set desired for an application (such as a game). They take into account whether the program will run on a single or a number of platforms. They define the overall architecture of the program, then pass the work off to other programmers to implement. Within the ranks of programmers there are junior programmers and senior programmers, depending on the degree of responsibility.

  Programmers work closely with the game designers, writers, producers, and directors to give feedback on what is feasible for the budget or what's not possible for technological reasons. In the case of our company, we have Windows and Mac programmers in-house, and we go outside for a 3DO port to the game.

How would you distinguish between a program designer and a game designer?

The game designer designs game play: Are balls falling from top or side? Does the user press the keyboard or mouse for play? It's the program designer's job to determine the best way to implement the functionality the game designer has come up with. Should we use sprites here? Should we have multiple soundtracks playing here?

How does being a programmer in a multimedia company differ from other work environments?

The job is the same, but working on a game or a title you have to understand the media involved: audio, video, animation, text, graphics. A lot of programming in multimedia is the integration of elements, taking sounds and videos and putting them together in one coherent piece so they flow together. When we hire, we look to people with a media background, like someone who has been a musician, or a video background.

What is your typical day like—what is the process?

It varies, which is nice. It might be a day of meetings (where things are being decided), or it might be a day of program design, implementation, and working with other programmers. Other days, it's just plain sitting in front of the computer and writing code: putting on blinders and staring at the screen. Then there are times where we spend time checking to see if things are done correctly, for example, if an animation starts and ends at the right place — quality control issues.

What is the best thing about being a programmer?

Getting something to work: the feeling of accomplishment when you've taken a complex problem and seen it work for the first time. It's a very focused job with small and big rewards. You're in control of making the thing happen, and when you do, it makes you feel good.

What are the worst aspects about being a programmer?

In a project, the artists and designers take as long as they need or want, and whatever time is left over is what the programmer gets. On a three-month-long project, we often work the most during the last couple weeks. With programming, either it works or it doesn't, so there's no margin for error. That comes back to the issue of time constraints. There is almost always a tight deadline, and that generally means long days and nights. A 50-hour week is a slow, relaxing week for me. Other weeks run 80 to 100 hours, and I've personally put in 120-hour weeks on deadline. Some programmers just live in their offices and go home once a week. They're hungry kids just out of college who can't be torn away from their work and who sleep and shower at the office. They don't take weekends off. But after five years, they get programmer burnout.

What are the best kinds of traits or characteristics to work in multimedia?

You have to be able to communicate. It's not the kind of job where you go off, sit in a corner, and do your stuff. The traditional picture of a bleary-eyed programmer looking at a computer screen day in and day out is not the case in multimedia anymore. There is so much human interaction in creating an interactive piece—writers, sound designers, directors—that everybody needs to understand what the other person is doing to make the pieces fit together. You're getting input from all kinds of people, and you need to communicate with them and they with you.

What is the best kind of education for this work?

I personally dropped out of high school, but other programmers went to college and majored in mathematics or computer science. There are various types of programmers, and for some things—such as real-time 3-D programming or for writing device drivers—you need to have a heavily mathematical background. More and more, it's a math-heavy job; I wish I'd devoted more time to studying math when I was younger. As the machines get faster, they are able to do more, so you need to be able to make them do more. Programs have become so complicated compared to a few years ago. The high-end programs keep getting more complex, and the low-end ones absorb the features of last year's high-end. But for interface programming, it's not so much about math as it is the art of programming. It's knowing how to make things simple for the user.

What about on-the-job training?

The nature of the job is that it changes. If you're going to be competitive, you've got to keep up. I read almost nonstop: books, magazines, manuals. I read *Byte*, *MacWeek*, *PC Week*, and *PC World*. I go to trade shows. I'm always calling up hardware and software vendors and filing away their literature. If you don't have the latest features in your programming, you aren't doing your job.

Tell me about being a freelance programmer versus being on staff.

Typically, there is an in-house team, but we bring in outside people for specific projects or jobs. Some people like the contract programming side, where they can take a job or not, take a month off if they want to. When I was working for myself, I'd work six to nine months a year, making more money in less time. Now I'm on staff; I got married and there's more stability.

What do you advise someone trying to get into programming?

Instead of only working at one place, get a lot of experience under your belt in different environments; learn more than one program. That way, you show that you are able to jump into something new and make it work. And it isn't enough to just know C or C++. You should also have experience dealing with sound or integrating video into a program. You should have exposure to authoring languages like Macromind Director, Visual Basic, or Asymetrix Multimedia ToolBook.

How fluent in these languages does someone need to be in order to be hired?

We try to bring people in at the bottom and raise them up, but that's not always feasible when we're on a project on deadline. It's hard to find very experienced people who have something to show that is exactly what we need. Entry-level people have to be thoroughly proficient, and we prefer seeing some commercial product experience other than a class project. On the other hand, if the need is great, if we can't find anybody else and don't have the time to keep looking, we might give someone with little experience their first break.

How did you get your job at MechADeus?

I had some friends who knew of this place. I had been working as a technical director for another multimedia developer a few blocks from where I'm working now. They knew who I was, so they didn't even ask for examples of my work. I haven't had a résumé in years. Better than a résumé is to walk in with a CD-ROM and say "Here's what I have done."

What programs have you worked on at MechADeus?

I did the Mac version of the game *Critical Path* and all the digital video production for both Windows and Mac versions. By that I mean I did the digital compressing, editing, and compositing. I also did some minor programming changes for the Japanese and German translation versions for both Mac and Windows.

For *Daedalus Encounter* I was the program designer, Mac programmer, and again did video production. There was a two-week shoot at a large blue-screen stage with a director and live talent. My involvement was from the technical side, telling them if lights were casting shadows or how the human characters would fit into our computer-generated world.

How do you see multimedia developing in the future?

More and more networks, on-line shared assets. Video will become standard issue; there will be more real-time 3-D and bigger, faster sprites. Everything is already well-defined for the near term, but it will keep getting better: crisper real-time 3-D animation with larger texture maps.

I also see multimedia becoming more mainstream in the corporations. Large companies will bring more talent in-house. It used to be that to finance a kiosk they'd take a little from one budget, a little from another. Now when companies plan a new product introduction, they budget from the start for a multimedia sales tool on the trade floor. So there's more assured money out there for developers, and that will continue to grow.

Are there any books you would recommend that give a good idea of what your profession is all about?

Just the classic, *The C Programming Language*.

What professional societies do you belong to?

None. In fact, I don't like them. If you're really busy, you don't have time for those clubs.

Quality Assurance

Marcia Watson
Independent Consultant
Los Angeles

Frédéric De Wulf, manager of developer relations for Microsoft in New York, calls Marcia Watson the "goddess of testing." At Philips Interactive in Los Angeles she oversaw a staff that grew to be as large as 100 people to test CD-I software and, eventually, hardware. She had originally gone to Philips as a multimedia product designer, reviewing titles that were under development, but became intrigued by an offer to work in the area of quality assurance. After three-and-a-half years at Philips, Marcia moved to another Los Angeles company, Davidson and Associates, a multimedia title developer. Marcia received her undergraduate degree in 1966 from the University of California, Berkeley, with a major in modern European history, and went on to teach world history and media development to high school students for ten years. After receiving her Ph.D. in history in 1984, she was introduced to multimedia while developing management training programs. She is currently a consultant in multimedia product development.

What is the role of the tester on a multimedia title?
It varies, but I see the purpose of testing as identifying the risks associated with a title. "Risks" vary from the speed of title performance to such issues as whether content has been cleared for copyright. We check to see if the credits are properly done. Is everything spelled correctly? A lot is swept under the rug during the production process, and sometimes the checks and balances haven't been working. It's the tester's role to say "What about that little pile of dust in the corner?"

Technical testing issues include:
- Error handling—if there is an error in the code, how sensitive or forgiving is the program?
- What happens when the input device receives multiple hits? (Said another way: If kids pound on the mouse, what happens?)
- If you have a "save" function in the title, does it work properly?
- Is there a dimming function? (Does the screen dim down after a while when when the program is in use? This is a desired feature, because it saves screens.)

- Are the hot spots big enough for the input device? (If the program uses a joystick, which is a lot cruder than a mouse, testers have to check if the hot spots are big enough.) [*Editor's note*: A hot spot is an area on the screen where an event happens when a cursor passes over it.]

Fixing things takes time, and performance issues usually come up at the very end, often past the market release date. It is not our decision which problems to fix or not—that's made at the strategic level by the head of production or the head of the company.

What kinds of things did your staff at Philips pick up?

Once someone noticed Disney art and asked whether it had ever been licensed. It turned out it hadn't, and a lot of art had to be created at the last minute to replace it. Another time, we had a CD-I music title on "how to play the guitar." One of the testers was a music notation expert—we had specifically hired content experts—and he noticed that the timing of the music being played didn't match the way it was notated. Every notation in that section had to be redone, art and everything. Another time, we had a piece that was essentially very chauvinistic and offensive; once there was blue language that had to go.

Describe the testing process.

About six to eight weeks before a title is turned in for testing on a grand scale, someone on the team is charged with the preparations. A methodology must be devised and written down. Too many companies approach testing with what I call the "any-monkey-can-do-it" method. This is like turning loose everyone in a football stadium with lawn mowers. They may or may not cut all the grass. To do it right, you have to make sure everyone is assigned a ten-yard strip to be responsible for. So testing has to be planned in advance. One of the things that differentiates testing organizations is the degree that they're able to plan the process as opposed to winging it.

This plan, then, is the blueprint for the testing team, which includes a group of testers and a supervisor. They go through the title and pull out the things they find wrong and write up "bug reports." [Editor's note: see the end of Chapter 5 for a sample "bug report."] These reports are organized and then turned back to the production team—the software engineers and the producer. They fix certain things, return the product back to us, and then the whole process résumés.

After x-number of passes, there's basically a mutual agreement about what mistakes everyone can live with. There is no title that comes out without some problems; it's just a matter of degree. There are, of course, some things that have to be fixed: timing issues (but "fast enough" is a judgment call), the palette displays (the colors), the legal clearances. And not only do we check spelling; sometimes we actually write the literature that accompanies the product.

Quality assurance is an entry-level position, isn't it?

Yes, and it is a good training ground. I think everyone who works in multimedia should get involved in QA for at least four months. It gives you a dual awareness between the technical issues, as well as the more global user perspective.

What is the difference between a tester and a program debugger?

Debugging is usually done by the software engineers who created the title. They take the bug report generated by the testers and fix the problems that were noted down.

What kind of background should testers have?

There is no formal training to do this work. People come to it with a large range of skills. We need editorial types, those I call the "T-crossers and I-dotters." At the other extreme are the "cowboys"—they have a sixth sense about which places to go. You don't even give them a test guide; you just turn them loose. You can't train people with this ability, but you can recognize someone who has it once they've been on the job a couple weeks.

The one thing that is consistent about good testers, no matter what their backgrounds, is that they are accustomed to building structures of ideas. Musicians, writers, software engineers, and graphic designers are all comfortable with the structure of ideas and make good testers. Being detail-oriented also helps.

What kinds of people did you look for when you were hiring the team at Philips?

There are three basic characteristics. They had to be just plain smart. Then they had to be the kind of person who not only works at a precise level of detail, but could also handle conceptual material; essentially, they had to be able to work at a low level and a high level at the same time. Then they needed persistence and the ability to work as part of a team. If all those things aren't in place, it isn't going to work.

We'd interview ten people and hire one, and of those who came on board, about ten percent wouldn't make it. But the ones who lasted were wonderful. QA became the recruiting ground for the rest of the organization, the first place managers came to when they were hiring.

Are testers of all ages, or does it tend to be a younger person's job? What about the issue of being a man or a woman?

Because of the low pay scale, testers tend to be people at the start of their careers. At Philips we had half men and half women, but I didn't see any difference particularly.

Tell me about the outlook for someone in quality assurance.

The life span for freelance testers seems to be about two years. The tester's frustration is that not everything gets fixed. The planner types get frustrated because they never get enough lead time to do the plans the way they'd like. So these people tend to move on to whatever their background was before becoming testers: film, video, music, marketing, the law. QA is a good steppingstone, not an end in itself.

The frustration for the supervisor, and what creates burnout at the top, is being the truth teller, the whistle blower. Often the message and the messenger get confused, and you get canned. It has nothing to do with diplomacy skills. The role has a fearful aspect, a certain amount of anxiety, because what you have to say is often unpleasant.

Are there any parts of the country where would-be testers might find the most work?

It's wherever the developers happen to be: Los Angeles, Silicon Valley, Boston, and, increasingly, Seattle. There is also a little activity in Washington, D.C., and Atlanta. It's not a requirement to be proximate, but it is convenient.

What magazines do you read in the field?

Communication Arts is the only one I read regularly.

Sound Designer/Composer/Voice Talent

Dave and Jennifer Evans
Co-owners, Digital Voodoo
Austin, Texas

Dave Evans received his degree from the State University of New York in 1981, majoring in math and physics. He worked as a scientist with an oil field company in Houston, then at the Jet Propulsion Laboratory as a systems analyst in Mission Control working on the Voyager spacecraft mission to Uranus. He became increasingly interested in business and accepted a management job at an insurance company in Austin. A professional bass player in rock bands through college, he came back to music in 1990, seeing it as a way to combine his love of music with running a business on his own schedule. He stresses that he had no formal computer background and is self-taught.

Jennifer's background is primarily in performance—singing, dancing, and acting. A member of a female comedy troupe called The Lemming Sisters, her training has included everything from standard voice coaching to improvisational work. Originally from Chicago, she went to the University of Texas at Austin on an engineering scholarship but graduated in 1986 with a B.A. in marketing after having managed retail stores throughout college. Later she ran a telephone customer service department for an insurance company, where she started thinking about the possibilities offered by networking.

[Note: Answers are Dave's unless otherwise noted.]

Digital Voodoo is an audio studio. What do you do there?

DE: First, we sound design: we conceive what sound or music is required for a given situation. We are also involved with performance. I work as a composer, using a bass guitar (where I have professional experience) or using an electronic keyboard, a drum machine, and the computer keyboard. Lastly, we are involved in production for multimedia applications.

JE: I perform voice-overs and create character voices. I also work with Dave while composing to define moods in the different scenes and the types of music or voices we'll develop.

What kinds of computer software or hardware do you use at Digital Voodoo?

We use Twelve Tone System's Cakewalk for composition, and in multimedia, to synchronize visual and sound components. For digitizing, we use Voyetra Technology's WinDat software, which we run on Ensoniq's SoundScape. (We are testers for Twelve Tone and Ensoniq.)

What types of computer products do you recommend for musicians just getting into multimedia?

To see if you're really interested, you need to do some basic investigating. First, you need to become familiar with the software and hardware. Get a sound card that plays digital audio and MIDI files, and then attach an audio CD player or tape deck. [*Editor's note*: MIDI—Musical Instrument Digital Interface—is a standard developed in the 1980s to represent sound in a form comprehensible to computers.] Bring the music or sound effects—or your own voice via a microphone—into the computer. Next, try using MIDI sequencing software. Using the same sound card and some inexpensive software—e.g., Twelve Tone's Home Studio—you can experiment with music in an electronic, digital format. You can get all this for under $300.

What kind of work have you done at Digital Voodoo?

DE: We started the company in 1994. We've composed and recorded original music for a series of screen savers for Electronic Arts. For a Comdex conference, we created the audio component for an interactive presentation for a PC manufacturer.

JE: I did voices for Origin's *BioForge II*, an interactive movie played on a PC. I created the voices for the standard military personnel and also for the character of Nursebot, a robot with hypodermic needles for hands who tries to sedate everyone throughout the game!

What's different about composing for multimedia?

Writing for video and traditional recorded performance is a linear process. You decide what you want to get across and how you are going to do it in terms of tempo, mood, etc. You think about it as a process from beginning to end.

With interactive multimedia, there is no beginning or end. You can't make an assumption about what has been heard before or about what's next. You're always thinking about that. The ideal situation is to work on an interactive title right from the start, with the scriptwriter, so the music and story can be developed together.

What is a typical day like for you?

DE: We start between 6 A.M. and 8 A.M. by taking a one-and-one-half-mile walk together, reviewing what needs to get done that day. When we get to the studio, which is in our home, we check our electronic mail (we have a direct Internet connection) and then start working on the project at hand. We may be composing music for a video or a QuickTime movie, or it may be a corporate logo. We might have a script or some notes. We'll look at these items, and then I'll start playing the keyboard or programming a piece of music. Jennifer and I work it out until we have it the way we want it. Is a drum too loud? Should we use a Spanish-style guitar here? I have no formal training in the piano, but because of my musical background I'm able to play a few notes or create a progression. If our job requires a traditional piano rendition, I'll hire a professionally trained pianist, but many of the pieces are very short and I'm able to create them myself. We work until we're happy with the sound.

JE: If I'm recording voices that day, I'll go into the sound booth in our studio. I'll give Dave three versions for every line, and we'll make selects as we work. Then we use software to edit what we've recorded, to shorten or lengthen pauses, etc.

DE: If we are not using MIDI, we transfer the music to digital tape. If I'm adding a bass track, then we start with a digital eight-track recorder, but we always end up with DAT tape. Next, we digitize what we have and create a digital file.

Once the music, sound, or voice is digitized, we can edit it again. You actually see a picture of the acoustical wave on the screen. We cut sections out, trim it, reverse it. Often, late changes introduced by the client can be solved by rearranging words or just cutting some out.

Alternatively, the other pathway is to write a MIDI sequence or composition. In this case, we don't digitize sound, but instead build a MIDI file, which contains the instructions about how to make the sound using a PC's sound card.

With music in either digital or MIDI format, we contact the client and arrange to deliver it using traditional delivery services or, preferably, electronically. (We have an ISDN line—integrated services digital network—that cuts the uploading time by a factor of 10.) Then we'll have a telephone conference with the client to discuss their reaction.

We eat dinner at around 8 P.M. but usually work afterwards until around 1 A.M. Multimedia is like the entertainment industry. If you're interested in a career in this field, you need to be prepared for irregular and extremely long hours.

Your studio is at your home?

The great thing about multimedia and networking is that as we get better telecommunication it won't matter where you're living or what you're wearing—it will be "What can you produce?"

There are four elements in our studio:

1. a sound booth, which provides acoustical isolation for voice-overs
2. electronic sound modules, the pieces of equipment that generate sounds—drums, piano, etc.
3. the computer, where the music is created
4. the mixing console, the sound center that ties everything together

Working at home is part of your philosophy about the virtual corporation. Tell me how you conceive the "virtual multimedia developer."

As urban areas become increasingly congested and commuting becomes more and more of a problem, we need to find smarter ways to work. One way is by having a virtual corporation in which a group of people each bring their own special skills together electronically without having to work in the same office.

I'm the president of a group we started here in 1994 called the Austin Area Multimedia Alliance. It's a virtual organization: it exists on-line. We have about ten to fifteen board members made up of representatives of technology-related groups in the area: the IICS (International Interactive Communications Society), the International TV Association, the Austin Software Council, the Virtual Reality Alliance, the Texas ISDN Users Group, the World Wide Web Users Group, the Visual Arts Association, the Texas Music Association, and so forth. Board members collect information from among their membership about their multimedia production skills and communicate it via this central forum. One important function of the group is to put on one-day workshops about their area of expertise so as to educate the rest of us. The idea is to prepare Austin so that if multimedia developers in this area need talent, the talent is here. And as the telecommunication capacity increases, people in other cities will be able to draw on the talent we've nurtured here.

So there's a lot happening in Austin?

A lot of content providers in multimedia have started to work here. The American Institute for Learning is creating self-paced multimedia educational projects for kids at risk. We also have something called the Austin Technology Incubator, developed in conjunction with the Austin Software Council and the University of Texas. They have a building with business services available to help entrepreneurs get started. And of course there is a huge investment community here: computer manufacturers, chip researchers, people making video compression hardware, etc. There are also a lot of video production facilities in town making the transition to multimedia.

What's your advice to someone wanting to get into the audio end of multimedia development?

You need to bridge two important skill sets: business and art. Sometimes you find in the creative community a mind set that believes that if you're in business, you're not an artist. In order to stand out, you need to understand what it means to be professional in business. Although a few of the larger companies such as Electronic Arts have full-time staff musicians and sound editors, I think most people in this field will end up working for themselves. Skills will be needed intensely during certain phases, but not during other times.

Be very, very professional about what you're doing. We wrote out a business plan when we started the company. We honor the commitments we make. When we go to a client, we're prepared. When we deliver a product, it's the best we can make it. When we work on a project, we make an attempt to understand the roles of the other members of the team so we'll be able to work with them better.

What kind of person is suited to this kind of work?

You have to have the desire and interest to learn something that is simultaneously very technical and very creative. I've worked with people at either extreme—the artist who feels that computers pollute art, and technologists who devalue the importance of choosing the right color. You can't be in either camp. Artists don't have to start out technologically oriented. The technology can be learned.

What do you read to learn and keep up?

JE: A book that helped me as a performer in the game area was *The Magic of Interactive Entertainment*. It helped me understand how developers create games and what roles the various people play on the team.

DE: In terms of magazines, at the studio we get *Mix* and *Electronic Musician*, and for interactive multimedia: *Wired* (for life style), *Axcess*, and *NewMedia* (for current industry information).

What professional societies do you belong to?

The IICS, the Austin Software Council, and the International MIDI Association.

Video Producer for Multimedia

Bob Hone

Executive Producer and President, Red Hill Studios
San Anselmo, California

Bob received a master's degree in chemical engineering from M.I.T. in 1980 and in journalism from the University of California, Berkeley, in 1985. He went on to become an award-winning associate producer for such public television pro-grams as Science Notes *and* The Machine That Changed the World, *a five-part series about computers for which he produced, directed, and wrote two hour-long programs. He is the author of two books:* QuickTime: Making Movies with Your Macintosh *and* Making Movies with Your PC. *In 1994, Bob founded Red Hill Studios, a multimedia production and post-production facility in the San Francisco Bay Area specializing in content development, inter-face design, 2-D and 3-D graphics, video production, and digital video editing. Red Hill also produces its own titles for the consumer market (an interactive CD-ROM,* Shoot Video Like a Pro), *as well as for museum exhibits (*Seeing Time, *installed at the Exploratorium in San Francisco, the Tech Museum, San Jose, and the Science Museum of Minnesota, St. Paul).*

As a video producer, how do you think video relates to multimedia?

The thing that video is good at is motion and emotion. It's dynamic—it records things that change over time better than any other medium. Also, video is good at showing faces, and people like looking at other people. In terms of human evolution, we've developed so we can read faces very quickly; they convey a lot of emotion, a lot of information.

How does shooting for a CD-ROM differ from shooting for a videotape?

Shooting video for a computer screen really requires a new bag of tricks and a new way of thinking. In video, you know you have the full television screen. But in shooting for CD-ROM you don't really know how big that video window is going to be: Is it 320 x 240? Is it 240 x 180? Will it even have a 4 x 3 aspect ratio? Once you know that, it really begins to define what you can do.

When shooting video for multimedia, it's important to do a lot of static shots and not to move the camera very much, then use editing later to create a sense of movement. Also, you have to shoot tighter shots. If the image is going to be in a small window, forget about wide shots. You're just not going to have the pixels to be able to show an interesting image in a wide shot, such as a person's face or an important foreground object.

When shooting for multimedia, whether it will be played back from a hard drive or a CD-ROM, it's good to have backgrounds that are going to be friendly for compression. That means backgrounds with less detail or the kind of detail that looks good even when blurred. A lot of people are shooting actors against blue screens and then later building a "virtual" background set or texture in a computer program. That way, the face looks better because it doesn't take as much data to reproduce the background (which means you can use the data for what you want to, namely, to make the face or foreground look better).

Are there any rules of thumb when you're applying digitized video and audio to multimedia? Any cautions?

If you're planning to include digital video in your product, make sure you pay close attention to production. You want something that is shot very nicely, with balanced light on the face. Don't just go out there and wing it. If you don't have good stuff in the can, or on tape, you're not going to have good stuff in your product.

How important to the viewer experience is the size of the digital video?

The size of the window depends on the content. If it's a person's face and if it's an interesting piece of information, you're actually going to pick it up even if it's a small window. If it's a big window and the content is boring, then it's just a big window and it's boring.

How is desktop video affecting multimedia?

Desktop video has provided a top-end tool for multimedia CD-ROM people to work with. For example, VideoVision Studio, the video digitizing and JPEG-compression board from Radius, is a wonderful desktop video tool. It happens to be great for developing CDs.

What do you see as the greatest challenge in developing multimedia applications?

It's making sure that the scope of work—your vision—is covered by your budget. You need to think ahead of time about the money, how much time you have, and that the equipment or tools you are using will actually perform. If you're developing a hybrid CD-ROM, you need to consider the transfer rate on the Mac side and for the PC.

What should the role of audio be?

A lot of developers overlook audio in building CD-ROM titles, and that's really a mistake. CD-ROM data transfer rates handle audio quite nicely; that's what it was built for. Audio can define a rich texture for your experience. Think of *Myst* and the sounds that are there. You're not really hearing them after a while; they're just in the background, but they're affecting your experience. People should be using audio more.

Given the storage demands of digital video, what do you consider an appropriate allocation on a CD-ROM? How much video should you use?

When using video in a CD-ROM product, you have to evaluate the value of the video versus other media. Some titles might require a lot of video. Generally, if you've got characters, if you're trying to show procedures (things that change over time), if you're trying to show action, then video is the best way to go. Video works well in a lot of role-playing titles, where the character talks to the user.

In other titles, it might be better to work with still images and audio. If you're trying to show a place, then very often a still will convey more information than video. The advantage of stills is that they invite you to linger and look for details. Video washes over you at 15 frames a second on the computer, so your mind is tugged by the brightest, fastest-moving, or largest objects. You're not going to catch the rich details. A photograph of an intense emotion, as seen in coffee table picture books, can in fact freeze that instant and focus our attention on it.

I'm sometimes frustrated by clients who say "I want 15 minutes of video," without stopping to consider if it is worthwhile. A better way to look at it is, What is the best way to convey the message? For example, the extremely popular game *Myst* uses very little video. They chose to use still images that created a richer visual environment than would have been possible with video at its current technological data rate on a CD-ROM.

What's the most frustrating aspect of multimedia production right now for you?

The most frustrating aspect is also the most interesting aspect, which is that there aren't any rules. Every project has a fairly steep learning curve. Now, why is that? Well, it's because we don't want to do boring things. We always want to push the edge. That leads to a lot of frustration because you miss your schedules, the project ends up taking longer than you thought, it ends up being more expensive. But it's also why I'm in this field.

What excites you about multimedia?

The allure of interactive multimedia is that it allows the user to control the experience, to control the interaction. That's very powerful.

What got you involved in multimedia?

I had an idea brewing to do a kiosk or a documentary about the change that exists around us that we can't see. This became an grant proposal in 1991 to the National Science Foundation, from which we developed a half-million dollar project for museums that we have now completed, called *Seeing Time*. It is an interactive exploration of the unseen world of natural change, events that occur too quickly or too slowly to be seen. By navigating a virtual time tower, museum visitors can view up to 180 different video clips in a kiosk showing changes that occur over a wide variety of time scales, from millions of seconds to millions of years.

What advice could you give to someone who wants a career in multimedia?

One of the things is to decide whether you are a producer or an artist, because the skills required are very different. If you want to be a multimedia artist, you should figure out what's the most important thing to you. Do you want to do 3-D, 2-D, digital video? Then look at the key artists in your field, find out what their tricks are, and emulate them.

On the other hand, if you like putting the whole thing together, then you want to be a producer, but you're going to have to have very good organizational skills to do that. If you want to be a multimedia producer, the main thing is get involved in a production. That means starting out by answering phones, doing grunt work, being a gopher— do it, because you're going to pick up what's involved in a production by osmosis.

Do you recommend any particular resources for someone starting out, such as a book that changed the way you think about multimedia?

The most important source of information in this young industry is other people. You know, books will provide you a certain amount of information, but they can become outdated. The most important thing is to network. Talk to people, get on-line, go to meetings—that's the best source of information.

What do you think of the seminal developments that have taken place in the evolution of multimedia during these past few years?

Seminal events are very temporal in nature. What we think is seminal today in the long view may in fact be quite minor. I think the key thing was the notion with the Macintosh that you could provide a metaphor. Once that idea set in, it opened the door to creating other types of metaphors. What you see now is that you're breaking the 2-D plane and moving into 3-D, and who first did that? It's hard to say. But moving from the idea of the computer as another kind of typewriter, or thinking of it as just a screen of letters, to the idea of a graphical user interface, then a 3-D interface . . . these are the major steps.

Where do you see the market headed for interactive media?

In the near term, I think you're going to see a lot more 3-D interfaces, Autodesk's 3-D Studio combined with QuickTime. QuickTime will begin to make an impact. More interesting things will come probably two to five years down the road. Two things will happen: either we will have the adoption of MPEG as the standard for playback, which will greatly increase the value of the CD-ROM, or we'll have a new storage medium entirely, like flash memory, which will remove this tremendous data bottleneck that CD-ROM has.

Where do you think multimedia will be in ten years?

In ten years we won't use the word *multimedia*. It just will be. We will be talking about interactive television or interactive books or interactive this or interactive that. But the word *multimedia*, which really came from slide shows with sound, won't be used to describe what we're doing today.

There's a lot of talk about the importance of interactivity. Do you think that people really want to be more interactive with their media?

That is one of the fundamental questions. The most focused, engrossing experience people have is going into a dark room, staring in the same direction for an hour and a half, and not talking. We call that "watching movies." That's a totally passive experience, yet people do it all the time. It may be that certain types of entertainment are going to remain passive. It's very age-related—as the population of game players gets older, you're going to find people wanting more and more active entertainment.

What hardware or software developments will make the greatest difference in the next generation in multimedia programs?

One of the wonderful things about this industry is that some of the basic limits go away every two years. It's Moore's Law: the price of chips drops by fifty percent every two years as the computing capacity doubles. It started in the early 1960s, and it's still going on today. No other field allows that kind of opening of vistas every couple years. So we know that CPUs [central processing units—i.e., computers] will get faster and memory will get cheaper. The big, big bottleneck still is the CD-ROM data transfer rate. What we really need is some kind of data storage device that will allow us to play back full-screen, full-motion video. At that point it will become a whole new business.

What characterizes a great multimedia program?

The ultimate test of whether a multimedia program is good or not is whether the people use it, whether that's in training, in education, or at home. If they don't like it, if they walk away, that's the ultimate test.

Can you describe your vision for multimedia, what you want to be doing with it?

Figuring out your vision is quite tricky, because if you get locked into that vision it's going to be obsolete in two years. The interesting thing is staying out on the wave—this wave we've been paddling on like crazy. Keep your eyes open, because as new technology comes upon you, your vision will need to change, because possibilities you haven't seen before could become real.

What are your thoughts about interactive TV?

Five hundred channels with nothing on is not much better than thirty channels with nothing on. Whether or not interactive television actually gives you true interactivity has to do with how the system is being developed. Personally, I'm not a big fan of interactive shopping. I think that's kind of a waste. Malls are interesting social places, not just places where you buy things. So I'm somewhat skeptical of interactive television in that it gives you more choices. We don't necessarily need more choices; we need better content.

Interactive Scriptwriter / Marketing

Sam McMillan

Independent producer/freelance interactive scriptwriter
San Francisco

Sam's background is in fine arts and poetry. After receiving a master's degree in teaching in 1977 from Duke University, he became a poet-in-the-schools in North Carolina for ten years. Then he was an assistant to the press representative of the American Dance Festival, which served as a springboard to a job in New York City at the Dance Theatre Workshop as an associate producer. Later he worked in the marketing department of Avon Books. He moved to California after five years in New York and worked in public affairs for the Berkeley Repertory Theatre. In the summer of 1990 he answered a newspaper ad for a job as a writer/designer with SoftAd, a company marketing products on floppy disks. After three years at SoftAd, he began freelancing for Vivid Publishing, Red Dot, and Interactive Media. Though still writing, he is moving into project management.

What background do you look for in writers seeking work?

Ideally, I look for people who have multimedia projects under their belts, or who have come through credentialed programs, or have experience using a prototyping tool, such as HyperCard or Asymetrix Multimedia ToolBook. They need to have shown an ability to organize large amounts of information. If they've never had any experience electronically, I'd like to see something on paper: sales data sheets, brochures, catalogues. If it were a marketing position, I'd like to see some ability to sell. In general, I look for evidence of working on project teams in the past. Also, a sense of humor is critical!

If they're right out of school, the best way to gain experience is by interning. Another way is to get on a project team and take a very small chunk of a project, even if it is only copywriting, because that will give them credit on a CD-ROM. They might not know much about interactivity, but at least they've been exposed to how their writing was taken by someone else on the team and turned into multimedia. The neophyte wants to get into the position as quickly as possible to be the one who decides the interaction scheme. You want to move from just writing copy to determining the structure and organization of information.

What traits do interactive writers need?

The creativity of a filmmaker or a poet, and the anal retentiveness of someone toilet-trained at two and one-half weeks—that's really what it takes! The more technical you are in this industry, the better off you'll be. My technical skills have come very slowly and have been very hard won. I've asked lots of questions and stayed up late trying to learn programs.

What are the tasks performed by a writer on a marketing-oriented multimedia title?

The simplest task is copywriting either the on-screen text or voice-over copy. But the more important thing the writer brings is an awareness of interactivity, an understanding of how the elements of multimedia—text, graphics, animation sequences—and content areas can be interlinked.

What is the process of creating a script?

In a paper-based marketing script, one way to start is with a content outline: text on paper that describes what the user will actually see or read or do on each screen. You don't explain how the information will be communicated (through animation or voice-over, etc.) at this point, or the functionality or branching.

The content outline will eventually match up to a flow diagram. The flow diagram charts out a screen-by-screen road map of the project. It's a view-at-a-glance written in enough detail so that anyone looking at it would essentially know every possible outcome of the user's interaction. Flow diagrams can be fairly elaborate, covering an entire wall. The idea is that the flow diagram will be used by several people: a programmer to get a sense of the program at large; clients or producers to keep themselves honest. It will help them keep track of whether they have done a section or not. It will illustrate how the user will go from one section to another. And writers use it as a way of organizing their thoughts.

At any place in the flow diagram, I should be able to turn to a page in the content outline and find out what the user will be either reading, doing, or viewing. When I first started interactive scriptwriting, I always began by creating the content outline, and once I had it nailed down, I would diagram it. Now I find it much faster to start with a flow diagram, knowing how the pieces fit, and then I write the content outline.

The next step could be a script, or if it's a complicated project, you might want to write a concept outline, which describes the interactivity. Where the content outline addresses "the what," the concept outline addresses "the how." The concept outline discusses the video, icons, the navigation schemes: "If the user chooses Button A, this happens."

You didn't mention the treatment.

Hollywood would call it a treatment; interactivity would call it a proposal or a strategy document. This is done before the content outline. Writers who know a lot about interactivity write the proposal. But typically it's created by the producer, with the writer's role limited to wordsmithing.

The first part of a strategy document summarizes the project in a couple of paragraphs—the main reasons we're doing this, the objectives. It will identify some of the tactics that the CD-ROM (or on-line project) will use. By tactics, I mean: Will there be video? Animations? Voice-overs? How will video support some of the content points?

The strategy document goes on to describe the target market to be reached and the system requirements. If there is a production team, you would want to include the members' biographies and perhaps a track record. Other components of the proposal would be the flow diagram, maybe a content outline.

Do you use any commercial software to help you in this process?

I use the brainstorming program Inspiration, from Inspiration Software, for making flow charts. You create little boxes or balloons and enter a description of a few words, like "sales video." You don't actually describe the sales video at this stage. Once I get my ideas flow-diagrammed, I push-pin it to the wall over my monitor and start writing screen by screen. There's also something called MacFlow, from Mainstay—and that's OK. It works. But my favorite so far has been Inspiration.

Another program is MacToolKit's Corkboard, which organizes information using the metaphor of the push-pin and 3" x 5" cards. It lets you cut and paste and arrange things. It handles word processing well. It allows you to write as many "nodes" — or branching choices — and as deeply as possible as you want to.

For people who can't draw, there's StoryBoard Quick from Power Production Software. Another program, StoryVision, gets you from flow diagram to script. It compresses some steps, because it links the flow diagram to a word processor.

For my scripts, I tend to use HyperCard, which is usually thought of as a tool more for programmers than writers. I write copy on the screen and bring in extra graphics. Then I will strip out an extra field in HyperCard that is just for script management issues. You never see this information on the screen, but it can be printed out. Script management issues include node numbers (a way of sequencing and organizing the information) and transitions: how the user got from one screen to another and what happened along the way. Was there a wipe? Did we dissolve? Did something pop out? It will include a thumbnail—just a name—of the graphic that we're on, because you don't need to describe the graphic anymore; you're seeing it.

I call these WYSIWYG scripts: what you see is what you get. They accomplish a couple goals. They're easy to read because they're highly visual. They require a little more work on the part of the writer, because there are now some graphic issues to deal with. You have to learn another tool—HyperCard—but once you get fluid at it, you can move fairly quickly. And it's a real short step for programmers to go from a HyperCard script to a prototype, and that will make you really valuable as a writer.

How does an interactive script compare to other scripts?

It's a shotgun wedding of the Hollywood film script and an interactive scheme. But there is no clear format yet, and many scripts are a mess. Some scripts contain programmers' or users' notes, but there's nothing structural about it. Many scripts I see are difficult to read. The script has to be written in such a way that everyone understands it: the programmer, graphic designer, project manager, and the client.

I want my scripts to reveal certain elements at every node: the node number (for example, 2-1-A.1 for Section 2, Screen 1, Sub-menu A, Revision 1), a thumbnail description of the graphic, the head or subhead on the screen. I want to see a transition: How did we get from the previous screen to the next one? Then there's the on-screen and/or voice-over copy. User instructions should also be included, such as "Use UP and DOWN arrow key to move Highlight. Enter to select."

What is a typical day working as a writer for a multimedia company?

At 9 A.M. I might have a "ramp-up" meeting with the Acme Widget Co., which some call a "kick-off meeting" or a "discovery meeting." This is not the meeting where they are being pitched; the deal has already been signed. They've flown out from Padooka, Kentucky, and want an interactive marketing disk for their ultra-widget. The project team sits around a table: project manager, writer, graphic designer, maybe a programmer if we can afford the time, and the client. The client essentially does a brain dump: they tell us everything they can about their product.

The writer's job is to absorb as much of this information as possible. The writer acts as the advocate of the computer for the client, explaining how they can solve their problems using the resources of a computer. It may be by creating a price comparison: cost of owning an Acme Widget versus an XYZ widget. Or they could do spec sheets at the push of button. It might be using animations; it might be a video, God forbid, of the president of Acme Widget welcoming the user to the program.

The writer needs very quickly to come up with a scheme to communicate the marketing objectives to the end-user. Not everything will be decided at this meeting, but the outline of the project should emerge. It takes a writer who can think on his or her feet.

Writers are so often ignored, but you make them sound central to the creation of a marketing title.

They are, and as the industry gets more sophisticated, the writer will take more of a primary role in consumer titles as well. As writers better understand interaction and information design, as they understand the resources of the computer, they'll take a more central role and drive the project forward. But also production companies need to get more sophisticated. Because there are some designers who work primarily in visual ways who don't come to own projects as much as the writer, who's responsible for creating a script that everyone can follow.

So back to our typical day.

After the first meeting ends, I might shift gears and start writing a script for another project that's further along. Generally, I try to block out my scripts a section at a time in order to get this stuff out the door. I have to be very focused and very goal oriented and say "Today I'll finish section one." And I just go from node to node to node until I get to section two. And that might take a couple hours, or the rest of the day, depending on the project.

Then I might be called into an "alpha review" on yet a third project that is moving into the production process. It might be about 60% done. Perhaps we've already shipped the client the disks, and now we're going to have a conference call. And we'll proceed together, screen by screen. Sometimes some of the functionality is in place, or else we're just space-bar-forwarding through each screen.

Who would be at the alpha review?

The writer, project manager, designer, the programmer. At this point, everything is up for grabs. The client can change copy, though it costs more money at this stage than when it was just a paper script. As a writer, I have my clipboard and paper, and I am taking notes furiously, because I am the only one who will ever take notes. It just seems to be the way of the writer.

I've sat in meetings in which programming issues were raised throughout the meeting and the programmer sat there looking at the screen, and I thought "Either this guy is really smart and doesn't need to take these notes, or we're in a lot of trouble." Weeks go by, and as a writer I manage projects by walking around. I sometimes think of myself as a professional pest. I ask people "Let's take a look at those art screens. Let's see how the program's coming." And I find that many of the changes the client requested have not been caught. So I get my notes, and we go through them. You start taking responsibility.

So, after the alpha review, the client goes through the project screen by screen, makes comments, and then the writer goes away and revises the script accordingly. Makes copy changes as needed. Designers make changes to art or colors. Many clients don't know what they want until they see something that approximates it, and then they're better able to communicate their needs and wishes. What can really be a problem for the writer is when a client says "I think Section 3 really should trade places with Section 7." Because then you have to renumber your flow chart and your script, and it's not easy to cut and paste. And everybody loses track.

Is the day over?

No, maybe the next thing is an internal "script review" on a different project. This meeting is designed to make sure that the first draft of the script is on track and on target. (Scripts in marketing run anywhere from 30 to 180 pages.) The client has not yet seen the script and is not present. The project team gets together—creative director, project manager, writer, and the head of programming—and charts the accuracy of the script. The writer is actually reading through it, line by line. They're talking about transitions, interactions, programming issues, and they're reading the copy. The subtext of the meeting is also to understand whether the writer has written a script that is doable. Is this going to be technically feasible? This is where the creative director and programmer earn their money. The programmer can say "This effect is going to cost several thousands of dollars, whereas if you try this idea, it will cost a few hundred." Or "There's no way that we can do this!"

It's a free-for-all. All of a sudden the programmer may be making remarks about your copy. You have to be pretty thick-skinned and enjoy the rough 'n' tumble of defending your ideas. You have to be able to explain why you're doing this and what the net effect will be. Ideally all the effects, all the razzle-dazzle of what the computer is doing, are supporting some marketing message.

So a writer creating a marketing disk really needs a marketing background? It's not enough to just be a writer.

You have to know how to sell. The marketing is done at the service of sales. Maybe you're not trying to close the sale, but you're trying to raise the profile of the company or perhaps give it some sort of technological advantage.

Now if you're writing a game or an educational title or a cookbook, you're not selling a product, but you're still selling a concept. And all the effects and techniques of computer interactivity still should be in support of that main idea.

Where do you see job opportunities for writers?

I think there's a tremendous market in "speech support," or writing multimedia presentations that run off a laptop and are projected behind speakers at seminars and conferences. This is especially good for writers who understand presentation packages. The one I like the most is the hardest to use—Director—but other writers use Microsoft's PowerPoint, Compel, and Astound, from Gold Disk.

What books do you recommend?

Understanding Hypermedia and *The Cyberspace Lexicon: An Illustrated Dictionary of Terms.*

CHAPTER 4

Industry Perspectives

Advertising

Mike White
....
Executive Vice President and Director, Media Department
DDB Needham
Chicago

Mike joined Needham Harper in 1983 as senior vice president and director of the department of media resources. In 1988 he was named "Media Director All-Star" by Marketing and Media Decisions *magazine. Before joining Needham, Mike worked for several ad agencies, including Cunningham & Walsh, Earle Palmer Brown, McCann-Erickson, and Leo Burnett. He graduated with a B.A. in economics in 1961 from Williams College and taught for several years at the American Association of Advertising Agencies' Institute for Advanced Advertising Studies. He has been a panelist at the New Media Expo in Los Angeles and a judge for the Interactive Media and Marketing Awards, sponsored by* Advertising Age.

Please tell me about the job of media director.
The media department of an advertising agency is responsible for planning and then executing how a client spends his money, so that the ads the creative department develops can be seen by customers. We plan and buy network television spots, magazine schedules, outdoor bulletin boards . . . or new media venues. Our responsibility is getting ads to the consumer. As director, I oversee a department with 80-some people who are account-specific in their day-to-day concerns.

What outlets are there for multimedia?
There are CD-ROMs, the on-line services, and in-store kiosks. One example of a promotional device using a CD-ROM was *U.S. News and World Report*'s annual guide to the top colleges. They've done this guide in the magazine before, and now they've created a CD-ROM version to be sold retail, which lets users enter SAT scores and other data about themselves and be matched up with the right schools. An advertiser could sponsor such a CD-ROM, not in the sense of a 30-second commercial, but in a much more subtle way—for example, on-screen billboards, messages that lead you from one area to another, or ID-logos. Additionally, if that sponsor had a field operation, those agents or dealers could be a

point of distribution. The dealer could invite parents of high school students to use the CD-ROM in the showroom.

What is your definition of interactive multimedia, especially as it relates to advertising?

Virtually anything that allows us to dialogue with the consumer, knowing full well that the prospect is now in control of the message. The consumer chooses the type of information or data that they want to get from us, which necessarily requires multiple paths on our part, as compared to traditional advertising, which is very linear.

What, in your opinion, are the hallmarks of an excellent multimedia advertising campaign?

One of the problems we're having with multimedia or interactivity is falling in love with the technology rather than keeping the focus on the marketing need. The question to ask is whether some form of interactivity can help solve a marketing problem. What might be right for our client Frito-Lay might not be right for State Farm Insurance. So the hallmark of a good multimedia campaign is finding a way to use interactivity to enhance your marketing effort in a way that solves problems. Either it goes beyond what you're currently capable of doing, or it addresses a problem that interactivity has caused for you.

Interactivity creates *problems?*

Consider on-line grocery shopping, such as Shoppers Express or Peapod. Package manufacturers invest millions in packaging that's meant to identify a product in a store. On-line, the product may only appear in a list with other similar products, without its logo or distinctive packaging. The question for our package goods clients becomes "How do I recapture my investment for packaging for grocery store distribution?" Wheaties' great orange color is gone, and it appears without a distinctive identification alongside Kellogg's Rice Crispies and Corn Flakes. And one of the lines that pops up on the screen is unit pricing—so now I've spent all this money to enhance my image in the traditional marketplace, and it's lost in the on-line shopping service. So the marketing problem is this: How do I invest in on-line promotion?

Another problem might be: What can we do for State Farm agents beyond what we do now with television commercials or magazine ads? Given that State Farm runs a Good Neighbor campaign, how can an agent be more "neighborly" using multimedia—be it on-line or with CD-ROMs?

How is multimedia regarded at DDB Needham?

We are in the development stage in a number of areas—we're still investigating things. We ran some ads for Rubbermaid on Prodigy—customers could go in and see a mini-catalog—but it wasn't that successful because customers couldn't order directly. (Rubbermaid doesn't want to offend its traditional distributors by competing with them.) In any case, Rubbermaid's primary goal was simply to make people aware that they make a very broad line of products beyond the kitchen, to lawn furniture and garbage cans. One problem with campaigns for products like this is that not enough people were interested in following the path. What is it you say in your ad at the bottom of a Prodigy screen to entice someone to go into Rubbermaid? Where's the fun here? It's a real challenge for packaged-goods companies. It's one thing for Chrysler to say "We'll give you a test drive." But what can a Rubbermaid, or Frito-Lay, or General Mills do to entice the consumer? Who wants to follow a path on the subject of hamburger helpers?

What are your thoughts on solving this dilemma?

You might try an "affinity" campaign. Let's say you have a TV campaign featuring a country music star as a spokesman. Maybe in an on-line service or a kiosk you bring users something more about that country music star, such as fan information, or allow them to download a song. As another example, a beer might sponsor sports scores or bring the user access to sports information. That's affinity advertising.

I'll give you another example of an affinity deal using a client of ours, Helene Curtis. We might someday create the ability for the customer to scan in a picture of herself to see what she looks like with different hair colors or styles. There could be a quiz about her hair type and frequency of shampooing, and an answer could come up about the correct shampoo and conditioner to use. This would be even more effective if it were done in combination with the beauty editors of *Cosmopolitan* magazine answering questions about hair problems. Meanwhile, we're running the normal ads on TV for Helene Curtis; the on-line activities would be affinity advertising.

You have to make the customers want to pursue your presentation. If it gives them interesting information or how-to information, if it's fun or there's some incentive (like a sweepstakes), then they'll engage.

Interactivity might provide another form of coupon distribution. An interactive kiosk in a store or a mall, or interactive TV set-top box, might have printing capability. The consumer could get a recipe, a coupon, or a game that could be sent in. There are a lot of possibilities. However, if the only way the packaged-goods people end up using interactivity is for a new form of coupon distribution, it will go away really fast!

What other challenges does multimedia present to ad agencies?

One of the problems is that there are so many forms of interactivity—on-line services, kiosks, interactive TV, CD-ROMs—and there are so many different players, you don't know which way to go. Should you cast your lot in with this new consortium in a particular multimedia form, or wait a bit and get the business of the partners in the next big merger who are using yet another form of interactivity? It's a high-risk proposition. Who is going to be successful ultimately—the media companies? The phone companies? We don't know the answer.

What we've done at DDB Needham is develop a "fund" formed by many different advertisers who agree to share their experiences using different multimedia approaches with other members in the fund. That way, a single advertiser can experiment with interactive TV while someone else tries an in-store kiosk, and they can share their information. That way, a single advertiser doesn't have to try four different things.

What new media forms are proving to be front-runners?

Advertisers will find ways to use CD-ROMs to their benefit the way they found ways to use videocassettes. For example, sponsorships will become more and more prevalent—instead of asking the consumer to pay $29 for a CD-ROM, they can get it for $9.95 with advertising included. That would be a rudimentary way of using CD-ROMs. Another way would be taking a character from an advertising print or TV campaign and creating a game featuring that character. That's a high-cost investment, but you'll see things like that happen. The *U.S. News & World Report* college guide I mentioned—people will find ways to participate in a subtle, acceptable way. There will be sponsors on services like that.

What is "acceptable," and what is "offensive"?

It would be offensive if you had to sit through a 30-second commercial to get into the program. People aren't going to tolerate that. Offensive advertising is when you show advertising in theaters—commercials at the beginning of movies. Offensive means something you have to put up with even though you don't want to.

The beauty of interactivity is the ability of the consumer to pick and choose. So advertisers have to find ways to participate that the public finds fun, helpful, tolerable—or thought provoking. The important thing is to provide a service while at the same time getting our message across.

Are there advantages to using multimedia for advertising?

That depends on the marketing need. If I have a product that is somewhat confusing, or I have a large line of products and the user needs to know which version to use, multimedia could give more information than can be conveyed in a 30-second commercial. If you could provide additional information, that would be helpful.

Another thing is to tailor the message. Instead of featuring this product in all my advertising, I change the ad according to who is viewing. For example, Videotron's interactive television project in Canada—Videoway—lets the customers know they're about to see a Ford commercial and gives them the choice to see one for a van, a truck, or an economy car. If the button isn't hit right away, there is a default commercial. But if the van advertising is more interesting to you, that's the one you get. Are you interested in peaches or pears?

If we do it right, interactive advertising can be more engaging. If you get somebody to go down your path, that's a whole lot more involving and hopefully more persuasive than something we just throw up on the TV screen or flip to a magazine. If we do it right, it can be much more powerful.

Are there certain types of clients or products that lend themselves to be advertised using multimedia CD-ROMs?

Products that are big investments—such as cars or financial services for clients with large portfolios—will be natural, because they can justify the expense of producing a CD-ROM. The problem for packaged-goods advertisers is cost per ad. It's one thing for an auto manufacturer to sponsor a CD-ROM that goes into a handful of people's hands via the dealers; it's another for a cereal maker who would need to get that CD-ROM distributed to millions of hands. You would be hard-pressed to see the impact for a cereal maker in the market; it would be difficult to amortize the expense of making a CD-ROM against a $3 box of cereal. You would hardly notice the impact of your effort in the market.

Other naturals are retailers with catalogues from whom you can already buy directly via modem or mail. There will be a payoff early on for catalogue sales companies such as Land's End, either on CD-ROM or on-line.

What are we seeing in terms of on-line advertising?

A number of clients are creating "home pages" on the Internet and supplying everything from information to affinity advertising to financial service advertising. It's almost more public relations than advertising. Others are putting catalogues on-line. Since the Internet is becoming increasingly accessible through the commercial services such as America Online, more clients will be willing to try it as a first step into investing in new media advertising, and taking the lessons they learn from it.

We're still learning which media work best for a particular client's marketing needs. Which one of the media forms performs as they say it's going to? Who will survive, and who won't? Who knows how to produce properly, and who doesn't? Then there's the creative dimension of getting people to follow down a path three to four screens deep into a message for a product or a service. We know how to make one-page ads or 30-second commercials, but it's a whole different ball game when you have to draw people four screens down and keep it fresh!

How do you find employees who know how to entice people in this new advertising medium? Are you retraining existing staff by sending them to trade shows, or are you bringing "techies" in who have no background in advertising?

We're finding you need to go from both directions—you need people who come out of a marketing/advertising background so they are sensitive to the marketing rationale behind a campaign. At the same time, you need the technology people who can give you a variety of technical solutions to a problem. Or who can tell you that you can't do it the way you wanted to, but could accomplish the same end by trying a different approach. There are few people out there now who know it all. The techies haven't had time to learn about advertising; the advertisers don't yet know the technology. And we don't know what's the right technology to learn about. Someone may know Internet but not CD-ROM production.

Have you hired people specifically for interactive advertising?

We have on the production side to a limited degree. We have hired people to run digitizing equipment. We can do Internet home pages and kiosk games, but we can't do full-blown CD-ROM production. The staff we've hired in this area also helps us grow and develop our expertise: What should we try, and what shouldn't we try? At the same time, we reach out to freelancers or work with movie studios (for example, to license characters to use in ads) and outside production houses (who can produce special effects).

What types of jobs are being created by new media?

Multimedia producers or creative directors, who are responsible for developing the idea and storyboarding the game or service. Then there are others who would be involved in the production, or overseeing the production if it's done by outside services. The model for this is our in-house producers for television commercials—they don't literally produce the commercial; they oversee the production when it's done by someone on the outside. So I suspect the same thing will be happening with multimedia, at least here. Foote, Cone and Belding created a new holding company, True North Communications, that has entered into a joint venture with Robert Greenberg's multimedia production firm, R/GA Media, called TN Technologies—so that's an example of a major ad agency that will have their own full-service, in-house production capability. We prefer to use outsiders, because then we can pick and choose who is best suited to producing different kinds of campaigns.

On the media side, I have a new position called "director of electronic ventures." He's the media/marketing person who finds out what various venues are for sale and how we might use them for Client X. It's the same traditional approach we take when evaluating a TV show or magazine: Is this a good medium for the client?

Beyond the advertising industry, I think the magazine industry has a tremendous potential for job opportunities for people who can turn hard copy into a consumer service. If content is key—which it is, particularly in things that consume a lot of content, like interactive TV—the question becomes "Who has existing content?" The magazine industry does. Right now, magazines are very perishable, but they can be evergreens if you put the information they contain into a service: fashion tips, recipes, hair care, sewing ideas. Hearst is looking at this. And we are working with them for one of our clients, *Cosmopolitan* magazine, providing a fashion/beauty service sponsored by one of our clients in an affinity relationship.

Would you hire someone who knew a lot about the new technology but didn't have an advertising background?

An interest in advertising would be critical. They would need to get pleasure from understanding why people do what they do, and then figuring out how to dialogue with them. Advertisers are interested in what makes people tick; we get paid for people watching! If that's the sort of thing you'd like, you might work out at a place like this. But if you know about this technology but you'd just as soon do it by yourself, this would not be a good place for you. Advertising is typically taught on the job, not by college courses. I came in with an economics major—hadn't taken one advertising course in my life. So if you understand the technology and are turned on by what we do, you don't necessarily need to know everything about advertising when you come in: we have media and account people who can help you with the marketing/advertising side of it.

What advice do you give to someone who wants to be involved in multimedia advertising?

Don't fall in love with one form of the technology, because it's always going to change. Don't be so narrowly focused that you learn only one computer application, or something that would only run on a kiosk. We're seeing the convergence of many industries, so it's hard to say whether in ten years we'll be able to tell the difference between the computer monitor, a television screen, or a telephone. Focus more on the customer than on the technology. What might people be willing to tolerate, and how might I make it as easy as possible for them? What would they be willing to do? What are they interested in doing? What would they find fun? What are they capable of doing?

The complexities of the technology are not what's going to make this a popular medium. It is going to have to be simple and user friendly. For consumers it's going to be "I don't know how it works; I just know that it does." Eventually we want to get to the point where customers could use computer programs without reading the manuals. It should be intuitive. So whether you're interested in the technical side, the production or the creative side, keep the focus on the consumer.

What do you see as the future of interactive advertising?

Convergence will have an impact on advertising. The way we're going to pay for all these new technologies so that it makes sense is to use it in multiple forms. You're going to have to develop an ad campaign that will work on interactive television, has a CD-ROM component, and a kiosk component.

One of the big areas of innovation is going to be on the production side. Right now we spend hundreds of thousands of dollars to make a 30-second television commercial. When you're making multipath messages, which might have to be updated regularly to be fresh, you can't spend $250,000 per path! We're going to have to find low-cost ways, and flexible ways, to produce the kinds of messages that interactivity will require.

The interesting thing is that once we learn how to do that, we'll circle back and apply it to developing traditional television commercials.

It's our feeling that TV as we know it—basically, free television—will still be what people spend most of their time on. We don't see people giving up a popular sitcom in large numbers for the Internet. There is a huge percentage of the population that will choose not to interact with the new technologies. Some people will always want entertainment dumped on them—it may be in the form of a pay-per-view movie—but whatever it looks like in the future, the big TV networks will maintain a very substantial share of media time.

What kinds of magazines do you read to keep up and recommend?

Advertising Age is the best trade magazine in our business and has a weekly section on interactive media now.

Are there any books you would recommend for someone who wanted to get into advertising in the new media area?

It's an older book now, but *The Media Lab*, about MIT, is still provocative. It is a must-read, Multimedia 101.

Which professional advertising societies are starting to have seminars about multimedia?

The primary one—the "4A's," the American Association of Advertising Agencies—has a new technologies committee, which is trying to form standards.

I understand you are on the jury for the Interactive Media and Marketing Awards. What do you look for?

I look for people who use these new media forms in innovative ways. One that stays in my mind is a French retailer who used a kiosk to sell fragrances. He created a game to help someone, such as a boyfriend or a husband, buy perfume for a lady friend. It took you through choices: if she were a gem she'd be a diamond; if she were a flower she'd be a daisy. At the end, they'd match the person to a fragrance. It was a fun marketing game.

What are your final thoughts about careers in this new industry?

From a career standpoint, the business is so new and so poorly defined that the people who get into the business in the 1990s are the ones who are going to invent it.

Distribution

Joanna Tamer

President, S.O.S., Inc.
Marina del Rey, California

Tamer received a B.A. in creative writing and literature, and a B.S. in the phi-losophy of science, both in 1971, from Oakland University in Rochester, Michigan. She says she studied philosophy to learn how to think, and creative writing so she could express what she thought. "I've never had a job; I never sought a career path. I've always been a consultant," says Tamer, who formed her company, S.O.S., Inc., in 1976 after a trip around the world. Initially, S.O.S. was a consulting firm to help inventors, artists, and entrepreneurs start their own businesses. (Her father was an entrepreneur.) In 1981 a client in Boston got her involved in computer retail consulting, and she has not left the computer indus-try since. From that time forward, S.O.S. specialized in new channel distribu-tion for software products. She designed and built distribution channels for high-tech (mostly software) products. In the early 1990s, her focus shifted to new media distribution—"For me it was simply the next new product that didn't have its own channel," she says, "and most software distribution had become very stable by then."

The distributor is the link between the publisher and the market. Briefly describe the functions performed by the distributor.

Distributors ship, warehouse, and act as a bank for the publisher. They collect the receivables from large chains and small independents and pay the publisher within 30–60 days, even though it may take them longer to collect.

The distributor is not responsible for marketing; that's the publisher's responsibility. The distributor will provide cooperative marketing pro-grams, which the publisher will pay for either in co-op ("soft" dollars) or in cash. But the publisher is responsible both for creating the "push mar-keting," which pushes product into the channels, and for creating "pull marketing," which pulls the customer into the store.

What kinds of entry-level jobs are there in distribution of new media?

The best entry-level position would be to work for a regional or national distributor. The pay is not high, but the distributors tend to hire from within. Therefore, an entry-level marketing person or administrative person could work within several departments throughout the distributor's company, thereby gaining valuable field experience in administration, telemarketing, marketing communications, and other divisions within the company. The infrastructure of distribution is very complex, and the ability to do several jobs within one company gives an entry-level worker a broad understanding of how distribution works in the marketplace.

Distinguish between a national and a regional distributor.

The big national distributors are Baker and Taylor, Merisel and Ingram, all of which happen to be in southern California. Then there is a range of smaller regional ones, such as Tech Data. It's very fuzzy distinguishing between regionals and smaller nationals, but all of them seem to ultimately "sell up" to the big three.

Is it possible to have a career devoted to new media distribution, or should people be prepared to be distributors of other media as well?

It will be possible in the next few years to specialize in new media distribution. It will help to have an understanding of the distribution of audio, video, books, and software in order to understand new media distribution. This is because new media distribution is in flux, and the business model will settle as a hybrid between the entertainment industries and the software industries by the turn of the century. So the more experience a person has in all of those distribution models, the more informed they'll be about new media.

Do people ever start out with a career in distribution, or is it something people move into from other areas?

Typically, people move into distribution from marketing, order entry, sales administration, or sales. I'm one of the few people who started straight out in distribution; I don't know anybody else who started out and stayed in it!

If someone is looking for a job in this field, what do they need to understand about working for an affiliate label versus working for a national distributor?

Affiliate label distributors function as the middlemen between publishers and national distributors, and so their function is very similar to a national distributor, but their business model is slightly different. They take a larger "distribution fee," and job seekers will need to understand the needs of both the publishers who work with affiliates and the national distributors who receive product from them. So you're standing with a foot in each place. The major affiliate labels are Electronic Arts, Brøderbund, and Compton's New Media.

If someone were interested in getting into distribution for multimedia, would you suggest they try to get a job at one of the big three nationals, or would you think they'd learn more working for the distribution division of an affiliate label?

It doesn't matter. If the job seeker is interested in new media, work for the new media division in any of those distributors. It would be wise to make certain that the distributor is committed to new media as a product category before you take the job. There's a lot of change going on, a lot of risk. You wouldn't want to start in new media and then have the division fold around you, or have it move to the book division.

What kinds of careers feed well into distribution?

Sales, marketing, telemarketing, telesales, and sales administration. Telemarketing is gathering information or making someone aware of the product, but you're not responsible for closing the sale, whereas in telesales, you're trying to close the sale. There's also a legal career to be made in distribution, and contracts administration.

What is the best academic background for working in distribution?

Business administration and marketing or sales training—any field that would get you into those entry paths mentioned above.

What is the most interesting thing about this field?

That it never stays the same. The business models keep changing, particularly in high-technology distribution. Because the product base keeps changing, the channels have to change to adapt to the new technologies which are invented.

How does that affect distribution?

You go from a very specialized distribution channel, with salespeople trained in the special technology, as well as in the customer base, and move into the mass market where the products are bought off the shelf without training, or with "help" tutorials built into the software. A product that ten years ago was bewildering to the end user is now taken for granted. As technology products become more common by category, as that category moves from a specialized distribution channel into the mass market, then new technology takes its place, which then requires a specialized channel.

What things are most aggravating about working in distribution?

If you're working for a distributor, the pay is generally lower than if you're working for a developer or publisher. The glamorous high salaries associated with "high tech" are not paid in distribution companies. There's less opportunity to own a piece of the technology or own equity in the company, because it's a service business and it's already established. You're not inventing any new thing, so the glamorous upside of creating a new product isn't available in distribution. Distribution is the movement of product from one place to another. If you build your own distribution business, then you could own that, but that's rare.

What kinds of problems and uncertainties will face those who decide to go into new media distribution?

There's the fact that it changes all the time. The distributor lives on a very small margin of moving product from the publisher into the marketplace, and has to be careful how he spends his money. Distribution costs a great deal of money to initiate, and there's more risk in building a distribution entity than most other kinds of businesses in general, but especially in multimedia. You need to build an expensive infrastructure for distribution, and then you need to fill the pipeline with product. And that's twice the risk of anybody else, because the infrastructure is expensive and recruiting the products in the face of a great deal of other competition from other distributors is difficult. The other risk is that as prices come down for new media titles, in order to create a mass market, the operating margin of the distributor becomes even smaller. And his risk increases if he is not significantly established.

Where do you see things evolving?

New media distribution is evolving straight into the mass market. By the late nineties, the major channels will be the superstores. These superstores will be of all descriptions—audio, video, book, office product, and software stores. They'll have warehouse facilities and the ability to buy in bulk and handle thousands of products, or as they're called, SKUs [stock-keeping units]. Superstores will be the major channels. They have very great buying power. And they may buy direct without any distributor in between them, which is another jeopardy for the distributors. It is a pretty risky business to be in, frankly.

What's your advice for those thinking about a career in distribution?

There's no way to learn distribution except by doing it—there are no courses in it. If you're going to enter distribution, with all its many facets—marketing, sales, administration—it would be best if you had some clear idea of where you want to end up. In many ways, distribution is a means to an end. So, if you don't ultimately want do sales, don't enter distribution by being a telesales person. If you don't want to do marketing or "mar com" [marketing communications], don't become the marketing assistant or the copy editor. There are so many pieces to working in distribution that it would be best to take a path through it to the kind of work you ultimately want to do. Even if you stay with a distributor to do it.

At the same time, you could try all of it if you are coming in on the entry level, to the end of learning what kind of work you really want to do, whether in distribution or in the broader field.

What kinds of places do people go to from distribution?

They go to publishers, to their own businesses, or to other distributors. It's very odd because distribution is not considered a separate business in software. You can go to work for distributors, but distribution is a function in the marketplace. It's moving product; it's a middleman's role, not an end in itself. Very rarely do people say "I want a career in distribution." They want a career in sales or marketing, and distribution is part of what they do.

For most people who are in distribution, if they are not the owners of the company or among the early founders, distribution is a learning ground and stopping place, and then they generally move on into more specialized areas. Because there really are very few top positions in distribution. Typically, people leave distribution to move to a smaller company where they have a larger role.

Distribution aside, what do you see for the future regarding multimedia?

Multimedia will become the common way of exchanging information and creating entertainment and learning, both on the computer and on the television. Multimedia interactivity will become commonplace.

What books do you recommend to help someone understand your business?

Demystifying Multimedia, Emerging Distribution Models for Consumer Interactive Media, Multimedia Applications Development, Multimedia Law Handbook, and *Multimedia Law and Practice.*

What magazines do you suggest?

NewMedia magazine, *Morph's Outpost, CD-ROM Professional, Wired, Multimedia World,* and *Digital Media.*

Which professional associations do you belong to and recommend?

The International Interactive Communications Society (IICS), the Interactive Multimedia Association (IMA), and in the San Francisco Bay Area, the Multimedia Development Group (MDG).

What are the best conferences to attend?

Intermedia, Digital World, New Media Expo, Digital Hollywood, and E3—the Electronic Entertainment Expo.

Film, Video Games, On-Line

Michael Backes
Screenwriter and computer entrepreneur
Los Angeles

Mike was an associate producer for Paramount Pictures on the film adaptation of Michael Crichton's novel Congo, *and he has scripted numerous films, including* Disclosure *and* Rising Sun *(with Crichton) and* Dead Drop. *He was the display graphics supervisor for Steven Spielberg's* Jurassic Park, *a technical consultant for Amblin Entertainment's* Twister, *and helped create the technical sequences for* Copycats. *He is a cofounder of a Silicon Valley multimedia entertainment company, Rocket Science Games; Vitrus Corp., developer of Walkthrough products; as well as a new venture to develop an "on-line infrastructure," Electric Communities. Mike consulted for the Advanced Technology Group at Apple Computer for five years, particularly in the area of 3-D computer graphics and scientific visualization. In 1990 he established the American Film Institute/Apple Computer Center for Film and Videomakers in Los Angeles, and he serves as its co-chair. He is on the board of Steven Spielberg's Starbright Foundation, which is dedicated to finding innovative applications of technology for children with serious health problems.*

In your opinion, what is the hallmark of interactivity that works?
A transparent interaction between a person and a computer. The game *Doom* is a pretty good example of transparent interaction: you don't look down at your hands much. You can concentrate on what's happening on the screen in front of you. So interactivity to me is seamless communication without having the interface get in the way.

What do you personally find most exciting or promising about these new technological developments?
I am fascinated by the idea of virtual space and creating something that you can navigate. Whether or not it necessarily obeys Newtonian or Einsteinian physics isn't as important as is the idea of some kind of new synthetic space that can be traversed, whether it's to gain information or for recreation. I think it's really compelling.

To me, the biggest drawback to the Macintosh—usually my computer of choice—is that in using the desktop metaphor, it became very 2-D, and I think the 3-D interfaces are the wave of future. They're what excite me most about using this technology. As far as creating games or multimedia for computers, I think what's really potentially cool is creating 3-D environments to interact, to play games and to do business.

Three-dimensional environments for doing business?

In business, the nice thing about the 3-D environment is that it is a lot easier to display very large groups of people on-screen — in the Stock Exchange, for example. You can do stock trades without 3-D, but it's the interaction with people—the deal making—that goes down better in a 3-D environment. A 2-D interface gets crowded really fast. So if you're dealing with a lot of large data sets, it's often more convenient to deal with them in a 3-D rather than a 2-D environment.

How would you compare the film experience to CD-ROMs or video games?

The thing to remember right now is that CD-ROM technology is in its infancy, so there's not much grammar, there's not very much sophistication, there's not much real emotional content. It's pretty primitive. The budgets are really little. It's a new business. So you have to be a guerrilla fighter to get out there and roll up your sleeves and get the kind of production values you really need to compete in the marketplace.

I think the idea of using CD-ROMs as ancillaries for films is boneheaded. They're totally different experiences, and you find out very quickly that the linearity of a film and the distinct singular point of view of a film doesn't translate well to a multiple POV [point of view], nonlinear medium.

What does Hollywood have to offer multimedia then if not making CD-ROM derivatives from films?

What they have to offer is production experience. And as these things get more complicated, the actual production tasks that are faced by the creators of CD-ROM are in many ways identical to what you see in the film business. So the kinds of things that producers do, the kinds of things that production designers, and art directors, writers for dialogue, special effects people, directors for actors, and actors—these are the roles that you find in conventional film production. We have big-time experience in that, and that's why the acting looks so good in movies and so crummy in CD-ROMs.

It's just like when people came out of vaudeville and theater to design sets for movies. The biggest transfer of talent from vaudeville to movies was in production talent. Multimedia is not, as they say in hushed tones, "a new kind of film making." It isn't. It's a totally new thing.

How would you characterize multimedia, then?

It goes back to multiple point of view, nonlinear story structures. You have to learn to tell the tale for the medium in which it's going to be delivered, and that's just starting now. The emotional grammar of CD-ROMs is incredibly primitive: none of them make you feel longing, or hope, desire, or love. People make fun of *Doom* as a stupid game, but it does one thing: it does make you feel a sense of suspense. When you open a door, you don't know what's behind it—it really flips you out. That 3-D space really makes a different. Pretty soon someone will make a game that will really scare the hell out of people.

Multimedia is a perfect medium for horror just as it is for film; scary movies were among the first things to show up in the movies. It's really easy to scare people, it's harder to get people to feel love. That requires a very distinct, very realistic performance, and synthetic characters just can't deliver those kinds of performances. Because they start looking robotic. But to scare somebody, you just need something to jump out at them, basically. I also think you can do humor, too. But that's harder. First will come horror, then comedy. I guess the adventure genre is already being used. Adventure isn't too hard: basically, take someone through an exotic locale, and a CD-ROM can certainly do that. It's going to be a while before we have *An Affair to Remember* or *Sleepless in Seattle* experiences in CD-ROM.

I think where the quality will become possible is in networked games, where we can play games with each other, fall in love on the 'net—that sort of thing. Then it's a matter of "let's pretend." But there's a real big business in that because it's been shown there are people who have an interest in pretending and not being themselves; these networked environments can really provide that.

How would you distinguish the approach to multimedia in the Hollywood community relative to New York or San Francisco developers?

The San Francisco developers are the most arrogant, and L.A. is probably a close second. I haven't come across too many New Yorkers in this field. The problem with L.A. is they think they know talent and "show biz"; the Berkeley attitude is more along the lines of "We know what REAL ART is." The truth is, to borrow a line from the screenwriter William Goldman, "nobody knows anything." The proof is in what you do, not in what you think you do. Everyone is walking around in the dark, and occasionally somebody runs into a wall and says, "Hey, I found a wall." And that's how the space is slowly being defined.

I think there's lots of room for humility in this business, because really if you look at most of these titles—even the ones that are put on a pedestal as being the best—they all are pretty much below the mark. They'll get better, and there's incredible potential, but they're not there yet.

But that's what's great: it is still early in the game; it still is the Oklahoma Land Rush. D. W. Griffith hasn't shown up yet. Even Edwin Porter—the guy who made *The Great Train Robbery*—hasn't shown up yet. Nobody has made any grammatical breakthroughs in this medium.

What would you say to the next Griffith or Porter?

I'm deeply suspicious of people who want to get into this who don't play games. Just like I'd be deeply suspicious of a film maker who didn't like movies. It's interesting that very, very few film makers have been able to make successful television shows. A lot of people who want to get into entertainment multimedia don't play games. People who come from Hollywood into the video or computer game business and say "We know how to do this" usually fall on their faces.

And who succeeds?

I think it's the people who really have the intense burning desire to entertain. I keep going back to *Doom*, because it is a good model. All those guys [who created the game] want to do is kill stuff in an entertaining fashion, and they deliver on all counts. I think the ones who have really got it are the ones who know what's fun. A big sense of fun is a really good thing for makers of games.

What are some of the problems of converting a movie into a video game or a CD-ROM game?

It's fraught with peril, because I think what makes a great movie is a distinct point of view, and the second you start to allow the person to change the action, you cause the point of view to become diffuse. And that hurts things. The reason that Roman Polanski movies are great is because he is obsessed with making a particular kind of movie. If Joe Blow enters the world of *Rosemary's Baby*, he's not going to end up with *Rosemary's Baby*.

Should video games or multimedia CD-ROMs attempt to imitate cinematic devices, or is that the wrong approach altogether?

Only the ones that are worthwhile. There are certain ways of composing and framing a scene cinematically for how to follow the action that might work. A good example of how to do it well is *Virtual Fighter*, from Sega. It purports to be a 3-D action game, but in fact you have very little control over your point of view in the scene; therefore, the action can be delivered in a cinematic way. Not to say that it necessarily is—it could be even more cinematic than it is. The game designers are controlling how you're viewing the action even though you're controlling the action. For example, the game designer puts the camera someplace, and then you control the characters fighting in that scene. So what happens is that the game designer can pick a particularly dramatic and aesthetically pleasing angle to heighten the emotion of the participant. In other words, the virtual camera is put somewhere for a reason, and ideally it services the emotional response that the game designer is attempting to elicit from the user.

MCA, Paramount, Warner Brothers, and Sony (owner of Columbia Pictures) are some of the studios that have invested in multimedia companies or set up their own subsidiaries. What pitfalls do they face in attempting to create entertainment in such a different medium?

Sony has their own game machine, the Sony Play Station, out of Japan. What's really interesting is they're designing good games, not just saying "How can we do *Prince of Tides* as a CD-ROM?" So I think they're going to be pretty successful. Everybody else is viewing multimedia as an electronic T-shirt to basically make some more bucks off their movies. The companies that actually start to bring their creative resources to bear on making better games, as opposed to just figuring out a way to make a few more bucks off their franchised characters with pointy ears, have the right approach.

Since you were involved with the movie Jurassic Park *as a technical advisor, what is your opinion of the game spin-offs?*

I just don't think there's much comparison between *Jurassic Park*, the movie, and *Jurassic Park*, the game. They're in totally different leagues. The movie is set in a very complex world that can't be particularly well simulated on a piece of optical real estate right now—a CD-ROM. It can't be done very well. It's much too complex a system. And given the time that you need to come out with a product, I mean, if you were going to do a "dinosaur terrarium"—your basic "Dino Park"—I think that's potentially a cool idea for a game. But it's going to take a long time; you're not just going to rush it out to be an ancillary. You've got to really think it through. The video games (for 3DO and Sega) based on *Jurassic Park* suffer from the fact that they had very tight development schedules and they weren't given the opportunity to really break the mold. They were just basic tie-ins—instead of fighting monsters, you're fighting dinosaurs. A simulation of the park would have been more compelling. It wasn't that the games were bad, it's just that they were what they were, and they weren't supposed to be any more than that. They weren't supposed to be breakthrough games. The pinball game of *Jurassic Park*, by the way, is really excellent.

Do you think these new opportunities will mean more jobs in Hollywood, or will there just be a reshuffling of existing talent?

There will be more jobs, just like there were more jobs after television came in after radio. But it will not only be happening in Hollywood. Multimedia will very rapidly become independent of Hollywood. They will use Hollywood resources and people who have worked in Hollywood. But I think the multimedia industry will develop all over the place. The nice thing about it is that there won't be any particular concentration of talent. If I were looking around right now, I'd get close to an art school, because that's where the real talent is. That's where you have people coming who are trained artists, who are trained to create art on computers: they're the gold mine.

Tell me more about your thoughts of why the multimedia business will develop independently of Hollywood.

Because the number of resources that are required from Hollywood are not as large as Hollywood would like to believe. I believe what Hollywood has that's applicable to the game business is primarily design talent.

Not the acting and directing?

Not necessarily. These multiple-plot-line stories—I mean, if you look at how actors are used in CD-ROMs, they're not used particularly well. They're used primarily to do bridge scenes; they're not typically featured in the actual game play. You cut back to some canned piece in the middle of your game that most kids and adults flip right by. You just want to play the game; you don't give a damn what the "bumpers" are. They don't care if you've got four actors who failed to get a pilot this year—you know, it was a toss-up whether they'd be in the game or a judge on *Star Search*. They're C-level and D-level talent; occasionally, you get an A-level actor like Ned Beatty or Dennis Hopper. But as a rule, it's low level.

Won't the quality of actors change as multimedia becomes more established?

I don't see any reason to, because I don't think good acting is required to make games better.

You don't think good actors could be brought into the game play as the capacity of the computer increases?

A performance is a very linear thing. It also represents the specific reaction of a character to a specific thing, and it's really easy to lose that if you start telling the actor to do something thirty different ways. What makes a performance compelling is when a Robert De Niro puts all his focus into doing it one way; he may take five different approaches to that one way, but it's still one thing he's trying to get across. He's trying to tighten, tighten, tighten the focus until he gets something that really works.

Who knows, eventually they may have Sly Stallone be the character in a game, but I don't think that particularly adds anything. It's just bringing the likeness; it's not bringing the character that the actor delivers to the game. And I don't think likeness is that important; performance is important, and I don't think you can bring the performance into multimedia.

In other words, Mickey Mouse isn't Mickey Mouse unless he acts like Mickey Mouse. And Sly Stallone can't act like Sly Stallone for too long in the game before it becomes very, very repetitive. Because you can't give him enough variation, you can't really capture Sly Stallone: it's not really like being with Sly Stallone in an environment and you're interacting with him. Instead, he's got prerecorded responses that you blast through very quickly. The thing about a game is that it's got to stand up to repetitive play, at least today. Eventually, there may be event games intended for you to play once—maybe that's one way that actors will become useful.

This kind of prognostication is fraught with peril.

As one of the founders of Rocket Science, what is your view as to what makes a really good video game?

Suspension of belief, just like in a movie. If you're there, you're in the game; it's good if it can command all your attention. You're not looking at your watch; you're not getting bored. In other words, if the game is doing what it's supposed to do, it doesn't matter what genre it is. Even the graphics can be lame, and you can still have a good game. There's this obsession with pretty pictures, but it definitely does get back to the game play. On the other side there are these jerks going around who say it's all about game play and that no one gives a damn about the pictures. And that's simply not true, either. Production values are incredibly important; they make your product more aesthetically pleasing. If you have both great production values and great game play, you're on the right road. And that's what we're hoping to do at Rocket Science. We're focusing on making sure that production design does not overshadow our game play, like I think it did to some degree in our first couple of titles.

There is a lot of debate about how to make video games appealing to girls. What are your thoughts on this?

It is a problem. I think one of the reasons is that the emotional content has been relatively limited. And I don't just mean stereotypical "girl" emotions. What I'm talking about is the lack of an emotional palette to appeal to women. As that increases, then women will be more attracted to these games. One thing I've seen is that many women are hooked on the Russian puzzle game, *Tetris*. It has a very distinct goal orientation. There is pattern recognition, and you have to think on the fly; these seem to be tasks women are very good at and find appealing.

As a film screenwriter, what do you see as the challenges in creating branching narratives that are interesting despite no traditional dramatic buildup, climax, or denouement?

My biggest issue is that I don't think branching narrative is interesting. The problem with branching narrative is that it is finite. What's much more compelling is this: How do you create an environment where characters have the mobility to do anything they want, and then still put what I call little dramatic "Easter eggs"—or the potential for things to happen—in that environment? Branching narrative is limited in the manner of interactive laser disks: As soon as you've exhausted the possibilities, you're never going to play it again. From a writing standpoint, I'd rather look at how you write for a game like *Doom*—how do you make *Doom* a richer environment from a verbal standpoint? No one talks in *Doom*; they just go "Grrrrr!" and shoot you. What if they talked—what do you do then? That's what they're dealing with at Spectrum Holobyte with their Star Trek products. They don't really have a branching narrative; rather, their characters have the potential to say things and the potential to interact. And I think that's the way to go: branching narrative is deader than a doornail.

What did you mean by "a dramatic Easter egg"?

It's the scene the character walks into. It could be the right place and the wrong time. Or wrong place, wrong time. You walk into the bank in a game to get into some money and happen to come across a robbery. How would that interaction come down, depending on what you do? Life has certain dramatic potential. How do you re-create that in a game? It's a really tricky problem, and I don't have the answer yet.

The problem with developing good stories for multimedia is that when you're dealing with synthetic characters, you very rapidly see that they're not real. In a movie, you can never question it, because you can never stray off the narrative path—you can't stop in the middle of the scene as an audience member and say, "Hey, Hamlet! Go through that door!" Hamlet's going through whatever door he wants to, and it has nothing to do with you. You're just dragged along. In a game you can choose: Does he go in the door or not? And that immediately diffuses the dramatic action. Therefore, what I think you can do is pepper a scene with "dramatic Easter eggs"—the potential for the bank to be robbed; you're involved or you're not involved.

But eventually, even that loses its savor. I think where this eventually goes is that someone like me will create an environment—let's say, derelict spaceship on the edge of the universe. Then you and a bunch of your pals, or people you don't even know, will come together and explore that environment. Some of you will play the inhabitants of the space station, and some of you will play the explorers. In other words, it probably has more to do with role playing than anything else. Then it's real human interaction and how well the people play their parts.

Now what eventually may happen is—and this is where Hollywood actors could lend something to the mix—what if you had big on-line games where you had big Hollywood stars acting in the game as characters? And so the player would actually get to be "in the movie." That's where Hollywood might be able to really give some talent, because then talented actors could act, or more specifically, do improv.

Have you written any game scripts? What technical challenges do they present compared to what you've written for film?

The technical challenges are pretty much the same in the sense that you're trying to make it entertaining. But you usually have to build more into a game and sweat the details, because you have to make sure that somebody can use it for many, many hours. With a movie they only have to use it for ninety minutes to two hours. With a game they might only stay in a scene for two minutes, but they might play for fifteen hours, and you have to make sure that everything will bear very close scrutiny. We don't yet know what the narrative "tricks" are for games the way we do for film.

The biggest problem in coming up with a compelling game design is just making sure the environment is really interesting. Because I think the environment—the setting—is more important in a game than it is in a movie. In a movie, it's the characters. In a game, you are the character, so the writer doesn't have to worry too much about that. The writer may have to do things to you, but more importantly, the writer needs to make sure the environment you come into is really compelling. That's the biggest difference and the biggest challenge.

How does one create a game that players will want to return to again and again?

Again, it's creating an environment rather than a narrative. With a narrative, once you've seen it, you've seen it. Even if you create five different narratives, the player uses it five different times, and then they've seen it. If you create a compelling environment, they'll come back. Look at what Disney has been able to do with the theme parks. Big Thunder Mountain is different every time you ride it to some degree, even if the essential charge is the same—because you're looking at different things.

What would be your advice to a writer who wanted to get into scriptwriting or game design?

Take some classic visual design classes. Understanding visual design elements can help writers understand the kind of problems they'll have to overcome to make a compelling game environment. If you look at something like *Gadget*, created by Shono-san from Japan, it's created by a visual designer/writer. It's compelling; it's set in this really dark creepy world that's brilliantly realized. And one of the reasons that it looks so good is that it has visual integrity. The people who are going to be most successful in this are not writers; they're designers who have some writing ability. If you can't draw yourself, at least learn how to talk to artists.

Aside from writers, what is your advice for someone wanting to get into this new field? What kinds of skills will most be in demand?

Computer animation, computer animation, computer animation.

What are your thoughts about being entertained at a computer terminal versus a television set?

To me, interactive TV is a matter of the emperor's new clothes. I think on-line systems will evolve into interactive TV; at the moment, they just don't have the bandwidth. Just the way people have hooked up their stereos to their TVs, I think eventually everybody is going to hook up their computers to their TVs. There won't be such differentiation.

What do you see for the future in terms of multimedia and interactive entertainment?

It's already developed into a new genre, but the entertainment hasn't caught up to technology yet. As it does, there is extraordinary potential for a lot of fun. That's the whole point of this: entertainment should be entertaining. And as multimedia gets more sophisticated in the kind of entertainment it's able to deliver, it will grab a wider audience. Some people will never like computers, though, just like some people don't like television or movies.

Looking at things in reverse, do you think interactive media will have an impact on what viewers demand from film?

Absolutely, just like MTV's rock videos have had an extraordinary effect on film making and television—the editing and the storytelling, how things are fast and loud, and information is presented in a shortcut sort of way. There are certain cutting and visual conventions that arise in any media, then pollinate into other media.

What do you recommend in the way of an insightful book?

Out of Control, by one of the founders of *Wired* magazine, Kevin Kelly. It discusses how computers are starting to resemble human organisms, how they are modeling our own innate creativity, which is important to understand by the image makers and artists among us.

Multimedia Law

Mark F. Radcliffe
Partner, Gray Cary Ware & Freidenrich
Palo Alto, California

Mark received a B.S. in chemistry from the University of Michigan and attended Harvard Law School, where he was the Notes and Comments Editor of the Harvard International Law Journal. *After law school, he clerked for Chief Judge Howard R. Turrentine of the Southern District of California. He is on the editorial board of the* Computer Lawyer, *a monthly newsletter, and has coauthored a book on multimedia law,* The Multimedia Law Handbook.

Please distinguish between high-technology and multimedia law practices.

I view the difference as being that high-technology clients cover a much broader range—from semiconductor or software to biotech industry—whereas multimedia is focused on this new incoherent industry and is a narrower class of companies. A multimedia client could be a content owner, like Time-Life Books; it could be the provider of some type of "engine," such as Macromedia (which owns the authoring program, Director); somebody who is providing a service, such as the publisher Mindscape; or a hardware manufacturer, like Media Vision.

You refer to the multimedia industry as being "incoherent."

To say there is a multimedia industry is incorrect; rather, it is a series of enabling technologies. I don't think things are coherent enough to call it an industry. So when I say "multimedia," what I mean is a product that includes either all or some of the following: music, text, video, and still pictures. To say "multimedia industry" is a little misleading, because Time-Warner is investing in multimedia, but I wouldn't call it a multimedia company. There are a lot of people who do a little bit of this. If a publisher like Random House puts out a CD-ROM, does that make them a multimedia company? No, not really. Moreover, the industry is still forming—the distribution channels and standard deal terms are still very much in an evolutionary state.

Is interactive TV part of the multimedia industry? Although multimedia generally means something that is interactive, a multimedia product doesn't necessarily have to be interactive. Interactivity is a very important part of what differentiates many multimedia products from other linear products, like TV programs or movies, but at the same time one can't say that all multimedia products are necessarily interactive.

In your opinion, has multimedia or new media opened up career opportunities for lawyers?

It's opened up the opportunities for lawyers serving the more traditional high-tech industries. For example, I myself dealt mainly with software companies, and am now handling more multimedia-type deals to gain new expertise. I'm doing a lot of deals that have more of an entertainment flavor than any software deal ever had. So I had to learn all sorts of new things both substantively and in terms of business. For example, there are substantive issues about music licensing, which is very complex and has a lot of industry traditions that are strong.

Most computer lawyers don't know much about "rights of publicity," which is a very integral part of working in multimedia. It refers to the right to use somebody's image in a commercial product—their voice, or their appearance, for example—to tell a story or narrate something. It could be an actual picture of somebody. Or it could even be their "persona," such as Vanna White, who won a suit against Samsung for using a robot in a blonde wig changing letters on a game show that suggested her persona.

There's something else called "the rights of personality." It is broader, because it includes some things like rights of privacy, the right to be left alone, or the right not to be shown in a false light (e.g., not to have your head put on the body of a chicken).

So I've had to learn a lot about the music, film, book publishing, and entertainment industries. Because when you're trying to clear a property using preexisting works, you have to understand how the other industries operate and what their expectations are. One of the most difficult problems these days is using preexisting music, because most of the music publishers don't understand multimedia enough to set reasonable rates. They try to find something comparable, and to them the closest thing it looks like is a videocassette. The problem is that relative to CD-ROMs, videocassettes sell something on the order of ten times as many for any given title. It gets pretty expensive to use licensed rights from somebody with those misconceptions.

Multimedia also offers opportunities for entertainment lawyers to cross over into technology and multimedia. There are many excellent entertainment attorneys who are learning new things about software. Multimedia draws on a number of disciplines: entertainment law, computer law, copyright law, and, to a lesser degree, patent law. And then there are all the subdisciplines within these, such as contract law, which is something that's applicable within almost any industry. Multimedia interacts with all these different industries with different traditions in terms of how copyright operates, and with very different expectations. So trying to mediate all of them to arrive at an agreement people will sign can be very difficult.

Do you have a real-life example of how this works when these different cultures clash?

The classic example is a movie company that has a character to license from a blockbuster hit. A game maker approaches who wants to make a game based on the movie. The movie mogul says, "I want $250,000 up front," because the movie industry is very focused on dollars in-hand. Unfortunately, the problem in multimedia is that it has more of an equity-based compensation structure instead of a dollar-based compensation structure. [Ed. note: Equity-based compensation means you get paid in stock, or stock options, as opposed to getting cash in-hand.] And second, multimedia expects to get its returns over time based on sales. So it is difficult to fit a large up-front fee into a budget when the success of a product is very uncertain. The net result is that many deals don't get made because the Hollywood people don't want to deal with the market realities of the smaller CD-ROM world.

Another example would be the music industry using their normal terms. In many cases, this leads to problems such as OEMs [original equipment manufacturers] needing reproduction rights—and most music rights don't permit sublicensing from the multimedia publisher to the OEM. Also, the music industry makes assumptions about how many units are going to be sold and sets the pricing with inaccurate assumptions. The typically successful CD-ROM in 1994 was selling about 30,000 units, whereas the successful videocassette normally sells in the range of 250,000 units. If multimedia producers want to use 20 to 30 music clips, they can't pay the music publishers the rates the music industry is used to.

Would you say that new media law is a subset of computer law or entertainment law?

It doesn't fall under either right now. You see practitioners coming from both, so it's real tough to say that it's a subset of one or the other. It draws on both of them almost equally.

The point is that there is an entirely new deal structure going on here, and that's critical. Because frankly, many of the Hollywood deals are fairly straightforward in the sense that there's not a lot of variance as to what you can get. For example, in the Art Buchwald case versus Paramount over his right to receive net profits from *Coming to America*, one of the things that came out is that the net profit definition for all the studios is the same. And we're not talking about a one-page definition for net profit; we're talking about something that goes on for six or seven pages. What it means is that even though you have five or six studios, you can't get a different deal by going to one studio or the other. The important thing to take from that is the awareness that the movie business is a mature industry with an established deal structure.

Can you characterize the new deal structure that's emerging for multimedia?

It isn't finalized, but it draws most strongly on the software industry model and on the film model, with elements of the record industry and its affiliate labels deals. It's a little difficult to say which one is going to win out.

The software model is generally that the creator of the project licenses it to the publisher, who in turn takes it out and distributes it. The film industry model is that you put a creative team together and the producer generally owns all rights to the product. The reason those distinctions are important is for secondary uses. For example, in the situation where a license is involved, the publisher or producer in that situation has to think through all the rights he wants—not only rights in this particular products, but also rights in remakes of it, rights in sequels, and so forth. To give the most graphic example, you don't want to be the software publisher who licensed the first *Star Wars* but didn't get rights in the sequels. So it requires a lot more thought and preparation if you're a publisher and you're only getting a license rather than an assignment.

What you've got is a convergence of the industries, and I don't think that any one industry will "win." But I do think we're moving more towards the movie-type model simply because the dollars involved in creating products continue to escalate. As the money becomes greater and greater, you'll see more of a film industry type of model, though there are a lot of film industry traditions that don't fit right now. One of the things about the movie industry is that distribution is fairly stable—there's a relatively limited number of distributors. All the methods of distribution are fairly well thought out. You have foreign rights, you have videocassette rights, etc.

Distribution is completely up in the air in the multimedia market. Traditionally, multimedia products were sold through computer stores, but that's changing. Now they're being carried in bookstores, in mass market outlets, and a wide variety of other venues—and that doesn't even account for the potential for on-line distribution.

So it's still very much up in the air. And as long as you have that degree of uncertainty in the distribution side of the business, then the development side is going to have to have equal degrees of flexibility.

Intellectual property rights are obviously important. Let's start by discussing copyright law.

The most important intellectual property right in multimedia is in the copyright area. Copyright covers a work of authorship (music, film, books, software) and includes five rights: the right to reproduce, distribute, modify (a.k.a. make derivative works), publicly perform, and publicly display. The copyright holder can license those rights or use them himself or herself. It protects works against being copied, generally proved by showing that the second party had access to the original work and that the works are substantially similar.

"Substantial similarity" is a qualitative, not a quantitative, test. So the more important the piece you took, the less you have to take for there to be a copyright infringement. For example, a major magazine was found guilty for taking only 400 words out of a 200,000-page autobiography of President Ford, because the words they took were about the Nixon pardon, the part that everybody wanted.

Copyrights arise automatically from the time a work is created, as long as it's "fixed in a tangible medium of expression"; in other words, virtually everything is fixed except for things like oral conversations or speeches without notes.

What about patent law?

Patent law is the next most important area for consideration in multimedia. Patents give you the right to make, use, and sell something, and they cover ideas, which are not protected under copyright law. Patents protect inventions that are nonobvious, useful, and novel. The government defines the exact scope of a patent, unlike copyrights where the scope is set by the principle of substantial similarity (which is based on the type of work). If somebody else designs around the patent, they're not liable. When patents are granted by the government, they tell you exactly what the claims are and how they're implemented.

Patents do not arise automatically—you have to apply to the government to obtain a patent. You go through a long administrative proceeding to prove that you meet the high standards. Patents are protected for a very limited period of time, only for seventeen years, while copyrights are protected for fifty years after the death of the author, or for a minimum of 75 years, in any case. (There are other terms depending on the author or time of publication, but those are the most frequent ones.)

Patents are expensive to get, anywhere from $4,000 to $50,000, depending on the type of technology. And they take three to four years to get issued. However, they are probably the most powerful form of intellectual property. In multimedia, they tend to come into play on the technology side—for example, how the software works (that's what the Compton's New Media patent was about).

Trademark law is also an important area in multimedia?

Yes, trademark laws protect words, symbols, devices, or sounds that indicate the origin or quality of a product. Examples of trademarks are Apple's logo with a bite out of it, the roar of the MGM lion, and symbols such as the Morton Salt girl. Trademarks permit you to prevent the use of a confusingly similar symbol.

"Confusing similarity" is based on two criteria: the appearance of the trademark and the difference between the goods or the products in question. So an apple and a pineapple were found to be confusingly similar in a case involving a trademark infringement of Apple computer, because the people coming up with the Pineapple brand were planning to sell Apple-"compatibles." The question is this: Would the public be confused by these two trademarks on these two products? A trademark doesn't give you the absolute right to use a particular word, symbol, or device for any product; it gives it for a particular product. So the fact that Apple owns the trademark for computer goods doesn't give them the right to stop someone from making earth-moving equipment under that name.

Is there any other important area of intellectual property as it relates to multimedia?

The final area to mention is trade secrets. Trade secrets apply to all industries; they protect ideas or inventions that are not widely known within the industry and which people have taken reasonable steps to protect. Examples of valuable trade secrets are the formula of Coca-Cola and certain types of programming techniques. Trade secrets tend to be something you don't see as much of in the film industry as you do in the software industry.

How much about CD-ROM and computer technology does the lawyer actually have to understand? In other words, how technical do you need to be?

I don't think a technical background in computers is required, though it helps to understand as much of the technology as possible. The truth of the matter is that if you get too wrapped up in the technology it can impair your ability to communicate to third parties as to what the agreements really mean. On other hand, you have to understand the technology well enough so that you don't do something that is nonsensical in the context of the technology (even if it's legally correct). I think the level of knowledge necessary would be what you see in the *PC World*-type of magazines. You don't have to be able to understand the *Byte*-magazine level of knowledge.

Is representing multimedia clients in their financial transactions different in any meaningful way from representing clients in other industries?

The actual financing work is not different, but the models for financing are constantly shifting. There is the typical Silicon Valley model—the startup with a bunch of engineers who hire management and start the company. They sell equity to venture capitalists, move forward, and go public or get sold.

That's the model that a lot of multimedia companies are using; however, there are an increasing number of people who are looking at the film model, where you create a publishing company of sorts. You have a series of independent developers with whom you have relationships, you take a look at their producers, and you finance—either wholly or in part. For the distribution you make money by selling the rights. There may not be a lot of equity—it's much more of a cash model. So far, there hasn't been a lot of bank financing in multimedia like in the film industry. So there's not a clear model of how all this works.

There's a lot of money sloshing around from the large content companies, the Times Mirror and Time-Warners of the world and other companies, trying to get into this for what they view as strategic reasons. There is a lot of strategic partnering going on.

The major difference between multimedia financing and other financing is that the due-diligence aspect of making sure that the deal is in a position to be financed (do people own the rights they claim to own?) is intimately bound up with intellectual property rights. So intellectual property rights, once again, take a primary position as to whether or not the deal is sensible and can obtain financing.

What are the most common misconceptions that lawyers not in this field have about new media law?

The common misconception is that it is just like computer law, or just like entertainment law. There is a lack of recognition about how different it is and how fluid the deal structures are right now. The other misconception is the degree to which you have to know about different industries. Attorneys coming at this from the computer software side, although they may be very capable and know copyright law as it applies to software, will be surprised by some of the things like performance rights, which is more of an entertainment law issue. Or "renewal rights" under the Supreme Court Act of 1909, a complex area of law well-known in the book publishing and entertainment industries, but not by software lawyers.

It's interesting: you're building a new industry and setting up the deal structures, so it's very exciting. You're painting on a blank canvas.

Is there a certain temperament or mentality that is particularly suited to the practice of multimedia?

I think you have to be flexible and curious because things are so much in flux. The attitude that "It's got to be this way" or "It's always done this way" will be difficult to carry forward.

Are there many lawyers who have developed multimedia as a specialty?

There's a handful of lawyers, and they tend to come out of the software side of the industry. I have been doing intellectual property law for thirteen years now, for example. Generally, they haven't come from the music industry, but rather from the more standard entertainment practices, like film and TV. The industry is fairly small: There are only a few lawyers who could claim that multimedia is all they do, and the ones who could say that are mainly solo practitioners with one large client. In the case of my practice, multimedia is around 60% of the total caseload.

Most multimedia law is done on the West Coast, since the multimedia industry is developing more rapidly out here, but there are some attorneys on the East Coast. It tends to be practiced in the major centers—places like the San Francisco Bay Area, Los Angeles, New York, and to a lesser degree Chicago and Boston.

Do you foresee the day when multimedia work would be sufficient for someone to specialize in that and that alone?

I think so, but that day is probably five to seven years off. Multimedia law today is somewhat similar to what software law was in the early 1980s, practiced by a few specialists scattered throughout the country. People thought software was an odd specialty, and now it's become ubiquitous.

As a matter of fact, interestingly enough, software has changed the way the legal profession is structured, in my opinion. It used to be that intellectual property was handled almost entirely by small, boutique specialty firms, called PTC firms (patent, trademark, and copyright). The large, general-practice firms like my own did financing and other things, but essentially handed all the intellectual property matters over to the PTC firms, with very few exceptions. However, because software mushroomed so rapidly, became so critical to people's businesses, and demanded such an enormous amount of legal effort, the PTC firms were eventually unable to handle it. General practice firms like my own began to work in the software area and do software contracts, which meant that we had to learn about copyright, patent, and trademark law. So gradually the lockhold the PTC firms had on these intellectual property areas has disappeared. And now general practice firms do virtually everything that the PTC firms do, with the possible exception of patent prosecution, which the PTCs still dominate for a variety of reasons.

I think that multimedia is likely to become just as ubiquitous, simply because people will be using it in business presentations, they'll be using it in education, for entertainment, etc. There's been a lot of focus on blockbuster hits, but the true money in multimedia is going to be on the training side.

For example, Holiday Inn, with the hostelry industry's typical turnover rate of 120%, is now saving millions of dollars training new employees wherever they are located, rather than flying them off to faraway locations.

Do many lawyers leave the specialty, and why?

It is an intense practice, and people may leave because there's too much uncertainty, or because they find their old specialties are more attractive. The problem is that in this industry you may not have a client for long—they are always merging, and shifting, and changing. So unless you're in a place where you spend a lot of time doing this, it's real tough to do it consistently. Being in the Bay Area, where there is a constant deal flow, is all right, but if you're in a place like Chicago, it's much more episodic. Somebody may look at it and decide that the learning curve for multimedia law is enormous and may not be the best use of their time.

How would you rank the financial compensation for this specialty as compared to other specialties within the legal field?

The incentive is less in terms of immediate dollars in pocket than the opportunity to be in an expanding area. In most cases, law firms do not pay premiums to attorneys because of their area of specialty; they tend to pay premiums for having large client lists. But I see an opportunity to be in an area that is growing, and to ride that growth into a long-term career.

What are the best and worst things about practicing high-tech law?

The best is that it is constantly challenging and you're doing new things. The worse is that everybody wants things yesterday. Until lawyers and clients become educated, they just don't understand how complicated this really is. I'll get calls from a general counsel or a businessperson who will ask, "Just give me your standard form." Well, in multimedia there is no standard form.

Here's an example: I have a client who is fairly sophisticated in this area, but who was trying to make a "go/no go" decision on a project that was brought to them, which was very complex from a clearance point of view. There were over forty video clips, which included music and a whole series of rights of personality issues. And basically they called us on Monday and said, "We need you to help us on this," and we didn't get the box of materials that needed clearance until Wednesday, and they needed a decision on Friday. That's the sort of situation where people are making demands which are unrealistic given the complexity of the issues. Depending on how risk-adverse the client is, they're pushing hard for a "yes" answer, and it's real tough to come up with a creative solution when you don't even know where the problems are.

Speaking of clearances, when should lawyers handle this versus these new specialty clearance houses that are cropping up?

It all depends on the nature of the project and how much is at risk. We actually refer out a significant amount of work to the clearance houses, because they can do it more cost-effectively than we can. Particularly in music rights, clearances is a very specialized area. You need to know the people you're talking to. These clearance specialists see a lot of deals.

In the movie industry, clearances are mainly done by paralegals. But the problem is that the deal structure in multimedia is much too fluid for that. You're not even sure what rights you need, because you don't know if you're going to put it on-line, or if you going to distribute it through OEMs . . . so there are all sorts of issues that are still open. You can't always just turn clearances over and have them done mechanically. I think, properly supervised, one of the most effective combinations is a lawyer setting out the standards and then letting the clearance people go out and do it.

For pure clearance issues—e.g., just using a 60-second video clip of King Kong—it's a toss-up as to who is more cost-effective, depending on the experience of the firm. Obviously, if you go to a legal firm that doesn't do this on a regular basis, you can spend a lot of money while they figure out what they've got to know, what rights they've got to clear, and who they've got to go to. But if you come to a firm like my own that does clearances on a more regular basis, we know whether it makes more sense for us to do it or outsource it to one of the clearance agencies.

What advice would you give to a law student who was considering entering multimedia law?

They should do their best to learn about intellectual property laws, which are going to be the core specialty of multimedia. Second, they should do their best to learn about the industries that are involved: the software, record, book publishing, film, and TV industries. Third, and this is probably the most important, is to go after graduation to where the work is. No matter how good a multimedia lawyer you are, if you are in Fargo, North Dakota, you're not going to get a lot of work. The fourth issue is go to a firm that is devoted to this area. Law students should not think they can build a multimedia practice on their own if they go to any firm. There are firms that have no interest in doing this, and they have to build an infrastructure to do it right. We have paralegals who specialize in copyright and trademark work. We have all sorts of books in our library—there is a large investment the firm has either made or is willing to make.

Finally, although this may be appear to be a glamorous profession, it really is a lot of hard work. There is a very steep learning curve if you're going to be able to practice effectively. The reason is that it covers so many industries, as well as so many legal disciplines. I've read probably 1,000 pages on music licensing alone, and it isn't light reading.

I notice you are a correspondent for the European Intellectual Property Review. In terms of a career in international law, do the intellectual property laws vary widely between European countries, Japan, and how we practice here?

International intellectual property laws vary quite dramatically, although that variance is becoming less so because the European Union is making the copyright law of its members all very similar.

But the legal tradition in intellectual property in Continental Europe is different than in the U.S. On the copyright side, the European tradition comes out of the civil law tradition and focuses on author's rights, whereas the tradition of the United States and the United Kingdom comes out of the government granting property rights. The way that plays out in the law is that authors have many more rights in the Continental model (France, Germany) than in the U.K. model.

For example, under the Continental model they have "moral rights," which are rights to prevent a modification of the work which would be inconsistent with an author's reputation. There's the "right of paternity," which is the right to have their name used with the work. That fits wonderfully well in the area of high art—sculptures, paintings, etc.—it works less well for more industrial products like software. And actually, a number of European countries have passed exceptions to moral rights for software, because the idea that you cannot modify a software program without getting permission of the original author forever—without a way to transfer the right—is not consistent with the nature of software, which is constantly being changed.

There is another point I want to make about international law. In the U.S., patents are granted on the "first to invent," so even if you invented something many years ago, the whole system is focused on the individual and his or her invention. That's not how it's done in Europe or Japan, where the patent is granted to the "first to file," irrespective of who made the invention first. That approach tends to favor large companies as opposed to individual inventors.

Is there much work in international law?

The international market for multimedia is still very unformed. Even some of my major publishing clients are having difficulty establishing distribution channels in Europe. That's going to change, but for the moment there are not a lot of international deals being done because of this uncertainty. There are always licensing deals being done, but I have not seen the sort of international flavor that the computer industry has, where you have people doing development work in Pakistan being financed out of Singapore. The installed base of CD-ROM drives is simply not as broad overseas as it is in the United States.

What books do you recommend to would-be lawyers who would like to move into multimedia?

J. Dianne Brinson and I have written *The Multimedia Law Handbook*, an introduction for nonlawyers or nonspecialist lawyers that has a lot of examples to help explain the underlying legal principles. It's been endorsed by the Interactive Multimedia Association. It has sample contracts as well as a list of multimedia organizations, and a list of people who provide multimedia components such as video clips, audio clips, things like that.

Then there are the traditional legal books: *McCarthy on Trademarks and Unfair Competition, Boorstyn on Copyright, Nimmer on Copyright*, and Peter Rosenberg's *Patent Law Fundamentals*.

Are there any good specialty magazines in this field yet for lawyers?

There are the traditional journals—*The Computer Lawyer, The Entertainment Law Reporter*, and *Entertainment Law and Finance*—all of which have columns on intellectual property issues or deal with them on a regular basis. There are also two new newsletters: *The Multimedia Law Reporter* and *Multimedia and Technology Licensing Law Report*.

I also read the trade magazines, such as *NewMedia* magazine, *Wired, Interactivity,* and *Multimedia World.* The newsletters I get are the *IICS Reporter* and *Interactive Content.*

What professional societies do you recommend for lawyers who want to focus on new media?

The leading professional societies are the Interactive Multimedia Association (IMA), in Annapolis; the International Interactive Multimedia Society (IICS), headquartered in Lake Oswego, Oregon, and the Multimedia Developers Group, here in San Francisco. There aren't any lawyer organizations focused solely on multimedia, but the closest you'd come is the Computer Law Association, which has programs in which multimedia is a featured topic. Their newsletter, *The Computer Law Association Bulletin*, includes articles on multimedia.

SERVICES OF A MULTIMEDIA LAW FIRM

Gray Cary Ware & Freidenrich is a San Francisco-based firm that does a significant amount of multimedia law. Here is a sample of the types of services a law firm with a multimedia practice might offer:

- Apply for and obtain patents, copyrights, and trademarks worldwide.
- Advise regarding the protection of intellectual property: trade secrets, copyrights, trademarks, and patents.
- Prepare confidentiality agreements and covenants not to compete; advise regarding proprietary rights of prior employers when beginning a new enterprise.
- Prepare software licensing and publishing agreements.
- Prepare product development, marketing agreements, and agreements for product distribution, including domestic and international OEM, distributor, representative, and dealer agreements.
- Advise regarding sales and use taxation of multimedia transactions.
- Advise regarding selection, protection, and registration of trademarks worldwide.
- Advise regarding strategic corporate partnering transactions and preparation of related joint venture, licensing, manufacturing, and/or marketing agreements.

Marketing

Frank Sabella

President and business manager, SABROCO Interactive
San Francisco

Sabella is a graduate of the University of California at Berkeley (B.S., 1979) and the University of Chicago (M.B.A., 1983). He has worked in high technology for more than a decade. His experience includes financial and product management for semiconductors and memory systems and, most recently, software marketing and product management with Hewlett Packard.

What kinds of traits are important for someone who wants to get into interactive as opposed to traditional marketing?

Tremendous patience! Making multimedia is difficult. There are lots of issues such as hardware incompatibilities or the "tyranny of the installed base." If you're an artist and you want to work in multimedia in marketing under deadlines, then you've got to know how to make art that will work! For example, there are technical issues with regard to palettes and file size. (The greater the color resolution and the bigger the file, the slower the application performs.)

You need many of the characteristics that you want for traditional marketing. It's basically about communication: you still have to have the right benefit statements, good graphics, and good copy. It's clear that there will be a lot of demand for people with traditional skill sets: copywriters, musicians, video people, animators. But you have to be a Renaissance person. You want to be creative with the content and at the same time be facile with a computer.

Tell me about your "digital marketing company."

SABROCO is a contract developer providing application design, media design and production, and engineering. We produce floppy-based demo disks, educational kiosks, CD-ROM title prototypes, and custom screensavers (featuring a company's logo or products, for example). We work as consultants as well, giving seminars on what multimedia is, or training in how to use Macromedia Director or Adia. Three of us who had been together at Hewlett Packard founded the company in 1993.

We target the business community, which is why we're located in the financial district and not near the other multimedia houses in what is called San Francisco's Multimedia Gulch district. Specifically, we help companies with their communication needs and sales and marketing efforts. Sometimes we are part of a team; we get hired to do specific services, such as programming. Other times we may act as the "executive producer." The range of products we produce is from simple floppy-disk slide shows all the way to complex CD-ROM catalogues. In between, we might produce speaker support materials for the president of a company, or a kiosk-based application describing a product that allows trade show customers to input information for lead capture (finding qualified customers).

I feel we are pioneering. We do a lot of "educational selling," explaining what's going on in multimedia. We are similar to a lot of multimedia firms in that we do a lot of different things. It's still "early days" for business applications.

What projects have you worked on?

We first did a pro bono piece for the local Randall Museum, a simple application that runs on a Mac dealing with the migratory patterns of Bay Area birds. It's a kiosk application and was done in HyperCard.

Another museum project that was very interesting was *Use Your Words*, for the Kohl Children's Museum in Wilmette, Illinois. We built a kiosk that dealt with nonviolent conflict resolution for young children. It was created in Director on a Mac Quadra 700 and included video.

Our early projects were for museums, but we have turned to the business community because funding is scarce for museums.

What nonmuseum work have you done?

For Clement Mok Design we created a small floppy demo disk of a Hewlett Packard leasing program. It allowed HP sales reps to show customers what leasing would cost them. Customers could type in the cost of the equipment, and the application would provide the per-month cost of leasing, given the existing interest rates. It also made a comparison of leasing versus buying.

We created a marketing CD-ROM for Soft Windows, Insignia Solution's software that lets Mac users run Windows applications. Our marketing application contained a contest with a grand prize of $5,000, which served as an incentive for people to watch the entire presentation.

We also did a multimedia floppy-disk demo as a "brochure" for our own services. A main menu comes up with four cameos of U.S. presidents (the graphic mimics paper currency to emphasize the business orientation of SABROCO) with the selections: Andrew Jackson for Increase Your Sales, Madison for Learn About Multimedia, Lincoln for The Bike Shop (an example of how multimedia would be used in a retail setting), and Washington for learning about SABROCO Interactive.

Tell me about the delivery medium for digital marketing.

A lot of business applications, or demo-type applications, run on one or two floppies and have to be small. The reason is because the attention span of most people is very short. Self-running programs that are sent to people traditionally contain only a few minutes worth of material. But things are moving to CD-ROM because it's gotten so cheap to produce, manufacture, and distribute.

What's the process of working with a client?

It's very much akin to an advertising agency doing an ad or a brochure. You have an initial meeting where people work on their strategy, talk about what they want. Then you produce some "comps"—design ideas, interactive design ideas, and so on. The client decides what sort of functionality they might like, what the look has to be. From there, you refine those ideas. You develop the graphic, or if you need sound bites, you develop the media elements for audio, video, and so on.

But there is this other angle as well, which is the technical side. It's not enough to simply produce a Quark file and get it printed. You have to be able to program and deliver an application, whether it's a portable application, like a floppy or a CD, or an on-line application that would be distributed through the Internet or America Online.

How is the business community looking at multimedia?

They're looking at it in two major areas: communication and training.

Communication is pretty broad but includes speaker support (multimedia presentations) and trade shows (kiosks that play an interactive slide show). It can be used to communicate internally within an organization or to communicate with customers. It reaches people you might not otherwise capture.

The second area is training. It's expensive to pull employees away from their desks to attend a seminar, and hire a person to give that seminar. If you can have an on-line training application or something that can be taken home, you can save a lot of time and money. And people can go through it at their leisure.

As an example of a training application, we did a kiosk for Stanford Blood Bank, in Palo Alto, that orients new employees to how the blood bank works. One of the objectives was to help people with diverse professional backgrounds—from nurses to lab technicians—understand what the other employees do and provide some common ground. It contained about 30 minutes worth of material, including video.

After the novelty of multimedia has worn off, do you think it will still be an effective marketing tool?

That's a good point. A bank in Louisiana sent out a disk and got an 8% response rate, which is very, very high—in direct mail, normally it's 1%–3%. And the feeling is that multimedia is sort of novel, now. Someone gets a disk or CD, and they're curious about playing it. But ultimately multimedia disks will be viewed more and more like other forms of traditional media. With junk mail, a certain percentage of the people are going to open it and use it, and a certain percentage won't. But disk-based brochures are pretty cheap to make; you can dupe a floppy disk very, very cheaply in quantity and mail it out for less than it would cost to print brochures. This is especially true for catalogues.

A lot of people on the networks tend to be very heavy users of computers, so I think it's hard to say if the kind of activity we saw at the beginning is going to continue at that rate. I get on-line because I'm curious and want to see what people are doing, what's worthwhile. So there's a lot of activity, but I think as we gain a better understanding of how to use these new digital communication tools, and as more people have the ability to access them—e.g., interactive TV, or multiple users in the home who are tied to the network—we'll see some changes in the kinds of things that are presented.

It's like the early days of advertising: What doesn't work? Over time you develop some experience with it and begin developing applications that are more appropriate for those channels. We see a wide discrepancy in some of these digital marketing tools. Some floppies aren't bad; they're well thought out, and they're reasonably attractive graphically. Others we think aren't very good. For example, a CD-ROM disk replication facility created a piece with a CD-ROM animated character that was very child-like, but we had a problem with the way the material was presented. It was too cute, and it wasn't designed for the audience. There's this fascination with the technology: "Let's put a 3-D talking whatnot in the application because we can." But it's not necessarily an appropriate element for the message. When we develop an application for somebody, it's very much customized for exactly what they want.

How can digital marketing best be used, especially in comparison to marketing channels that already exist and will continue to exist? What are the advantages?

First and foremost, you have a new channel, which means you have a new audience, which is numbering in the millions. There are a lot of people who are at their computers and not watching TV. They will get product information and news and everything else on their computers. And, demographically, they are well-educated, with a lot of spending power.

Secondly, as the infrastructure is put in place, people will be able to talk back. For the company, there are several advantages. They can use interactive technology to help them capture a lot of demographic information about their customers (such as the I-Touch stations, where record-store consumers enter information about themselves in order to hear playback of songs before spending money to buy music). You can get a very good picture of who your customer is. It also appears that these digital channels are cheaper on the transaction side, as compared to taking a phone order over an 800 number. The order goes right to a company's server; it's cheaper and more accurate.

Advantages for the customer?

First, you can get the information you want. You're not bombarded with advertisements you don't care about. Second, one of the things that research has shown is that people are looking for what they call "clutter cutters"; in other words, if you want to purchase a VCR, it's an extremely complex task. There are a large number of manufacturers, and you've got a number of features. The idea is this: I want some way to cut through all this nonsense and find the product that's right for me at the best price. Interactive technology lets customers do that. And you could apply this to a lot of products.

You think people would bother looking through manufacturers' information on-line rather than just going to hear what the salesperson has to say?

There's going to need to be a behavioral shift until people are comfortable using computers to buy products. It is going to be a very long time before a vast majority of the population is operating in a virtual world, though the younger generation are already comfortable with logging on and talking with their pals somewhere else. But it will take time for the population at large to get comfortable using the technology and feel secure with it. There's always going to be paper, I think, and there will always be shopping in the physical world. But there are a growing number of people who will begin to transact and shop on-line.

MULTIMEDIA MARKETING STRATEGIES FOR MULTIMEDIA GAMES: A CASE STUDY

For a glimpse at what marketing is going to look like in the multimedia age, consider the strategy of Toronto-based Discis Knowledge Research in the release of its first game, *Jewels of the Oracle*. The product consists of a 24-game 3-D archaeological quest in the "historically authentic" pre-Sumerian era. According to Sid Oziel, product marketing manager, the multi-pronged approach was as follows:

- Four months before product release (and in time for Christmas): A preview sampler CD-ROM containing three games was made available in a "merchandiser" pack for a point-of-purchase display near the cash register. The hybrid disk (MPC Windows and Macintosh-compatible) was available to consumers for $10, with a $5 manufacturer's rebate toward the full version.
  Strategy: Not to miss Christmas buying season, spark interest before game ships.
- Three months before product shipped: Target computer user groups. Sampler disks given out at large pre-MacWorld conference attended by Apple user-group representatives from around the country. On the PC side, same strategy directed towards largest PC-user groups: Boston, Sacramento, Houston. User groups could distribute sampler in any way they desired—as raffle items, or just given away to membership.
  Strategy: Develop good word-of-mouth among industry movers and shakers.
- Two months before shipment: Single "dazzling puzzle" from the game made available free to subscribers of America Online, e-world, and CompuServe, in their game forums, and AppleLink in the Discis company folder. In addition, a "slide-show tour" available allowing players to explore the pre-Sumerian city with artifacts and hieroglyphics, plus showing the interface for the game, a Well Room. A game sample was also available for downloading from the Internet, though this distribution channel is considered more of a free-for-all since there isn't the editorial selectivity of the commercial services' Hot Games sections. Discis was able to monitor how many times the puzzle was downloaded; an 800 number was provided on-line for customer game support and to direct customers to retail outlets that will be carrying the game.
  Strategy: Generate pre-publication excitement.

- At time of release: *Jewels of the Oracle* made available with games from other developers on a sampler CD-ROM demo disk put together by and distributed as an insert by industry magazines *Electronic Entertainment, CD-ROM Today*, and *Computer Life*.
  Strategy: Consumers get a flavor of what the game looks like and how it plays before they plunk down $69.95 at the retailer for the full game.

These new media marketing strategies were accompanied by traditional magazine advertisements and public relations efforts. As Oziel notes, "The LucasArts-type companies of the world can just put an ad for a new game in a magazine, and the public will buy it based on the company's reputation. Although Discis has released thirty entertainment and education multimedia products, this is our first game and we don't yet have recognition in that category in the marketplace. That's why we came upon the mixed strategy of conventional and unique marketing methods."

"Seventy percent of game buying is based on the recommendation of a friend or from having seen or participated in a demonstration," he says. "The best thing we could do was get a taste of the product out to as many people as possible before it went on sale."

Publishing

Randi Benton
....
President, Random House New Media
New York City

Randi's background has focused on children and children's products. After getting her undergraduate and master's degrees in biology and education (M.A., 1978, St. John's University), Randi went on to become a science teacher. She unexpectedly entered the field of textbook publishing when she inquired about a job that involved writing test questions, and she walked out with an assignment to write a chapter for a science textbook. Soon, she was an editor in Harcourt Brace's School Department, and then she set up an electronic publishing division. In the mid-1980s she worked at Bantam Doubleday Dell, developing children's titles with Disney and Sesame Street and directing the development of consumer software products. But, as she notes, "It was the right idea at the wrong time," so she returned to the world of print at Fisher-Price's children's media division. After leaving there, she became a children's publishing consultant for Reader's Digest *and Scholastic Books. She is the author of several* Print Shop *handbooks. "My career is eclectic," she says, "but each thing led to the next."*

What is Random House doing in the area of multimedia?

We know new media has the potential to be big, and we feel the children's market is particularly important. We want to evolve the publishing business into electronic publishing. Our New Media Division is developing the vision, helping the publishing group, and looking for alliances as to where to position Random House. Our goal is to evolve the new media business and then integrate it into the existing divisions, not keep multimedia titles isolated into a separate division.

I should distinguish our new media division from the electronic publishing division, which is a trade book group that puts out computer and reference books. For example, they have the *Random House Dictionary*, which comes out in a print and a CD-ROM version.

Tell me about the alliances you're making.

We are finding partners who can help us evolve specific aspects of our publishing program. We created a separate company with Brøderbund

Software called Living Books, which acquired our characters of Dr. Seuss and the Berenstain Bears. They will be marketed and distributed into the book channels through the juvenile division of Random House and through the software channels by Brøderbund.

What else are you working on?

We have numerous titles in development. We have formed an alliance to co-publish titles with Knowledge Adventure, including the *Random House Kids' Encyclopedia*, which is a completely new title. With our imprint Del Rey Books, we will be developing computer games and software through an alliance with Legend Entertainment, the publisher of science fiction and fantasy games, floppy disks, and CD-ROMs. We have also formed a joint venture between Ameritech and our subsidiary, Fodor's Travel Publications, to gain a majority of Worldview Systems in order to deliver up-to-date and electronically accessible travel and destination information to consumers and travel agencies. There is also a multimedia version of the *Random House Unabridged Dictionary* in the works.

How are you staffing the New Media Division?

We have an acquisitions manager, whose job it is to go to trade shows, find talent, and help coordinate projects. Her background is in marketing and video. Then we have a new media manager within each of Random House's imprints. We all come together monthly, about ten to fifteen of us, in a New Media Committee, which I chair. We're taking people out of our book publishing divisions and assigning them new media functions, so they're for the most part learning on the job.

I know we are going to need product managers to oversee new products; marketing specialists, to get new media products into the bookstore channels; business managers to make projections for this new industry; and PR people. Although we might hire technical people to help advise us, we won't be hiring programmers in-house.

What's your advice for getting a job in publishing in the new media area?

First, you need to know the publishing business in general, and the best way to learn is to become an editorial assistant. Other good entry-level positions include assistant producer or assistant marketing manager.

You should also think about what aspect of publishing you're interested in: the product side, marketing/sales, public relations, or finance. It's the same whether you go the book or the multimedia route.

On the other hand, you don't already have to be in the publishing business to get into this new area. New media will have a life of its own. Someone can come to us who has product experience developing new media from another industry.

What kinds of skills do you look for?

I want creative thinkers, people with a fresh view, people with no fixed expectations of how things have to be done. You have to be flexible because what's true today won't be true in six months.

I also look for those who understand teamwork. In multimedia, you can't own a project all on your own. Making CD-ROMs is like making movies, and like the early days of film, we have needs for creative people: writers, musicians, and so forth.

What's your prognosis for multimedia?

It's been over-hyped, and there has been very little discrimination about what's been produced. There are more bad than good titles, tons of titles that people don't need and won't pay high prices to buy. But it's clearly a relevant publishing format, and we need to learn about it. I'm excited even if my competitors produce good titles, because it contributes to the industry.

We also have to clarify the distribution channel so consumers can find what they want. We're all learning.

EDITOR JANE METCALFE ON THE POWER OF KNOWING AND NOT KNOWING

When Jane Metcalfe hires for *Wired*, the magazine of the cyberset, she doesn't necessarily look for writers or designers who know a lot about computers. She prefers people with a vision about how the converging technologies are going to play themselves out, and what role they envision for themselves in that process.

"I look for people with something very specific that they want to accomplish," she says. "You've got to come in with an attitude, an idea, a perspective, and then run with it."

She doesn't believe people should let their lack of knowledge about the technology or business aspects of new media be barriers preventing them from knocking on doors. "All that can be learned."

"In a world where obstacles have not been built, anything is possible. Look at some of the things that have been created out of nothing: *Wired* magazine, for example."

In 1992 Jane and her partner, Editor/Publisher Louis Rosetto, got the idea for a new kind of magazine that would not only cover this emerging phenomenon, but in design, layout, color choice, and typography visually reflect its nonlinear mindset. The idea germinated as she attended Richard Saul Wurman's Technology, Education and Design (TED) conference in Monterey, as well as the Computer Freedom and Privacy Conference in San Francisco. She was intrigued by the fact that so many people from different perspectives and industries were coming together around what she calls a digital toolbox "that can liberate people's imaginations in really astonishing ways."

Inspired by the "garage start-up" spirit of Silicon Valley and the "question authority" attitude from the 1960s, they set about creating a forum that looked at technological development from the perspective of its political and social impact on the culture and on people's lives and art. They saw not only the convergence of disparate industries around digital technology, but also the democratization of communication brought about by the relatively low cost of sophisticated tools—such as the Hi-8 camera— that turned everyone into a potential publisher.

Jane is also interested in issues of privacy versus national security, and intellectual property in the age of digital publishing. While being excited by the possibilities of e-mail for enhancing the emotional bonds between people, Jane's editorial vision for *Wired* doesn't shy away from exploring the downside of the digital revolution. She encourages writers to consider where the technology may be leading us.

Wired went on-line with *HotWired* in 1994. The intent was to invent a new media form using original material, not simply to shovel the contents of the hard-copy magazine into cyberspace. "We asked everyone involved to think about how to create something in a three-dimensional space with two-way communication," Jane explains. She compares the bringing together of people from various backgrounds for the *HotWired* staff to a stew: "We have highly technical people familiar with the HTML-formatting required to put things up on the World Wide Web, as well as people like Howard Reingold, who have been instrumental in building on-line communities in the past."

What books does Jane recommend to those interested in working in the high-tech world reflected in *Wired* and *HotWired*? She starts off with two books she says changed her life: William Gibson's *Neuromancer* and Stewart Brand's book about MIT's innovative laboratory, *Media Lab: Inventing the Future*. "Brand is a visionary and an incredibly insightful, clear, and thoughtful writer who imparts a perspective as to what's going on," she says. She also recommends Howard Reingold's *Virtual Community: Homesteading on the Electric Frontier* and Don Pepper's *One-to-One Futures*, which investigates the evolution of the one-to-many marketing model spawned by the Internet and interactivity.

"I think it's really important to acknowledge what you don't understand at every step along the way," she says. "No one at this stage understands everything—even the experts don't agree—so it's a perfect opportunity to display your ignorance in all its beautiful glory in order to get the answers as fast as possible. I think that's one of the best tips I can give to anyone: admit what you don't know."

Recording Industry

David Blaine

Senior Vice President, Business development and new technology
PolyGram Records
New York City

David Blaine attended Stanford University, where he majored in anthropology and minored in English. Upon graduating, he attended the management training program run by CBS for the large chain of music stores it then owned. Eventually, Blaine became a partner in a music store in Washington, D.C., gravitating eventually towards the distribution/manufacturing side of the business. A friend who had moved to New York called Blaine in the late 1980s about an opportunity to develop the distribution channel within PolyGram. In recent years, Blaine has become increasingly fascinated by the emerging new technologies, and he has been investigating how his company could enter new markets. PolyGram Records is part of a larger PolyGram family that includes such record labels as Mercury, A&M, Motown, and Classics & Jazz, as well as a film division, a sales/marketing/distribution arm, and a division that manages musical concerts (such as Woodstock '94) and underwrites Broadway plays.

How important is it for someone wanting to get into the multimedia end of the music business to be in New York or Los Angeles?

New York and Los Angeles are still the two primary points of entry for the record business and will continue to be for the foreseeable future. But, depending on what part of the evolving business you want to get into, it may not be necessary. There are hundreds of software developers spread out all over the country. Also, in time, with things like video conferencing for business and telecomputing, it may become less and less necessary for everyone to be in the same place.

What is PolyGram Records doing in the area of new technology?

First, we've gone on-line. We developed a site on the Internet and have also joined the commercial on-line services like CompuServe (in the Music Hall area) and America Online. We are doing this for a couple reasons. It's a good research tool for us to exchange information with consumers about which of our products they like and which they couldn't care less about. Also, it's a good way to expose the breadth of our catalogue in an organized and systematic way. It reaches people who are not traditional record-store buyers. They might be willing to spend a dollar getting a CD-ROM sampler and then buy the music at a store, whereas without the CD-ROM they might not have gone to the store at all. (Downloading music, such as Aerosmith experimented with, is still a ways off because it is too time-consuming.)

Our domain site on the Internet's World Wide Web (polygram.com) was set up in early 1995. The PolyGram home page lists all our companies and affiliates, and provides options for consumers to go to a contest, game, music, film, or video section, a newsletter, or a feedback section. Making use of graphics, video, and audio, additional home pages for different labels contain a catalogue of music release plans, tour dates, and fan information. A Blue Plate Special page highlights different artists in different genres. There is an animated "help" character named Frank, who supposedly works in PolyGram's mailroom, to assist with navigation; he was designed by some of the animators who created the Simpsons. It's a very colorful and engaging area, and since information will be changed frequently we believe it will be rich enough to encourage re-visits. Someday, consumers may be able to order products directly on-line.

Are you also producing CD-ROMs?

The information we're putting out on the Internet is also going into CD-ROMs for the retail music-store buyers. Called the Interactive New Release Book, it is basically the traditional comprehensive compilation of our audio products, our catalogue, but with the added ability for the retailer to sample 30- to 60-second snippets of songs, to index their purchases onto an order form, and to fax their purchases directly to our Indianapolis distribution center. It contains more marketing information than what we put out on the Internet.

One of our first retail products for consumers was classical violinist Gil Shaham playing Vivaldi's *Four Seasons*, with the "winter" segment made interactive using video shot on the streets of New York. This Deutsche Grammophon disk plays as a music CD in a standard audio CD-player, and as an interactive CD-ROM when played on a computer. Also included on the CD-ROM is a discography for Shaham, Deutsche Grammophon's catalogue, future products, and so forth. It's been extremely popular.

We're also doing a product to teach people about classical music through the life and music of Leonard Bernstein, who has an extensive catalogue with us and who has name recognition. This career retrospective would be an edutainment piece incorporating his correspondence, video from his TV appearances, his concerts, etc. Another project we're considering is doing something associated with the WNET production on the Civil War. We published the original score for that show, which consisted of a lot of period music.

We're also thinking of doing what might be thought of as more straightforward CD-ROMs about current pop groups, like Rusted Root. It would be like a music video, but provide additional material such as access to lyrics, liner notes, album credits, film of the band playing live, clips showing a "day in the life of" the band members, and so on.

We're working closely with Philips, our parent company, to select the developers to create these CD-ROM products so we can continue to learn as the technology changes.

Finally, a lot of what we're doing in this division is research. For example, there is the issue of how to handle the distribution of CD-ROMs. We should be able to sell to traditional music dealers, traditional video stores, and software dealers. We still don't know how this issue will resolve itself.

Tell me about your staff.

We have four people, including me, the cruise director. The director of technical planning, a guy in his late thirties, is basically involved at the nuts-and-bolts level of new projects. Once an objective has been agreed upon, he works out how it will actually happen. He has been working at PolyGram for about seven or eight years in the in-house computer division. He had come from a background in finance and economics, and had moved into systems from the analytical and programming side. Then he moved into the broader issues of technology and how the changes applied to our industry, ways in which the organization had to go through change.

The other hires were from the outside. One is a woman who is the manager of our on-line services. Her background is in marketing and marketing research. Luckily for us, she is a geek—playing with technology is something she does on her own and just brings to work with her. She manages the day-to-day administration and coordination of our on-line service. She helps decide how to approach it and when to launch things. Once we're all comfortable with the new technology and see it as just another way of doing the things we've always done, we'll see cyberspace as another way of marketing and exposing our artists. At the moment, she isn't dealing with the typical record-buyer customer; she's interacting with the wizards on-line who are more interested in the technology than with the things offered by it.

The other new hire was my assistant, a woman in her mid-twenties, who had been the head of administrative affairs at the chemistry department of a university. She is a desktop publishing wizard and also happens to be dedicated to the network. She had been supplying content to a local BBS before coming here. She has an abiding personal interest in the Internet and has a talent for using technology. She also has good creative writing skills. She's writing and creating a monthly company newsletter, *The Digital Inquirer*, that we send out to increase awareness about technology so it won't seem so alien. For example, one issue was all about CD-ROMs, what they are, what the good ones are, what the vocabulary is.

What kinds of skills are important for someone wanting to work in your area?

First, they need to have a high-tech awareness. They need functional capabilities on all of the standard PC application programs, such as word processing, spreadsheets, e-mail, and to some degree, desktop publishing. In our company knowing how to use a PC is more important than the Mac. They should be familiar with using the on-line services.

It isn't as important to me if they have a record industry background, which wasn't always true. It might be more important at the PolyGram holding company or at a distribution company.

What were the record industry's first forays into new media?

The range of artists who have put out CD-ROMs has gone from standard pop artists, like Todd Rundgren, to stars, like Prince. Todd's fans tend to be technologically oriented and buy CD-ROMs whether it's one of his or someone else's. But Prince's fans don't necessarily buy CD-ROMs, but will do so just because Prince has made one, even if they don't yet own a CD-ROM drive (keeping the CD-ROM as a memento in a "Prince collection").

The material released so far is good, but it's only a first effort. There is no model or template yet about how this will work. Each release is standing or falling on its own merits.

Peter Gabriel's piece didn't live up to my expectations, for as creative as he has been in sound and visual efforts, his 'ROM effort was less about his music and more about him as a person. I'm not sure this is what people expected.

Todd's piece offered almost solely the ability to manipulate the music: to re-edit it, re-sequence it. I think this would only appeal to other musicians or interested fans, a small market, but I don't think the majority of people want to manipulate a creative product. They might want to interact with it, but not by changing the artist's creative output. I think the public is looking to interactivity for information, not to change how the sound is made.

What is some of the jargon developing in the music industry relating to multimedia?

There is the distinction between regular CD-ROMs and a standard devised by Philips and Sony called CD Plus. Technically known as multisession disks, they can be played either in an audio CD-player or on a computer. Sometimes referred to as "enhanced CDs," they contain music plus a little more, such as the lyrics to the songs that can be read on a computer monitor as the music is playing. They went on sale in music stores in late 1995 for under $20.

The more expensive product is the CD-ROM sold through software stores and mass merchandisers. These feature major stars, cost in the area of $49.95, and contain much, much more than CD Plus disks—such as video interviews, behind-the-scene segments, extensive discographies, and background on the musicians. They would be products that would endure. Our feeling is that someone who has spent the money on an expensive piece of equipment with a CD-ROM drive is not going to be put off by paying more. Whereas the record-store buyer purchasing the CD Plus may not even own a computer. I call the more enduring CD-ROMs "icon products," because the production budgets upwards of $250,000 to produce these disks can only be justified with the largest stars in the music business—the icons.

There is also the word *labels* to refer to the affiliated companies who sign artists and produce music, which PolyGram then distributes. But now these affiliated labels are doing more than simply producing music; they're making videos and films and soon will be making CD-ROMS, so I prefer using the term *repertoire labels*.

What is your general opinion about multimedia: Is it a fad, or is it a viable new medium?

I couldn't believe more strongly that this is going to become an integral part of the record industry; it's only a matter of time. But we have to be prudent and careful as to what we produce. We can't just throw product out; we need to release things that the market will support. There are a lot of new products every year that don't succeed in the record business, so we need to be careful when we start adding CD-ROMs to the mix. They are expensive to produce and require a long development time and a lot of creativity. It's not a business yet, but it will be.

What publications do you recommend people read who are interested in getting involved with the record business?

For product awareness, there are the traditional sources: *Rolling Stone, Stereo Review,* and *High Fidelity.* To learn something about the industry, I heartily recommend a book, *This Business of Music* by Sidney Shemel and M. William Krasilovsky, published by Billboard. Another good book is *All You Need to Know About the Music Business,* by Donald Passman.

What do you read and recommend that is specific to new technology?

My personal favorite is *Wired.* I also read *PC Week, Computing*—all the standard computer periodicals. A good book about the body of law that is starting to govern use of material on the network and how to protect intellectual property is *SysLaw* by Lance Rose and Jonathan Wallace.

Recording Industry / Graphic Design

David Karam
....
Cofounder, Post Tools
San Francisco

Post Tools, a design studio that produces graphics for print as well as for digital media, took its name from an industrial shop on the ground floor of its building with the sign "post tools" in the window. Karam and his partner, Gigi Biederman, founded the company in 1992 after meeting at design classes at the California College of Arts and Crafts (CCAC). They have created interactive portfolios for industrial design firms and photographers, as well as an interactive kiosk for an office furniture company. Karam has a technical and music background, while Biederman brings a fine arts expertise, and, as David says, "we both do a little bit of graphic work." Karam was born in 1969 and studied music and computer science at the University of Texas before coming to San Francisco and studying basic graphic design at CCAC. He met Gigi in a class where students had to make a project in response to the word passion. *He created a piece about the role of food in the culture of his Lebanese grandparents. When food was placed on a scale attached to a computer various impressionist, nonlinear images came up on the monitor that captured the passion for food in this family's tradition. He left school without getting a degree and worked variously for a service bureau, a design studio, and Winterland (the late Bill Graham's company), designing T-shirts. The "brochure" for Post Tools is a series of accordion-style postcards of their designs, bound by a "band" of graphics they created for the Swatch watch concern.*

I understand you created some interactive promotional products for Warner Brothers Records?

We have made several IPKs, or "interactive press kits," on floppy disks (1.4 megabytes) for various albums—*Stone Free*, a tribute to Jimi Hendrix; *Split*, by the band Lush; and *Maybe You Should Drive*, from Bare Naked Lady.

Tell me more about making IPKs.

Stone Free was an album from the Reprise Records label containing sixteen songs by various artists singing Hendrix songs. For the floppy, Reprise supplied photographs, liner notes, and the music, and we created the device of presenting the information like an interactive version of one of those late-night TV ads, a "sounds of the '60s" kind of thing. You'd click on the name of an artist and get a few seconds of the music, and it would then cycle you back to the list. We did this in Macromind Director and Abobe Photoshop, using a Mac IIci.

On *Stone Free* we used hard cuts, but on *Split* we used fluid loops of music so it flowed a little better. We purposefully created an interface that wasn't clear. You aren't sure how it functions. Clicking has no function, other than making the image twist to show you that nothing is going to happen by clicking. You'd play it like a musical instrument, and eventually you'd come across the functionality. You'd learn how to work it on the fly. What you'd see after a while is that things would happen when you passed in proximity to certain things on the screen—lemons, twigs, numbers. You are controlling a layering of objects and sounds and space. And some of the space you are controlling is "space" to the left and right of the screen that you might enter inadvertently. Things have relationships, like characters in a play.

Maybe You Should Drive used the metaphor of a screen saver. We had a theatrical-style spotlight swinging wildly over the band members, and if you clicked on it, the spotlight would enlarge and various quotes about their music would appear. You could page through lyrics, notes regarding the group, dumb facts.

I guess since you're using floppies, there isn't room for video?

That's right; we use animation, still photos, music, and text.

At what cost to produce?

They run from about $6,000 to $15,000, which I would call "the developer's cost," because it doesn't include distribution costs or marketing. Also, since they supplied us with the music, there is no licensing fee included in that figure.

What's the process and time frame for making an IPK?

They have taken us from three weeks to two months. First we'll get the content and create a prototype of our concepts, the interactive program. Then we show them and get feedback. Afterwards we make the first revision, then get the okay on that, and after more work, give them the final disk. We only met with Warners once, and the rest was done over the phone and through the mail.

How did you learn about multimedia?

I've had a computer from the age of 14. I learned to program in BASIC and wrote a goofy adventure game that was at the level of a sixteen-year-old putting together a lot of images from sci fi movies.

The way Gigi and I got into multimedia was to create an invitation on floppy disk for the American Institute of Graphic Arts for a lecture they were sponsoring on a technical subject. The theme was "moving design," and we showed the way various images have moved over different eras, starting with a flipbook of a person from around the turn of the century doing calisthenics. We did this work for free, and within a couple weeks people were calling us from New York and Australia. We didn't actually get work until a year and a half later, but in the meantime we kept making interactive things because it was fun.

What advice would you give to someone who wants to do what you do?

Make some pieces that are based on a single contained idea and see what that is like. Distribute it by modem or give out floppies, and get feedback. In other words, develop something like what you want to do and send it around.

Which magazines do you read?

The English magazine *Eye; I.D. (International Design)*, which awarded us a Design Distinction award; and a local magazine, *On-Line Design.*

Interactive Art at MOMA

Barbara London's career path is instructive for those who hope to "get into" the museum field—or any field—but don't know how to begin. She invented hers. She initiated the first ongoing video program at a museum and, in doing so, created for herself the job of video curator at the Museum of Modern Art in New York.

After receiving a master's degree in Islamic art in the early 1970s from New York University, she originally joined MOMA as a curator in the area of print and illustrated books. In putting together a painting and sculpture show that was traveling to Australia, she saw that many artists worked in video, and she decided to include some in the exhibition. On her return she set about obtaining grants that eventually resulted in MOMA being able to develop a major video art library complete with related historical and theoretical publications.

"I've always been attracted to areas that need a lot of defining, which is also what drew me to Islamic art," she says. Video artist Nam June Paik has joked that while Barbara started out studying the trade routes between China and the Near East, and ended up working in electronic media, there's little difference; in one case, the information is traveling on the backs of camels, and in the other, over the airways!

Increasingly, video artworks are incorporating elements of interactivity. In the summer of 1994, MOMA mounted its first interactive piece, *Family Portrait*, by Montreal-based artist Luc Courchesne, which consisted of four kiosks, each containing videotaped portraits of two people. The museum-goer interacted with these eight "people" through use of a trackball and a HyperCard program that brought up questions and created pathways of conversation. Standing at the midpoint between the cluster of four pedestals, the museum-goer might have found a conversation "interrupted" by one of the other characters from a neighboring kiosk chiming in with a comment based on what had just been said. Glass plates over the pedestals reflected the activity below, so groups could gather around and watch the interaction, which Barbara said gave the impression of a lively cocktail party.

"People would spend a lot of time with each character, getting to know them the way you would a real person," she explains. The museum staff initially responded to the work positively because the kiosks, which were constructed by the artist out of metal, were clean and minimalist in design, but ultimately because the content of the art piece raised profound questions about the meaning of portraiture in this day and age.

"Just as traditional oil portraits 'capture' a person, so does this electronic artwork communicate the essence of these characters," said Barbara. What was as interesting for her was that it did so using technology that has become so familiar as to be banal—TV monitors and computers with trackball interfaces—which are no longer as intimidating to the public as they were when the technology was first introduced into the museum environment. She believes that we have moved from the phase where artists were fascinated with the technology for its own sake to where the technology is merely another tool, like the paintbrush, to generate art and ideas: "The medium is no longer the message. The content is what's important."

"The video and interactive pieces we are seeing now are very complex works, things you want to come back to again and again, like you do good poetry."

In the summer of 1995, Barbara curated another show, *Video Installation: Eight Artists*, which included many interactive pieces. One work, *The Lovers*, by Japanese artist Teiji Furuhasi, was set in a large gallery with black walls in which a stack of video and slide projectors revolved on a metal shelf at the center of the room. Onto the wall were projected running, jumping, and walking naked figures who looked eerily drained of their humanity because they were shot in color but projected onto a black surface. The piece examines the meaning of romantic love in our day and age, as the image of one person is laid over another without a sense of interaction between the two. It suggests how we can be with someone and at the same time feel alone. Interactivity is provided by a sensor in the ceiling that tells the computer and projectors where you, the viewer, are in the room—the figures seem to be performing for you personally. Barbara said she appreciated the fact that the interactivity was transparent, happening without the user having to click buttons or touch screens.

Another piece, by video artist Bill Viola, is set in a gallery with a fragment of a wall revolving on a pole in the center of the room. At either end of the gallery, video projectors send images onto this wall, one side of which is a matte "screen" and the other of which is a mirror. One projection is of the artist's own face, and the other side is of various images—landscapes, cities, and interiors—suggesting the mind or thoughts of the person whose face is on the other side. But when the images are projected onto the mirror, they are shattered and reflected onto the walls. People interact with the piece by trying to find the best vantage point from which to view it, which is impossible since the best place would be precisely where the portion of wall is. In the process, they inadvertently become the third element of the artwork when they suddenly realize that they are being reflected by the mirror, too.

Just as artists continue to incorporate interactivity into their work, so will museums themselves increasingly turn to new media techniques for archiving their collections, teaching the public, and, eventually, as more and more museums go on-line, for sending their artworks into cyberspace, into the museum without walls.

THE MINT MUSEUM GOES DIGITAL

"As more and more museums decide that technology is a good bridge to new audiences, they're going to need to find people to develop these applications," says Bruce H. Evans, director of the Mint Museum of Art in Charlotte, North Carolina, which has a collection of 20,000 works, most notably a major 15th- to 18th-century English porcelain display and North Carolina folk art pottery collection.

"The coming of multimedia will result in a new class of museum jobs. Of the interactive applications that exist now, my sense is that they tend to be either developed by museum curators who don't understand technology (so the installations look stuffy because the curators are basically talking to each other), or they're developed by "techies" who don't understand museums (so the installations look more like video games). Until people come into the field with both backgrounds, interactive applications won't be popular with the public."

The Mint Museum is in the process of digitizing its entire collection for the day when visitors will don headphones attached to non-tape, random-access, hand-held sets that will allow them to hear presentations about any work of art they happen to be standing in front of, no matter which route they took to get there. (Transmission will be from audio sensors embedded in the walls.) The device will contain either a microchip or a CD-ROM that makes a record of which artworks are viewed so that at the end of the day, the visitor could take it to the museum store for downloading onto a personalized CD-ROM for a memento.

Addressing the idea that museums are meant to be visited frequently, The Mint is creating ten different random-access tours, such as "The Artist's Viewpoint" or "Cultural History," so the same exhibits can be viewed from different perspectives on different occasions.

Another use envisioned for the new technology is to assist the scholars who frequently call the museum about its pottery and porcelain collections. Director Evans sees the day when he would be able to send someone a CD-ROM containing, say, images of black Wedgwood basaltes from 1760 to 1770.

Using Kodak's Photo-CD system, which permits four grades of resolution, he also plans to make low-resolution images available on the Internet, and when people become interested in downloading a higher quality reproduction of a work, they could get in touch with the museum about royalty fees.

These new technologies mean new jobs for those graduating with the typical background for entering museums—art history or art education—

who also happen to be familiar with using computers. Evans says practically every museum in the country is entering its collections into electronic databases. There is a tremendous need for people to enter and manage that data.

As for multimedia, some museums are starting to digitize their collections, though the Mint is outsourcing this process for the time being. There is also going to be a need for people who can manage museum on-line sites and for those who can conceive the as-of-yet unimagined interactive applications that will break down the barrier between the public and the enjoyment of art.

Evans suggests that those interested in art and multimedia contact the Museum Computer Network, which has a publication called *Spectra*, and the American Association of Museums, which has a bimonthly newsletter, *Museum News*. The Mint's Interactive Roadside Gallery is found on Charlotte's Web, a local BBS (Tel: 704/336-8013. Password: Webguest).

Executive Recruitment

Joel Koenig
....

Executive Director, Entertainment Industry Practice
Russell Reynolds Associates
Los Angeles

Joel, a New York University graduate and a licensed CPA, was for over 26 years with Deloitte & Touche, one of the Big Six accounting firms, becoming partner-in-charge of the Century City office in Los Angeles. At one point in the 1980s he did a two-year stint as the president and chief operating officer of a privately held video game company. Koenig was recruited by Russell Reynolds Associates in the early 1990s, and he has conducted searches for mid-level executives and higher for Sega, Disney, MCA/Universal, Paramount, and Times Mirror Corporation, among others.

I understand you lead what your firm calls the Convergence Practice, which is making placements in technology, telecommunications, and content providers. What is your definition of multimedia and the kinds of jobs that are being created in this field?

It's a confluence of the distribution and the technology—whether it's cable or telephone, fiber optics, wireless—along with the content providers, whether it's the studios or CD-ROM publishers. It's the coming together of these industries along with the software companies that make it all happen. I don't use the word *multimedia* in making placements because it's too generic for me. I use the word *interactivity*, or information services, which is used to mean everything that will be coming through the fiber aside from telephone calls.

When looking for executives to run newly minted multimedia companies, the ideal candidate would be someone who has a background in computers, entertainment, and media, and hopefully had a good head for business, as well.

The ideal person is somebody who has a technical background to some degree, maybe an undergraduate degree in computer science or engineering, with three to four years' work experience in a consulting firm or a corporate environment before having received an MBA. We look for people who can marry business and technology.

A good example of what we're looking for is a résumé I have right on my desk of someone in his early thirties who has an undergraduate degree from a New York school in electrical engineering. He spent a number of years in Silicon Valley and then got a MBA at Stanford. His last eight years have been at major technology corporations, starting out in the technical area and more recently moving into a business development and marketing role. His current position is in the international marketing arena. The guy's a hotshot.

Do you think that someone who hasn't worked in at least one of the key "feeder" industries— telecommunications, software, entertainment, or media—should attempt to enter one of the new multimedia jobs?

Not in an important position. Once in a while, it can happen. For example, one of my clients—Sega—was looking for someone for a top marketing job, and they wanted someone out of classical packaged goods. But it can't be someone from a company that's too traditional, too linear in their thinking. In general, you can't take someone from a company where the products don't change much from year to year and put them into an industry where things seem to change hourly. The person wouldn't have to necessarily be from a computer company—the toy companies, film studios, or athletic shoe markets also have product lines that change rapidly. It's a youth-oriented environment, but, more importantly, it's just frenetic. Fast-faced, pressured. To make a direct entry at mid-level or upper level from a traditional business is very hard to do.

Beyond professional skills, what personal traits are important for those who want to enter this industry?

Flexibility, open-mindedness, intense curiosity. They look for someone who is a risk taker. Energetic, innovative.

How important is it for an executive who is hired to run a new media division to have produced a diskette or a CD-ROM title?

I don't think that's necessary at all. The chairman of General Motors hasn't made a car. You have to understand how it's produced from a content standpoint and the technical point of view, but you don't have to have done it yourself.

From the point of view of the companies looking for talent, what skill set is most in demand?

At the senior levels, that individual who has the broadest vision of what's going on around the world is in demand. What's really happening in Silicon Valley, in the Research Triangle in North Carolina? What are publishing companies doing? What's happening in Australia? They want somebody who's got a pretty good vision and network.

I get many calls from around the world to do searches for U.S. candidates. It's clear to me that we are so far ahead of the rest of the world in this area. That doesn't mean there aren't exciting things happening elsewhere. But we are very far ahead. Russell Reynolds has offices in cities in most industrialized countries. Yet our clients recognize that the talent pool is here in the States, which is gratifying. It's not only the content side. It's clear that Hollywood films and television have been in the forefront: that's a given. But now in this whole multimedia area, the same thing is true. We're more advanced technologically, plus the markets here are more advanced in terms of cable, and pay television services, direct broadcast satellites and wireless, and so on.

In general, what kinds of skill sets are in oversupply?

Oversupply? Marketing . . . people who profess to be marketers.

What can you tell me about résumés?

They should give me crisp, short bullets about what they've accomplished. Also, if they've worked for one of the smaller companies I may not have heard of (or divisions of bigger companies), they should describe the size of the company or division, what they do and who their customers are—in a couple sentences. Don't just put down the XYZ Publishing Co.—tell me what that is. Is it a billion-dollar company, or is it somebody working out of their garage? Give me some help on that.

I personally don't care about their hobbies, their grades in high school. People spend too much time worrying about format. To be honest, I don't pay that much attention to résumés. I just use them as a starting point for conversation. As far as cover letters, it's helpful to include your latest compensation and what position you're looking for. I don't read letters that are longer than one page. We're all too busy.

What's your best advice to job seekers?

I would caution any middle management applicant or higher to do as much research as possible about possible employers. Talk to competitors, talk to customers, suppliers, talk to current and ex-employees. How well capitalized is the company? What's the track record of their management? If a company doesn't permit that kind of in-depth research, then I'd wonder about them.

Who's hiring? Where will the jobs be?

Those who create content, or the software to create that content, or the ability to deliver it, are in demand. The RROCs [Regional Bell operating companies] are hiring, the long-distance carriers. The studios are building divisions; all the cable companies are expanding.

What do you see for the future for multimedia?

Everything is evolutionary, not revolutionary. The consumer doesn't react that quickly. The checkless society hasn't happened like they predicted, but on the other hand, ATMs have proliferated. I think multimedia will happen; it just takes a while. Interactive gambling will be the "killer app." for the on-line services at home, sanctioned by the state governments. Home shopping will grow, for sure. I'm still not clear about video on demand. I don't think people will read their newspaper on TV.

I think it's just beginning. There will be a lot of mistakes. There will be a lot of winners and some losers; it's hard to know how to pick. We'll see continued consolidation. Most of what we're reading about is hype, not in the sense that it won't happen, but that the dollars invested will be flowing a bit more judiciously than we've seen in the early 1990s.

Tips from Multimedia Recruiters, USA

Ronn Rogers of Dallas-based Multimedia Recruiters, USA specializes in placing people in jobs in the multimedia industry. He provides recruiting and placement services to members of a trade association, Interactive Multimedia Association, of Annapolis, Maryland.

His calls come in from companies looking for staff members in such metropolitan centers as Minneapolis, Chicago, greater Washington (including Philadelphia), and Atlanta. (He notes that the most jobs in multimedia are in the San Francisco Bay Area and New York City but that the companies do not need to call recruiting companies to find applicants.) His most frequent requests are for graphic artists, multimedia programmers, and instructional designers.

- Graphic designers or computer graphic artists who know authoring languages such as Director, Authorware, or Quest, in addition to graphics software programs, are most in demand. Their job can lead ultimately to art director.

- Instructional designers typically help develop computer-based training (CBT). They often have degrees in instructional system design or the "science" of instruction.

- Programmers in multimedia know such high-level authoring languages as Macromedia's Director and Authorware, and Allen Communication's Quest, as well as the more traditional programming languages: C, C++, Microsoft Access, and Visual Basic.

Here are some tips from Ronn Rogers:

1. Write your résumé with the awareness that it's being read by people outside your company. If you're looking for a job in marketing and sales, for example, it isn't as meaningful to say you received the award for "manager of the year" as it would be to list what you accomplished in general terms that can be assessed by anybody: What kind of business volume did you generate? What percentage of your quota was this?

2. In your résumé, in addition to indicating an objective clearly at the top, also prominently indicate the computer platforms and applications you are familiar with. Multimedia is a part of the computer business, so don't bury your knowledge of computer hardware and software deep in the résumé where recruiters or companies have to search for it. Also, Rogers recommends "grading" your expertise in various programs, but don't over-hype your skills. Don't say you are at the "expert" level if you

are really at the "intermediate" level; you'll only embarrass yourself when grilled by the real experts.

3. When sending your résumé to a recruiter or company, don't send a demo floppy or videotape showing examples of your work until you are asked to do so. Rogers has over 1,000 résumés in his database and would not have room to store floppy disks or VHS tapes. He does not view or return unsolicited demos. However, if a company is interested in a candidate, he'll ask the individual to send the demo directly to the interested hiring manager.

4. Most recruiters deal primarily with people who have at least three years' work experience. If you are looking for an entry-level position in the industry, Rogers recommends two strategies: join the local chapter of the IICS (International Interactive Communications Society) to network with people in your region, and continue taking courses in multimedia at local community colleges. *NewMedia* magazine periodically prints lists of schools that are offering courses in multimedia. (See also Appendix V—Multimedia Educational Resources.)

5. Subscribe to an on-line service, most of which have career forums or help-wanted sections. Both recruiters and companies advertise extensively in this manner, since it is more focused than newspaper advertising. Search through the use of such keywords as *jobs, careers,* and *multimedia.*

6. Multimedia aside, as you consider your career, ask yourself two questions before calling recruiters or answering ads: Are you (and your spouse, if you have one) willing to relocate, and what salary level are you aiming for? Rogers finds a lot of people go through a long process of job hunting and interviewing only to discover they haven't thought these two issues through.

7. Keep résumés to one or two pages in length. Rogers says company personnel managers don't have time to read five- to ten-page résumés. "That's a core dump," he says. "I once got a résumé that was 50 pages long, listing every project the guy had ever worked on in his entire career!"

8. If you have a fair amount of work experience under your belt and want to contact a recruiter, make sure that the firm you're dealing with has a working knowledge of multimedia and is actively making placements in this area. Many companies have experience in the high-tech industry but still are not even really sure what multimedia is all about (though they might say they are). Do your homework about which recruiters are specifically active in the area of multimedia.

Technology Licensing

Trip Hawkins
....

President, The 3DO Company
Redwood City, California

After graduating from Harvard College with a degree in strategy and applied game theory, and receiving an M.B.A. from Stanford University, Trip became one of the early managers at Apple Computer. In 1982 he founded Electronic Arts, which has become the largest supplier of computer entertainment software in the world. In 1991 Trip founded The 3DO Company, a pioneering multimedia venture that is establishing a new interactive multimedia standard for playback hardware and game experience.

What is your vision for multimedia?

In the last twenty years we've had the home computers that are really more like an appliance, and we also have had video games that basically are glorified children's toys. My dream has always been to create a new product category that's somewhere in between that has enough power to have the same kind of audiovisual realism as television and yet be interactive. It isn't just a medium that you watch and listen to, but is in fact a medium of doing.

What advice would you give to someone who wants to build a career in multimedia today?

There are two different ways you can come into this. One is if you're going to approach it from a business standpoint, in which case it's good to study the industries and the history—really learn the background. I think when I get into business situations I find that a knowledge of history is really valuable. And of course, it doesn't hurt to know some things about business, but the best place to learn about business is in the real world.

The second track is more of a technical or a creative approach. If you want to have your hands on the medium itself and be able to create things, then you should go get a good technical education, either in engineering or computer science, or a technical arts background. I think the scarcest resource in the industry is really talented professional graphic artists who know how to use the state-of-the-art-graphic workstations and the software tools for making 3-D models and rendering artwork.

Is there one piece of advice you give if somebody asks you how to get into this business?

For anyone looking to get started, the best thing to do is to work for free, initially. Figure out exactly what you want to do, where you want to do it, and who you want to do it with. If you go to those people and offer to work with them for free, how can they turn you down?

There's a lot of difference of opinion about the term multimedia. What's your definition?

Multimedia is an overused term. But one of the problems when you're creating a new medium is that people want to describe it using terms that were used for a preceding media. Maybe there's going to be a new term that no one knows yet.

To me, multimedia implies something that's interactive and has the kind of audiovisual power and realism to create a mass-market experience. It does use multiple media, so it's not a totally misleading term to use—multimedia—but the word really doesn't convey enough about the fact that it's interactive.

How would you define interactivity in the context of multimedia?

For something to be interactive there has to be a stimulus-response; there has to be a cause and effect. As a person, I have to be able to use the controls and cause some kind of response within the context . . . not just change channels, not just turn it on and off, or turn the volume up and down, but to really change the nature of the experience.

What do you think is the greatest strength of multimedia?

It's as a learning tool. People learn by doing. Having a medium that is interactive, where we can do things and can learn from doing them, see the effects of our decisions and act out our fantasies, is very consistent with exactly how we learn.

What technical limitations of multimedia frustrate you the most?

The biggest frustration I think for the whole industry has been the lack of standards. It's not like television, it's not like music, it's not like video—multimedia has different formats, all these different technologies that are incompatible. This means that every few years the rug gets pulled out from underneath everyone—the consumer, the manufacturers, and the software companies. The best thing for the industry in the long run would be to evolve standards so that it was really like a mass medium.

What are the characteristics of good, interactive software?

I've always said that great software should be simple, hot, and deep. It has to be something that's very accessible. People have to be able to pick up the controls and start using it right away, be able to find their way around and get some immediate positive feedback. Then at the same time it has to be exciting and have a realism that draws them in and makes them feel like they're going to have fun and be entertained. Then, of course, it has to be deep so that they keep going, and that they get some educational value out of it, so that it makes them think.

Can you describe how you see the markets for multimedia products breaking out?

I think first and foremost this is going to be an entertainment medium. It's going to be driven by people's desire to have fun and relax. The secondary use is going to be educational, because since by its very nature multimedia gets you interacting; you end up thinking, learning. Finally, there is simply using multimedia just to find out some information that today you might get from a newspaper or the yellow pages or some other source.

You have a background in game theory. What principles can be effectively applied to multimedia, and why?

In any multimedia application there's an engagement between a human being and a machine, and so a big part of the challenge of multimedia is to teach the machine to engage the intelligence of a human being and to respond to it. What you're really attracted to as a person using a multimedia product is that engagement and the feeling that this machine has some intelligence, that it is aware of you and that it's responding to you.

Could you describe any people or resources that have influenced you the most?

One group is the big thinkers about game theory, decision process, and decision making—people like Tom Schelling of Harvard University, who is a mentor of mine. An important book for me when I was in college was Graham Allison's *Essence of Decision*. It was a matter of studying, from a purely intellectual standpoint, how people think and make decisions, and how organizations think and make decisions. You have to learn all those things to understand how to model decision-making behavior inside a computer so it can seem real to the people that are playing a simulation.

Then, of course, there's the presentation. You have to be able to convey this information in a telegenic way; there are a lot of famous thinkers from the history of film, television, and radio who have pioneered this, starting with Walt Disney. It's knowing how to evoke an emotion through an image, through music, and through the portrayal of a scene. Of course, a lot of that has to do with the big thinkers about the narrative form—people who know how to tell a good story and know how to use audiovisual media to do that. So what you're combining in this new medium is these two disciplines.

Are there one or two books that you would highly recommend?

I don't think I could really name just one or two books; I could probably name ten or twenty. But a great resource would be to look in a library and find autobiographies of people from the film industry or the music industry to understand how they managed the creative process and how they created original organizational structures to deal with new technologies.

There's interactive multimedia on the PC, interactive multimedia on the TV. Where do you think we're going in terms of the convergence of the two?

I think it's a two-step process. The home market for products that are based on CD-ROM is something where there's already an infrastructure. There are retail stores where you can buy the products; there are technologies that you can use to make the products work.

The concept of the information superhighway is very exciting, but many of the technologies are still being developed and still being proven. After they have been, you will still need to build an infrastructure. There's a lot of equipment and a lot of networking that will have to be put into place before any consumer could benefit, and so for that reason it's just going to take more time for us to get there from here.

Where do you think multimedia will be in two, five, ten years from now?

We're going through a formative stage that's a bit like the end of the Dark Ages just before the start of the Renaissance, and that's going to go on for the next few years. It's a battle of the titans, a lot of big companies throwing their weight around, trying to force the industry to adopt their technologies and their product approaches, and frankly there's going to be a lot of wasted money and wasted motion for the next few years. Out of that, hopefully, some truth will surface, and the industry will gravitate towards a model, a way of doing business, a set of technologies that we can really use for a long period of time. And that's when I really think a cultural renaissance will start, because then it will become more of a creative problem, a creative opportunity.

If there's one thing that you know now that you wish you would have known back then, what might it be?

I think it's a good thing that I didn't know everything then I know now; otherwise, I probably wouldn't be here.

Training

Brandon Hall, Ph.D.

Editor, *Multimedia Training* newsletter
Sunnyvale, California

Hall has had over twenty years in the training industry. After getting his doctorate in educational psychology from West Virginia University (specializing in behavioral psychology), he was a performance management consultant for a firm in Atlanta. He moved to Silicon Valley in the heyday of the early 1980s to join Wilson Learning Corporation, the second largest training firm in the United States. Wilson was involved in the traditional seminar-based training business, as well as videodisks. In 1985 Hall started his own corporate training seminar business, which taught management and personal skills. By the early 1990s, "when multimedia started delivering on its promise," he decided to publish a newsletter for trainers about new products and trends. He also gives a seminar to teach trainers about the new technology: "Getting started in multimedia training."

What is "the training industry"?

It refers to the training that is provided to employees of corporations. I break it down into two categories: management skills training ("soft skills") incorporates interpersonal skills, communication, negotiation skills, and customer service training, and technical training teaches people how to perform a specific task, such as using a desktop computer or how to execute a particular manufacturing process.

Before using CD-ROMs for training, what was available?

Before multimedia, there was programmed instruction, a brilliant but ultimately not very fruitful idea from the late 1960s to provide course material in a self-study book-based format. Information bites were followed by questions in an early form of interactivity.

This was a precursor to CBT, or computer-based training, which was then text only. CBT was the same idea as programmed instruction, but it was on a computer instead of in book form. Some very large corporations still use CBT over wide-area networks today.

In the early 1980s came interactive videodisks, also called "interactive video." It was basically analog video delivered on 12" platters, hooked up to and controlled by a personal computer. You'd do the search on the computer (or give the test) and access visual and text information from the videodisk.

What proportion of the multimedia business is devoted to training?

I would estimate that five to ten percent of multimedia titles being made today are for the training sector. This can be broken down into three areas: titles that are internally developed by corporations; titles that are custom-made by developers outside the corporation on contract; and commercially available titles, or off-the-shelf products, which are sold to the business market at large.

Is multimedia training a growth market?

Business is always looking at better and cheaper ways of doing things; multimedia training is a way to achieve this. Multimedia is cheaper than traditional classroom or workshop-based training. To develop a course using traditional training methods is relatively inexpensive, but it is expensive to deliver it over time. It costs money to send employees to seminars and also to give them the time off.

With multimedia training, the cost of development can be high, but the cost of delivery is minimal. There is a real cost savings: reduced time off the job, no travel, and also course compression. An eight-hour workshop might be done in four to six hours in a desktop training program. Initially, employees resist it because they like going to seminars, but after they've experienced CD-ROM training they appreciate the privacy, flexibility, autonomy, and convenience. So if a corporation has relatively stable content and at least 100 or 200 people who need the training, they are often justified to start thinking about delivering that information by CD-ROM.

How much does it cost to develop CD-ROMs for training?

The range is from $30,000 to $1 million, but the high end is rare. On the low end, most internally developed programs cost $30,000 to $60,000 to develop, but this doesn't include cost of the people's time, because they are on salary. For custom-made projects made by outside developers, it may cost more, but on the other hand, the quality might be higher.

Higher-end titles with high production values and at least one-third of their content as video would cost more, of course. We use a measure called "dollars per finished hour of multimedia training."

How much time does it take to develop a training CD-ROM?

One ballpark figure I've heard ranges from 100 to 400 hours of development time per hour of user time. User time can range from a couple of hours, to eight hours, or in the case of some training CD-ROMs produced by Anderson Consulting, several days.

Which authoring tools are recommended for developers in multimedia training?

The following programs are used in the industry because they contain specialty templates for educators and other features, such as more interactivity and branching, as well as the ability to determine who is logging on, what scores they're getting, etc. This latter functionality is called CMI, or computer-managed instruction.

- Macromedia's Authorware Professional and Authorware Star (which is used by educators)
- AimTech's IconAuthor and CBT Express (CBT has less functionality but is easier to use and has more graphical templates for educators.)
- Asymetrix's Multimedia Toolbook
- Allen Communication's Quest (specialty program for education market)

What are the opportunities for instructional designers?

With the advent of CD-ROMs, instructional design is going to be a growth area. Instructional designers existed before multimedia, because they are important for the development of any training program. But the field is going to come more to the fore with multimedia for two reasons. One, multimedia requires more design up front. If you roll out a workshop and discover it's not working, you can modify it on the fly, or certainly retool it before you deliver it again. But with the expense of making multimedia, you want to hit the target by doing your analysis up front. The other reason is that there is more of a team focus with multimedia development, and with so many tasks to perform, there is a function for the instructional designer. Workshop training is not something typically developed by teams.

What do instructional designers do on a CD-ROM development team?

The instructional design process is called the ADDIE model:

- A—analysis. They analyze the audience and what it needs to be learning.
- D—design of the title. What is the overall budget, what platforms will

it play on, how long will the program last? What is the pre-test, the post-test? How will the users enter their ID numbers?
- D—development. Clarification of the instructional objectives. This is where they work with the others on the team—programmers, audio people, SME's (subject-matter experts)—to make sure that the learning objectives will be met. At this stage they'll look at the flow of the content, any quizzes or tests that should be inserted along the way, simulations, etc.
- I—implementation. The CD-ROM is tested by users and then evaluated before the final rollout.
- E—evaluation. Once the training has been implemented in the organization, we ask this: How are people actually using it? How much did it end up costing? Are people really learning?

How do people learn to become instruction designers?
They can either learn on the job, take seminars, or read books on the subject, which is how it was done traditionally, or they can attend one of the fine graduate programs around the country, such as San Diego State University, Utah State University, Florida State University, or some of the others.

What other kinds of careers do you envision?
There is a new specialty called a "knowledge engineer" that's an outgrowth of a developing field called EPSS, or Electronic Performance Support Systems. Someday EPSS could replace training as we know it. It's a technical solution for helping people perform better on the job. It includes embedding training in software, intelligent coaching, access to on-line information or company databases, and often it includes communication with peers. It teaches the employee just what's needed, "just in time." Large corporations are already using this. For example, salespeople in the field needing to put together client presentations might be able to draw up documents from the company's computer that have already been created by others—charts, statistics, examples of how the same problem was solved by others, etc.

EPSS may be delivered by CD-ROM but is more likely to exist on-line. It needs be constantly updated, and that's where the career of knowledge engineer comes in. These are people whose expertise is to figure out what information is needed by the company's employees to perform specific functions. They filter out what's needed from all the data out there, structure it, make it useful and easy to access.

The role will become increasingly important in the future as we move into an information-based society where knowledge is a competitive advantage. The question is going to be how to get information to people faster.

What's the best application of multimedia in training?

Simulation. The best training brings you into an immersive environment. It's the difference between reading a book on city management versus playing SimCity and seeing the impact of changing the variables. Simulations are the future of training.

What kinds of companies are using CD-ROMs for training?

Traditionally, CBT or interactive videodisk training could only be afforded by the largest corporations or the military. With CD-ROMs, there is a move towards mid-size companies developing training programs. This is an example of how multimedia has changed the training industry.

What's in the future?

I see a consolidation of platforms in training from videodisk to CD-ROM on the desktop, which will continue for about three to five years. Then training will go on-line once there is sufficient bandwidth to deliver it over the network.

Since multimedia training programs are developed by corporations, it isn't possible for the general public to have access to them. How could someone who wanted to enter the field get some to study?

ICD Publishing has a catalogue containing training programs. An alternative is to find titles sold through retailers from Wilson Learning Systems, who have converted a lot of professional and business-to-business titles into consumer products. [ICD: 508/685-4600; Wilson: 800/328-7937]

Are there any books you'd recommend?

I've written a book, available through my company, *Getting Started in Multimedia Training: A Resource Guide*. It has all the things trainers need to know to get started in multimedia. [Ed. note: See Appendix II.]

What professional societies do you suggest?

The group whose national conferences are the most active in the area of multimedia is NSPI, the National Society for Performance and

Instruction. The largest professional training society in the country also has programs, the ASTD, American Society for Training and Development. I'd also recommend a general professional group, the IICS, International Interactive Communications Society.

CHAPTER 5

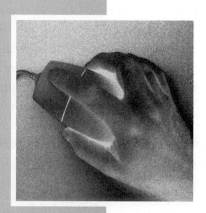

Case Study

*The Judson Rosebush Company,
New York*

This is the story of how a CD-ROM title comes into being. First, we'll meet "the players"—Manhattan-based multimedia developer Judson Rosebush and his staff of in-house and freelance production people—and learn about their backgrounds, their job responsibilities, and how they came to work for Judson. Then we'll investigate the process of how a CD-ROM title is created—from initial concept to gold master—by looking at two titles developed by the Judson Rosebush Company.

The War in Vietnam is an in-depth reference work combining film footage from the archives of CBS News with news articles and photographs from the *New York Times* selected by correspondent R. W. Apple, Jr. *Ocean Voyager* is an "edutainment" game intended to increase awareness among children ages 8 to 13 about the oceans and their importance in everyday life. Judson produced it for the Times Mirror Magazine division of Times Mirror Corp., in conjunction with the Smithsonian Institution. The chapter ends with an interview with the game designers for a third product, the animated game called *Gahan Wilson's The Ultimate Haunted House*, which was developed for Byron Preiss Multimedia and sold through Microsoft.

The Players

The Judson Rosebush Company was founded in 1986 to produce and consult in the field of computer graphics, placing it in one of the seminal "feeder" industries that have contributed to the development of multimedia. At that time Rosebush created for the Japanese corporation NEC some interactive sales material for its multi-sync computer display. He also created a HyperCard-controlled laserdisk for *Visualization: State of the Art*, a video program codirected by Laurin Herr for SIGGRAPH (Special Interest Group for Graphics of the Association for Computing Machinery).

After Judson Rosebush began developing multimedia titles in 1992, the company grew rapidly from a handful of employees in a studio above Carnegie Hall to, three years later, a staff of about ten employees and eight to ten regular freelancers working out of two offices.

Judson did not come to multimedia by chance; everything he had accomplished in his career and studied as an avocation led to the opening of his own shop. As a "SIGGRAPH pioneer" he had for twenty years owned and operated a successful computer graphics and animation company. He is a skilled software developer, as well as the author of numerous technical and popular articles and books, including one of the standard textbooks in the field, *Computer Graphics for Designers and Artists* (coauthored with Victor Kerlow), which includes a chapter on interactive media and virtual reality. He holds several hundred copyrights in software, film, and music.

Judson received a Ph.D. in the 1970s in TV and film production at Syracuse University. He worked his way through college as a disc jockey at a commercial radio station and by writing record reviews for *Rolling Stone* and the *Village Voice*. He also owned his own record company, releasing a couple of singles and about four albums.

After directing films for the then-Department of Education (HEW) in the early 1970s, he entered the public relations department of the Everson Museum in Syracuse during the era of "process art," perhaps better remembered as "happenings." Process art was the attempt by modern artists to illustrate the process of things rather than the object: for example, an empty canvas in a frame, or bodies covered in paint and rolled across a canvas. This experience attracted him to the world of computer animation because, as he explains, "one wasn't manipulating the image itself, but the process that made the image."

After some early experimental films and museum shows in the mid-1970s, he created a 3-D graphics system called Visions and founded a company in New York City around it, Digital Effects Inc. By the early 1980s he had built the first paint system and frame buffers in New York and was creating animations for industrial and feature films (including the character of the "Bit" in the movie *TRON*), TV commercials, videodisks, and laser holograms for museum exhibits.

By the late 1980s his company had metamorphosed into the Judson Rosebush Company, and he continued doing computer graphics animation, working with Hammond Inc. on digital cartography software and codirecting a series of one-hour videotape specials with Laurin Herr for the *SIGGRAPH Video Review* on the state of the art in computer graphics, HDTV, and virtual reality. This multifaceted background, touching on so many of the elements that go into creating multimedia, gave him the broad skill set required for becoming a multimedia developer. Multimedia is at least one industry that heralds the end of the era of the specialist and embraces the polymath.

Judson Rosebush:

I come to this industry with a developed sense of writing and publishing skills, graphic arts management, photography, film and video production, basic sound skills, and extreme fluency in computers and computer graphics. So I'm technically savvy, not only in computers but also in print, photography, videography, cinematography, sound, etc. I also have spent much of my adult life making content: books, magazines, giving interviews, directing software development, and shooting video. I mention this to show how a diverse background contributes to being a player in this industry.

The best way for young people to prepare for a career in multimedia is to attempt to acquire a broad set of media skills. They should be proficient in writing and knowledgeable in the graphic arts, sound, film. They should have been exposed to such programs as Adobe Photoshop, Illustrator, and Premiere; Microsoft Word; Sound Edit; and object-oriented programming languages such as HyperCard, Macromind Director, or Visual Basic. They should play video games and look at products critically, not only as consumers.

Midlife career professionals should take stock of their skill sets. The first challenge is to be able to use a computer, because that is the crux of multimedia. If they are already computer literate in a narrow area, they should broaden their computer skills. There are a few people who can specialize, say in Photoshop, but most people would benefit by exposing themselves to as many of the programs used to create multimedia as possible. After years of working, you might need to go back to school for a tune-up, attend a few classes. If you're already a corporate executive, you could re-create yourself within your organization as the head of the "new media" department or become the resident "technical specialist," although it might help if you knew what you were doing.

In putting together a company, Judson hired a staff of people in their twenties and thirties with similarly broad backgrounds: Matthew Schlanger as senior programmer and assistant director, Michael Smethurst as director of technology and new projects, and Sandy Streim as director of business development.

In addition to those interviewed here, Judson employs three additional programmers, a producer/project manager, four graphic artists, a writer, and an administration/production assistant. Additionally, he hires freelancers for every conceivable function as needed—from editorial copy editors, color correctors, and researchers to videographers and photographers. He prefers hiring people in the earlier phase of their careers—entry-level programmers, writers, or graphic artists—a policy he finds mutually beneficial: he doesn't have to pay a premium salary, and they get to learn how to create multimedia.

Judson Rosebush: *The key to understanding multimedia is being aware of what I call "the five axes of multimedia," namely text, sound, still pictures, moving pictures, and "code," or computer programming. The multimedia titles with the most depth and breadth, the ones that are informative, engaging, as well as entertaining, are the ones that incorporate as many of these five elements as possible.*

These and other areas of content are referred to as "assets," because content has to be thought of in terms of its cost in the budget as well as for its creative contribution. Photographs your grandfather took of the Grand Canyon in 1925, a song someone has written, film of the Hindenburg explosion, or Hitler's speech at the Olympics: these are assets from other media that can be applied to multimedia. Other assets might be a character, like Bugs Bunny. There are many CD-ROMs coming out now which use the asset of a brand-name, recognizable character, though the content is totally new and created expressly for the multimedia product.

Judson met Matthew Schlanger in the early 1990s at a faculty meeting at the School of Visual Arts in New York City, where Matthew had been teaching for about nine years. At that time, Judson, who also taught a course in the Master in Fine Arts program, was working on one of his first multimedia titles, *Isaac Asimov's The Ultimate Robot*, for Byron Preiss Multimedia (distributed by Microsoft). Judson was looking for someone who could help him who also was a Macromind Director programmer. Matthew started working for Judson as a freelancer, ultimately completing a section of the product called the "robotoid assembly." Eventually, Matthew, who never showed Judson his résumé ("I've mainly gotten work through word of mouth"), became a full-time programmer and director.

Matthew Schlanger:

Simply put, multimedia is combining different media in one integrated piece, each coming from different traditions. But the parts have to transcend each separate tradition to create one new genre. And the new genre is this thing that we now call interactive multimedia, which I think needs a new name. Because once it establishes itself as a separate genre, it shouldn't be called something that looks back to how it was created—the mixture of media. That's just semantics, but the point is that the final product must transcend the different traditions and become something new that does what all the separate parts alone couldn't do. Multimedia on the computer is still in its infancy.

The metaphor I use for this medium is early film making. They would take the camera, set it up in front of a theatrical stage performance, and shoot it. Early films were made with this single-shot, proscenium point of view. The language—the syntax—of cinema hadn't yet been created. Now we have a new medium again, and we're still seeing the same tendency to borrow from earlier traditions, though the syntax for multimedia is developing much faster than film did.

Interactivity is about the user getting to make choices. It's nonpassive. It's active engagement. There are different levels of interactivity. There's "click and watch," where every now and then you get to click, whereupon the machine takes over and does some kind of animation, and then you have another chance to click again. That's less interactive than a high-speed video game, which has so much interactivity that it's measured by interactions per minute. It doesn't really matter. The point is that the interactivity should suit the piece you're trying to create.

Matthew came to Judson Rosebush Company with a background in cinema (B.A., State University of New York at Binghamton, 1981) and after a career (still ongoing) as a video artist. He has had numerous shows and exhibitions in France, Israel, Holland, and Japan, and in this country his work has appeared at the Whitney Biennial, the American Film Institute's National Video Festival, the Everson Museum, and Tibor de Nagy Gallery, to name a few. He was an artist-in-residence from 1981 to 1990 at the Experimental Television Center in Owego, N.Y. Schlanger wears at least two hats at the Judson Rosebush company: senior programmer and assistant director.

Matthew Schlanger: *As senior programmer, I design the architecture of the software. I keep track of all the minutiae, like global variables and handler names, and all the parameters. I also divide up the work and manage other programmers, cre-*

ating methods of consistency in the way things are written so the whole thing fits together. I have also defined the animation and sound.

One of the best things about being a programmer is those days when you're enjoying what you're doing. You say to yourself: "I can't believe they pay me to do this. This is exactly what I want to be doing." It's when I'm able to use creativity to solve problems. Programmers like to solve puzzles, and get a thrill creating things. I like it when I create interesting systems that work, or make animations that are good. That's when it becomes art again. Speaking in general for programmers— and everybody who works in production—the worst aspect is the deadline pressure, especially when it gets outrageous. Sometimes, clients want everything yesterday.

My responsibilities as assistant director have included writing the technical specification and definition of program architecture, as well as shaping the product to meet both deadline and aesthetic goals. I can only speak from my own experience about directing; I can't tell you what directors do generically. In my case, I often create animations on paper, and sometimes I write storyboards, including artwork orders. When the graphics and sound come back, I give the work to the programmers to sew together. Also, I get material from the game designers and interpret it. They might write something like: "Birds do this, this, and this." From that I design a work order that communicates to the graphic people to animate the bird in a certain way, to give it a certain personality.

Direction for dialogue is very easy: "It's a bird, and it's angry." But with sound effects I usually get more involved. My philosophy is that nothing happens on the screen that doesn't also have a sound attached to it. And no sound occurs that doesn't have animation attached to it. I sometimes have to break the rule, but that's something I really emphasize.

One of my abilities as a director is to be able to see the whole product—to see very large structures, entire animations—and then write out in great detail all the steps that need to be done to get that big picture. And to delegate the minutiae out. That in a nutshell is what directing is about.

Directors also have to know how to delegate responsibility and deal with budgets and deadlines. I have to own the deadlines I am given. Part of my responsibility is to estimate how long a job will take. I guess I also function as a project manager.

Michael Smethurst met Judson through a mutual friend before Judson started his multimedia company. Michael started working in the evenings and weekends as a volunteer, writing public relations releases and brochures for a SIGGRAPH event. While still holding down a day job at a design firm creating presentation graphics, he began volunteering on various projects, using Judson's computer in off-hours for photo retouching. Judson hired him as a freelancer to input text and to add hyperlinks for the Asimov project, and then for about three months as a freelance programmer, working from 6 P.M. to midnight. Finally, he was hired full time in March 1993. The first thing Judson told Michael when he said he wanted to get into the field of multimedia was "Learn HyperCard." He also never used a résumé, rather was hired through what he calls "proof by competence."

Michael Smethurst:

In my job I do some programming and also manage freelance programmers. A lot of my time is spent overseeing projects, which involves everything from pitching clients to execution to beta testing. I am involved in teaching clients about the potential of multimedia, and what's possible, so we can generate some enthusiasm about the project.

I also am in charge of technology assessment. This involves reading MacWorld, *staying current about issues such as scripted languages versus compiled languages, talking to product managers and getting beta copies [of software] to test. I have to decide when it would be cost/effective to go into certain areas. I'm always looking for a better multimedia engine.*

I also deal with the business direction from the production perspective: What is our mix and balance? What are our internal strategies? How can we take code that we've worked on for a year and re-purpose it for another title?

Michael graduated from Hampshire College in Amherst, Mass., in 1987. He started out wanting to be a lawyer or a sociologist, but with his love for writing and music, ended up focusing his studies on English and French literature, creative writing, and philosophy as it related to modern authors. Before entering school, he had put out literary magazines on the Macintosh (in the days before desktop publishing programs), and upon graduating in 1987, he started creating the newsletter for the Association for Retarded Citizens. At the same time, he was managing a bar, booking bands, and creating promotional ads on the Mac for various groups.

Soon he switched gears and began building houses as a carpenter, first in Massachusetts and then in California after the earthquake of 1989. While building, he taught himself Filemaker Pro and started doing small consulting jobs; he also temped in offices using Quark, Excel, and Word. In the early 1990s he moved to New York with hopes of becoming a magazine writer, and then started producing catalogues for art shows.

Michael Smethurst: *You need breadth to do a good job in multimedia. Building houses was the best thing I ever did to prepare for multimedia because I learned an important lesson. There are three ways to solve the problem: the fast way, the cheap way, and the proper way. I learned that the best way is not to take shortcuts. When something breaks down, I stop and fix it. I don't work around the problem. If the printer doesn't work, I figure out why.*

You need strong skills in abstract thinking to work in multimedia. When you're designing hypermedia, you need to forget all that you know. At the same time, you need to understand what's gone on before, what other media do best— for example, knowing what television does well, understanding what video games are about, and what computers can do best. Why should we make a CD-ROM about Vietnam instead of a book or a videotape? The answer is that by providing hyperlinks and searchable text, users can find a concordance of ideas based on threads they're interested in following. With multimedia, you can come closer to escaping the editorial process. This is a core concept someone wanting to create CD-ROMs needs to understand.

Secondly, you need strong written and verbal communication skills. A lot of this job is presenting, pitching to clients or investors. You need to be able to talk about the technology well, combining the technical aspects with the popular and content side. If you only refer to technology, it scares a lot of clients. You need to have a marketing feature set. You're always dealing with so many people from different backgrounds: TV people, programmers, writers.

Finally, you need a lot of enthusiasm. You need to be psyched up about this medium.

Sandy Streim, the company's director of business development, first read about Judson in *NewMedia* magazine in 1993. At the time, Sandy was working as a marketing consultant and was interested in becoming involved with interactive media.

Sandy Streim:

There wasn't a lot out there then about multimedia from the finance and business side. So I researched what I think of as seven key industries: publishing, the record business, the magazine business, film, general software, specialty interactive software, and distribution. No single business model holds up one hundred percent. The movie model works well for production; the record business is a good model for distribution, though the distribution models are unsettled. The affiliated label model didn't turn out to answer the problems of distribution, because the pie couldn't be cut so everyone would make their money back. Will we sell these things in a CD-ROM store? Maybe. Through direct mail? Not yet. Bookstores? Record stores? This industry is changing every six months.

Sandy believes the multimedia business would have been considered too risky by many of his fellow students in Columbia University's M.B.A. program in 1991. But after graduating with a specialty in marketing and international business and working for a small New York magazine that placed entertainment databases into kiosks, he became intrigued with what was happening in CD-ROM and on-line development. He started attending trade shows and reading up on multimedia in *The Wall Street Journal* and *The New York Times*, as well as in such trade magazines as *NewMedia* and *PC Magazine*.

Sandy Streim: *To work for an independent multimedia developer, you need to be able to handle something new on a regular basis, to be unstructured and work in a more chaotic environment than many people coming out of business school are used to. No one works nine-to-five in this industry. This is a ten-hour-a-day business, plus weekends. And when it's time to launch a new product, the hours are longer. But I like the freedom and flexibility. A corporation is more structured. I believe the smaller outfits is where the action is. You need to be able to take a risk with a small company. You have to go out on a limb.*

You have to be persistent to get a job in a company like this. Multimedia is another arm of the entertainment industry, and there's a lot of glamour associated with it. This industry still has a lot of hype and not a lot of profit. You have to be willing to take less financial reward for something further down the road. In the smaller companies, you have to expect a salary of between $30K and $50K. You'll earn more in the larger companies, but even there, if you're working in the new media area you might not be earning as much as your corporate colleagues in other divisions. Programmers earn the money in this industry, the business types less!

I like to do something I'm interested in. I have friends who earn a lot of money but who aren't happy. I didn't want to just crunch numbers. I was attracted to the hands-on aspect of multimedia. I wanted to produce something and learn how to run a business out of it.

Sandy started working one day a week for Judson as an intern, but within six weeks started being paid when Judson said he wanted to make more demands on Sandy's time. He went on a per-diem basis as a regular consultant for a couple of days a week, writing business and project plans, doing market and financial research, and looking into branding schemes. Eventually he began handling business development as a full-time employee, including generating internal cost/cash flow analyses.

Sandy Streim: *I create marketing plans for our business (consumer and business promotion CD-ROMs) and for our upcoming self-published products. I also generate business plans to present to potential investors and work to increase the exposure of the company within the multimedia publishing community and the press. I have to advertise our services with a soft sell, sending out press releases to magazines, inviting people to our studio to see what we're doing. I sell our skill sets—the creative and technical services of a developer.*

Attending the meetings early in the planning process for *Ocean Voyager* was New York-based freelance designer and animator Kathy Konkle, who provided input regarding budgeting for artwork, a sense of how long the artwork would take, and whether the expectations of the producers and developer were realistic. Kathy is a rare bird—a designer who actually has prior experience in multimedia—having created illustrations for museum kiosks, 2-D and 3-D animations for advertising agencies making commercials, and technical and scientific drawings for federal agencies. She had met Judson about five years earlier when she introduced herself to him after an evening sponsored by the New York chapter of SIGGRAPH.

Kathy prefers working at home because of the flexibility it gives her, although she maintains regular work hours (9 A.M. to 7 P.M.) in order to be available to the rest of the team when they're at the office. She also likes working on her own computer, which she sees in the same way that a chef sees blades or a carpenter sees tools.

Kathy Konkle:

Animation and painting require a lot of hours and a lot of concentration. At home I can use my custom-rigged system set up the way I want it. There are fewer errors that way and fewer interruptions. The idea of someone monkeying with my computer makes me shudder.

Anyway, I need my computer at home because I use it not only for creating illustrations, but also for running my business, billing, and staying in touch with past clients. It's easier for Judson having me work at home, because if my equip-

ment breaks down it's my headache, not his. My advice to illustrators wanting to get into multimedia is to get your own computer: it's the best way to become accomplished and makes you take responsibility for your own system.

She works on a Macintosh Quadra 840-AV with a one-gigabyte hard drive and a scanner. Although the Quadra has built-in video capabilities, for more professional-looking video she is hoping to get two video cards, a FWB Jackhammer, a high-speed disk controller, and a Radius Spigot Pro for JPEG compression of full-screen, full-motion video. She is also planning to get a disk array (two hard drives linked together) with 40 megabytes of RAM. In addition to the Quadra, she keeps an older Macintosh IIci on hand as a backup, a second workstation in case her main computer goes down. She also uses the IIci as a fax modem and for times when she hires an assistant to help complete large jobs.

For the temporary storage of large files, she uses Syquest removable disk cartridges, but when she's completed a project and wants to archive her work, she goes to a local multimedia company with mastering equipment and for $150 has a CD-ROM "one-off" made.

As the associates of the developer are putting the product together, there is regular interaction with a project's financial backers—the producer or the publisher—to see if the project is on track.

Dominic Schmitt, CD-ROM producer, Times Mirror: *My job is constantly checking to see if the content of* Ocean Voyager *speaks to our audience and if the information is accurate. I am the person connecting the CD-ROM to the Smithsonian exhibit—which will travel to five cities ultimately—so I make sure that Judson's writers and illustrators are creating something that will blend well with the museum show. The purpose of the exhibit is to let children know that the problems of the environment are within their grasp, that the oceans are their individual responsibility even if they live in Iowa and their only connection to the oceans is through agricultural runoff.*

The Process

Planning, Content

Creating a good multimedia title starts a sense of what will succeed in a still-undefined market, as well as a group of people willing to work as a coherent team to bring disparate bits of visual and verbal information into a compelling, unified whole.

Judson Rosebush: *The ideal CD-ROM title must be massive in both breadth and depth. Our product,* Isaac Asimov's The Ultimate Robot, *does this, as do Microsoft's* Cinemania *and* Musical Instruments. *These products are focused and use many elements, or assets, of multimedia well. They are broad, they are fun, they are well-thought through.*

Too much multimedia lacks what I call "immersive potential." You can lose yourself in the paper edition of the Encyclopaedia Britannica; *you can spend days with it researching, browsing. I find I reach the edge of the multimedia space in most titles within five to ten minutes. Their content is thin: a few articles, a chronology, some biographies. This shallowness produces bad press, the "so what?" titles.*

My idea of a good title would be the one we produced on Vietnam with CBS and The New York Times. *It is a comprehensive reference work, a classic research tool. It will be the definitive compendium of information on the subject for decades. Yet it also reaches out to a popular audience by creating a rich tableau of materials that were shaped editorially, not just thrown together. The mapping section contains names that were included for a reason. It is built with knowledge to educate, to inform, and to engage. You don't have to be a Vietnam scholar to find it compelling.*

There is a tendency to substitute art direction for real content in a lot of titles. These are the pretty-but-shallow products. Few titles exist on the market that take advantage of the real content of media. In addition, the ones that don't succeed are trying to use design principles from other media. They aim for the lowest common denominator—adults with a seventh-grade education; their content is at the level of USA Today. *They are throwaways because there is not enough content that is useful or worth saving. Just because a lot of money is spent on production values doesn't guarantee an interesting product.*

Content in multimedia comes from two sources: original and existing. Original content includes work based on one's own media resources, such as the collection of photographs taken by Judson at the Nevada nuclear test site for a CD-ROM in process he's producing about atomic testing in the 1940s and 1950s, or, the compelling Next Exit multimedia performances of San Franciscan Dana Atchley, which are based on memorabilia and photographs taken by himself and family members going back to the 1850s.

Existing material, such as paintings, a cartoon character owned by a movie studio, or photographs from *Life* magazine can be licensed by developers from the copyright holders. But more ideally, a developer is hired to produce or co-produce a CD-ROM by the owner of a large number of media assets, thus eliminating the potentially considerable expense of licensing rights and also maintaining some degree of control over the material.

Such was the case in the creation of *The War in Vietnam*. Apple Computer approached CBS News with the idea of making a multimedia product using its extensive film archives of the war and the era. The computer maker, hoping to stimulate the production of high-quality CD-ROM titles for the drives it was including with computers, suggested teaming up with a newspaper, so CBS went to *The New York Times*, which assigned correspondent R. W. Apple, Jr. to select articles. The additional existing materials for the program were obtained without licensing fees: Rosebush Company and CBS staff created and researched original maps, and the National Archives in Washington supplied photographs of Vietnam-era weaponry. In the end the team gathered 950 newspaper articles and 300 still photographs from the morgue of the *The New York Times*, 150 photographs of weapons, and 57 video clips totaling about an hour from the CBS archives, and shot a six-minute introductory segment of Dan Rather and R. W. Apple, Jr. The only licensing fees were paid to composers of contemporaneous "Vietnam songs" that are included in the product.

Ocean Voyager came about when the Smithsonian Institution asked Times Mirror to create a media campaign in conjunction with an exhibit about the oceans it was organizing. In addition to the CD-ROM, Times Mirror developed the special souvenir issue to accompany the exhibit, and is cross-marketing the exhibit and its spin-off products in various Times Mirror magazines (for example, *Popular Science for Kids*), radio spots, and in co-venture programming for The Discovery Channel.

The CD-ROM is a game in which the player must use 30 databases embedded in virtual books, computers, and videocassettes to return Arpo, the seal, back home. The animal and the rest of the crew—a South Sea island boy, a girl prodigy scientist, and a crotchety old engineer—are on a high-tech submersible exploration vehicle.

Dominic Schmitt: *I have a 500-page binder with all the words contained in the databases. We hired a marine specialist as a content expert to help us with scientific accuracy. The databases contain enormous amounts of information to help the players research the questions that solve the game—everything from marine life databases of whales, seals, and bioluminescent fish, to databases of different kinds of boats, knots, charting symbols, semaphore codes, and seafaring songs. We have images from microscope slides, sounds of humpback whales, and information on chemicals and toxins in the ocean.*

Though the project was still in production as this book went to press, Judson estimated that the media allocation for *Ocean Voyager* will end up being 2,000 lines of dialogue; 500 text blocks, captions, and headlines; 1,000 sound effects; 100 video clips; 300 photographs; and 2,000 drawings/illustrations.

For all the advantages of co-producing multimedia with a copyright holder of interesting content, there is still the matter of "repurposing." This is an area of obvious interest to the book and record industries, as well as the Hollywood community, with its nine decades of material literally in the can. Such footage is of interest for nostalgic reasons (Kate Hepburn, Cary Grant, and Jimmy Stewart in *Philadelphia Story*), for its visual power as a cultural icon (King Kong holding Fay Wray at the top of the Empire State Building), or sociologically as a visual representation of a particular, forever lost period in time (postwar Berlin in Billy Wilder's *A Foreign Affair*). Most fundamentally, though, the material represents a mother lode of creativity—thought-provoking and lively entertainment. While existing content provides powerful imagery to enhance a multimedia production, it is not enough in and of itself to create a powerful work.

Judson Rosebush: *There is no such thing as ready-made content for CD-ROMs. Repurposing is an overestimated value. Material can be repurposed, but repurposing a good book doesn't necessarily mean you'll have a good piece of multimedia. Yes, you can take a character from a novel, but you really have to write from scratch. Repurposing is not a trivial task: consider what's involved in repurposing a book into a movie.*

Sometimes people come with a core brand name and think they're re-purposing an existing franchise. If you throw a lot of old Donald Duck cartoons onto a CD-ROM, you might have an excellent archive, but it isn't necessarily a good title. You've got to work on a CD-ROM from scratch. Shovelware is OK if you have a lot of archival content: thousands of pictures on a cultural or historic theme. It's a collection of data, it's valuable, but it is not necessarily interactive multimedia.

My feeling is that the superheroes of this new medium will not be repurposed from older media; they will be indigenous to multimedia. This has been historically true. The Disney and Warner Brother characters were indigenous to the cartoon world; SuperMario Brothers and Donkey Kong have been the most successful characters in the video-game milieu, and they were indigenous. So I wonder if the existing assets from the publishing industry will be worth the billions the publishers are hoping for. It's a free-for-all. The big guys in existing media may not necessarily be the winners in multimedia.

Writing

Once the content for a multimedia production has been determined, it must be organized in a thoughtful way. Just as a movie is developed on paper before a frame of film is shot, so a CD-ROM is developed first by organizing everyone's thinking in a treatment, then a functional specification, followed by a technical spec, and, finally, in some cases, especially for complex games, a design document or final script. (The terminology is not consistent from developer to developer and often depends out of which tradition the developer is coming from: the world of film, computer game design, etc.) These written documents (as well as the graphics that will eventually be created) are typically called "deliverables": items delivered according to a predetermined schedule to the client.

Judson Rosebush: *Deliverables in a multimedia production include the contract at signing, the functional and technical specs, the game design, the alpha, the beta, the gold master. The "alpha" is a working shell, a structurally complete prototype, but with very little content. The "beta" is the code-complete, content-complete product, but it still is in the testing phase. The gold master is the final disk before duplication, free of all programming and content bugs.*

There are also deliverables that might be considered internal to the project—in other words, what we as the developer buy from people supplying media assets: a piece of artwork, a "copy block" (on-screen text), a sound file, a photograph, or a piece of animation.

A treatment is generally a three-page-or-less summary of the concept, including the ideas to be conveyed, the characters to be created, and thoughts about the tone or mood of the piece. It outlines the amount of video, text, and graphics that will be included, and also includes a schedule specifying the "milestones" that must be met at each step of the way. It can be written by someone from the team of the financial backer, or it can be created by the developer. It is written at the earliest part of the production phase and will usually be discussed and dissected by many members of the team: producers, directors, writers, developers, and programmers. Once the treatment is approved by all parties, the functional specification is written.

Michael Smethurst: *A functional spec describes the functionality of the product—the interactivity and the non-interactivity. For example, "on clicking the desktop icon, the user will be presented with such-and-such an experience, which will dissolve into an animation leading to a screen where there is a decision." The functional spec can run from 50 to 60 pages.*

This evolves into a more detailed document known as the technical specification, which can sometimes take months to create.

Judson Rosebush: *A functional spec is a description of the product as it appears from the outside; the technical spec is from the inside. More specifically, the functional spec describes how the product will look and feel to the consumer, while the technical spec describes the computational functionality; it looks inside the procedure in terms of variables, subroutines, and parameter passing; architecture of the code; what language is chosen; and implementation methodologies.*

Matthew Schlanger: *The technical spec is a document written before production starts that outlines the program architecture. It can be as specific as to include every systemic global variable and handler, every essential global subroutine and function. Once you have the technical spec, you have the map to create a program; from it other things grow and are added. The basic structure is defined — the template. Then all the animations are created based on that template. The navigation of the piece is defined. The comparison in video production is to having a very carefully constructed storyboard.*

Michael Smethurst: *The technical spec describes what will play on what code. It's the blueprint for programmers. Technical specs are a good exercise to make sure that everything has really been thought through. It will be read by producers on the client side. If the client happens to be a computer company, they'll back it.*

In some productions, the technical spec is the blueprint for the project from which the writers, programmers, and illustrators work. In other, more complex programs, such as games or products with narrative continuity, characters, and dialogue, there might be a final document, the script or design document (the latter being the term in the game world). Even in a fact-based product such as *The War in Vietnam*, there was a small script for the introduction, an editor's note, and the help section.

While in film the typical length of a script is one-page-per-screen-minute (thus 90–120 page scripts), it is not uncommon to have 600–1,000 page scripts for multimedia games. They indicate line by line what happens with characters and objects, depending on the user's choices and interaction. It is the branching feature of multimedia—all the "what if" scenarios that give interactivity the depth and breadth it needs to be satisfying—that results in such tome-like scripts.

Michael Smethurst: *The game design will tell you "If doing this while this is happening, and something else happens (like a storm), then a certain sequence of events will occur." It adds game play to functionality. There are a lot more conditions than in a purely information-based product such as* Vietnam *or* Asimov. *In info-based products, you can just describe the screens and what happens when the buttons are pushed. In games, there is more going on.*

Production Heats Up

Production is too expensive to undertake until all the ideas are well-thought through and well-organized. Once the planning and thinking/writing phases are complete, graphic designers, illustrators, media gathers, rights and permissions staff, researchers, and programmers can start moving forward. It is not a linear process, but rather a complex web in which many people start working in tandem.

Judson Rosebush: *I'm of the school that you build things in parallel. You sketch the product in a programming sense before you build it. You build screens and sections with elements, using "Greeking," or the addition of nonsense copy. The idea is to start building the functionality, the look and feel, the shell. Even if a photograph hasn't been taken yet, you can outline where it will appear. You start building the grid of each screen: the design lattice of the product, similar to a book or newspaper, where you determine the width of the columns of text, the size of the margins, the fonts, the rules for boldface and italicizing, where the headlines will appear, where pictures will be placed, and so forth.*

In an early phase of production for *The War in Vietnam*, two freelance researchers worked full-time for six months creating a 1,000-word glossary, collecting photos of weapons, and working on maps. The maps were particularly difficult because since the 1970s many province and city names have changed. The glossary words, which are bulleted in on-screen copy for hypertext searching, include definitions for such words as *flak* or *anti-aircraft*. In addition, the researchers tracked down many of the documents that complete the product, making it a valuable asset to Vietnam historians: the Pentagon Papers, presidential papers, lists of battles, all the names that appear on the Vietnam War Memorial wall, and the words to Vietnam-era songs (which were written by G.I.'s and are sung by professional singers within the product).

The researchers also assisted CBS Executive Producer Joel Heller in writing the original text for a chronology that starts in 1940 and runs through 1994. It contains two columns: the left side are all the events taking place in Vietnam while the right side shows parallel events happening back in the United States, such as Super Bowl winners. After this chronology was completed, *New York Times* staffers combed over it and adapted it to better reflect the information from the news stories they were providing.

Visuals

After the initial planning meetings on *Ocean Voyager*, freelancer Kathy Konkle received from Judson some rough sketches regarding the basic layout of the product—four rooms in a submarine—that she proceeded to interpret.

Kathy Konkle: *As the illustrator, I designed the background plates for the rooms and animated the objects in them. We have the bridge, a pod (where you can pick up samples from the water with a robotic arm), a lab (to examine specimens picked up in the pod and from diskettes with databases on them), and the crew quarters. I designed how the lighting would look, the angles, and the instruments—the throttle, the joystick, the periscope, sonar, radar . . . and in the lab, the buttons that control the computer and monitor. I also came up with the design for the main character, an animated seal, which was based on scanned-in video footage. I had to draw this seal in many moods—happy, sad, worried—so that there will be different reactions if he is given a ball, or falls sick and needs to be taken care of.*

Kathy worked at home, coming into the office about once a week, or not, depending on where the project stood. If she didn't go into the office, she sent her illustrations in by modem as they were completed. The graphic elements she supplied were placed in the program Director, which uses the metaphor of a theater in describing its "cast members." Matthew provided her with what he calls work orders.

Matthew Schlanger: *Work orders could be thought of as instruction documents for people to create "code," graphics, and sound. The latter would be called sound work orders, or graphic work orders. Work orders can be one page, or ten or twenty. A graphic work order basically details every sprite (a Director term referring to a "cast member" of the show), every background that needs to be created, and exactly how I wanted it prepared, down to where the registration point should be. (In Director the registration point determines how the sprite is placed on the "stage.")*

Kathy Konkle: *I receive the work order section by section, but by the time the project is completed it might run 100 pages. The work order is based on the script and contains instructions on every single thing that needs to be animated. For example, in the case of an animated character, the body, the head, and the mouth might be treated as separate pieces. For a single sprite I might end up with one body, six heads moving in different ways, and four drawings of the mouth in various expressions. The same would be true of an inanimate object such as a book—which I might have to render flying across the room, opening up to be read, or sitting on a shelf.*

Kathy's method of working is to design or draw on paper, scan it into the computer, and, using this image as a guideline, manipulate it in a software program. Kathy uses Adobe Photoshop for such tasks as pulling forth color, mapping in realistic textures, and adding special filters. When she's completed the project, she turns it in on a diskette in a Macromedia Director PICT file.

Kathy Konkle: *Each individual piece is aligned, named, and ready for the programmers. Every pixel is in place: every posture of a character or angle of view is correct. The programmers then take these images and essentially animate them so they will move according to the script.*

As an illustrator, you need a simple grasp of Director—the more you know the better able you are to talk to programmers and understand the jargon they use. But, frankly, I don't have the time to learn it as well as I'd like; I'm too busy working full time creating the hundreds, maybe thousands, of drawings that go into a complex piece of multimedia like the ones Judson produces.

Programming

At Judson Rosebush Company, there are four sources for programming code: HyperCard (which was used for *The War in Vietnam*), Macromedia Director (used to create *Ocean Voyager*), a large library of additional programming components (for example, X-commands or routines from assembly languages C or C++), and finally the custom-designed collection of programming functionalities called RVAT (Rosebush Vision Authoring Tools). Created over the years, these tools include such things as automatic table-of-contents filters, hypertext systems out of Judson's own so-called Hot Text library, or dynamically positioned pop-up boxes. (*Dynamically positioned* means that the pop-up boxes would come on to the screen in strategic locations relative to the other information being displayed at a given moment.) Other examples of the capabilities of RVAT are the ability to import text already coded so that it is in italic or bold; artificial personality models; and a virtual mapping system, which in *Ocean Voyager* showed users their location at any given moment in the game.

Judson Rosebush: *I design code and oversee programmers, though the way I think of myself is as a software architect. When you build a building, there's an architect and a brick mason. Each may not happen to know how to do the other's job, but two jobs are involved: one is designing and planning the building; the other is building the building. Most people are aware of the side of software in which programs are written to accomplish a certain task, but aren't as aware of the architectural function, which is really the architecture of the CD-ROM that must be created in advance. In the Vietnam disk we wanted to build: hypertext capability, the functionality to turn from virtual page to page, the ability to take notes or leave a bookmark. We wanted a pop-up glossary, "zooming pictures" and help capabilities, a volume control, and a video play/pause/rewind mechanism. All these are examples of software architecture.*

Most software architects are self-trained since there are not a lot of schools that have these kinds of courses yet. Computer science departments at universities tend to be focused on technical applications, theoretical issues of software, operating systems design, or natural language analysis. This does not prepare someone to create code for multimedia applications. The computer science departments tend to produce people who are analytically strong but media weak. And this industry of multimedia is at its very essence a fusion of media and math, or said another way, consumer electronics and computing.

Programmers in multimedia need to have a creative side. They need to have had some contact with the other aspects of multimedia, such as painting, writing, film/video, or music. Media is what we're involved in. We're not making The War in Vietnam or Gahan Wilson's The Ultimate Haunted House to advance computer science. It's a media art. It's a communicational activity more than a computing activity.

Matthew Schlanger: Programming for a game is different than programming for a reference work: you're trying to achieve different things. The game is more creative, more animation-oriented, and contains more sound and feeling. It all comes down to creating feelings in people—you make them laugh, you remind them of something, you create characters. This doesn't have a place in a reference title. Here, interface design is more about navigating through a large amount of information in an elegant, intuitive way. You want to be able to get between the information quickly and easily and be able to go back to where you were. So there are different interface issues. In a game you may not want the interface to be obvious. Maybe the interface is part of the game. You have to figure it out. The question is then: What is the game play? How hard or easy should it be?

The whole production process is different because the assets are shaped differently and what drives the assets is different. With reference works, the assets are driven by the scope of the references material and how you decide to organize it. For a game, the assets are driven by the creativity and design—the creative elements.

In both cases, though, you want to have elegant interface design. The interface must work; it must make sense. I am not dogmatic about interface design; there are other people who are. Some people say "Never include anything with two clicks." That's crazy. Part of designing an interface is being creative—you want to make it intuitive.

There is a lot of misinterpretation about the job of interface designer. I've noticed that on some projects, the person who gets credit for it is the graphic designer, when I know they had nothing to do with the interface design. Interface design involves graphic design, but it is more concerned with how the program works.

An interface designer can be a graphic person or a programmer. They can both be working together. And it could also be a game designer. Or it could be a team of all of them. It really depends on the project. But it's a point of confusion in this industry to think of a graphic designer as an interface designer if all they're doing is building the graphics. Interface transcends graphics. Interface answers "How does it work? Why is it intuitive?"

Product Integration

It is axiomatic in the production world that the last twenty percent is often the toughest. In multimedia production, once all the elements have been received, designed, and programmed, the process enters the final assembly phase in which the actual content is integrated into what is now becoming the final product. Greeking must be replaced by the actual on-screen copy and empty boxes filled with the photograph or sketch that belongs in them. The reason is that if there is functionality associated with an element, it must get built at this point. If a certain word is meant to be designed as hypertext, the pathway to where it leads would need to be created now. For example, in *The War in Vietnam*, if you click on the word *Danang* in a news article, you're taken to a map.

This title used the interface metaphor of a book, so screens with material from *The New York Times* needed to have the articles, pictures, photo captions, and headlines installed as if on the page of a book. Each one of these was considered a separate element, because they came through separate pathways—text through the editors, pictures through the art department, and so on. Other things going on at this final stage include copy editing and inputting the sound.

Joel Heller, executive producer, CBS News:
One of the difficult and unanticipated issues regarding searching on key words was that midway through the war, the English-language spelling of Chinese-language-based names and places was officially changed. Mao Tse-Tung became Mao Ze-Dung. Then there were changes motivated by politics: Saigon became Ho Chi Minh City. So we had to go back and change all the words from the older Times *articles to the newer reference style, for the sake of consistency.*

Getting Product from Developer to Market

Once a product is complete, it goes through extensive testing, first by the on-staff programmers, then by specialty "bug/fix" testers. The testing company composes a strategy of what it proposes to test, functions that "exercise" the product. Depending on the contract, this could include proofreading the product, making sure that buttons lead to where they're supposed to, and inspecting to make sure all the pictures, captions, and "callouts" go together. (A callout is a notation such as *Refer to Figure 1*.)

The testing company also performs configuration testing to make sure the product runs properly on different machines or different peripherals.

(A peripheral is something, such as a video card, attached to or inserted into the computer.) There is also "environment checking" to discover what happens when the product is used in machines that don't have enough memory or don't have QuickTime installed, if that's what's called for. The company will return to the developer a list of suggestions of error messages or screen prompts to implement. After the developer has fixed the errors from the "bug list," the product goes back yet again for regression testing to see if the bugs the developer says have been fixed actually got fixed. (See a sample "bug report" on the facing page.)

When the product is finally finished, a gold master is created, also known as an RTM or release-to-manufacturing disk. The gold master is a physical disk used as the starting point of the manufacturing process; duplications will be made from it. When the product is sent to an outside service bureau for gold mastering, the content is often transferred to a DAT tape so the developer does not have to entrust the extremely valuable hard drive to anyone outside the office. If developers have a compact disk readable machine (CD-R) in-house, they have the option of making the gold master themselves, transferring the information directly from a computer.

Another step that is taken by some developers is to make the products capable of being played on either the Macintosh or the Microsoft Windows platform. This can be accomplished in one of two ways: by creating two separate gold masters, one for each operating system, or creating a single disk that runs on both types of machines. Sometimes the second option is not possible, but developers increasingly have more choices about how to handle the issue of cross-platform compatibility.

The final product, packaged and shrink-wrapped, can be distributed by the producer, as was the case with Time Mirror's *Ocean Voyager*; by a financial backer, such as Apple Computer through its education distribution channel in the case of *The War in Vietnam*; by a distributor affiliated with a publisher, as was the case with Microsoft's distribution of *Gahan Wilson's The Ultimate Haunted House* for publisher Byron Preiss Multimedia; or by the developer alone as is the case in Judson's distribution of an archival disk of nineteenth-century engraving for Wild Side Press.

Joel Heller: *Creating a product as complex as* The War in Vietnam *with all the parties involved—CBS, the* New York Times, *the Judson Rosebush Company and his freelancers, plus others such as the Pushpin Group (a design studio he hired to do some artwork)—you find that creating a CD-ROM is a very fine balancing act. Everyone has a point of view that wants to be expressed, and there are different*

Ocean Voyager
Bug Reporting Form

Bug #OV _____

Logged By: _____ Date: _____

Version #: _____ Platform: **Mac**   **Win**

Section Name:

    Opening   General

    Bridge   Pod   Crew Quarters

    Lab   Database   Control Panel

Action Taken _____

and/or

Plot or Subplot Location _____

Nature of Bug:

Content   Programming   Function   User Expectation

Content Bug:

Spelling   Major Text Error   Dialog   Display

Please Describe:

_____

_____

Assigned To:

    TMM   JRCo Art   JRCo Writers

    JRCo Tech   M Weber   Smithsonian

Resolution:

_____

_____

By: _____ Date: _____

Approved By: _____ Date: _____

corporate sensibilities that come into play. Making a CD-ROM is more complex and takes more time than most people anticipate.

You must have a good idea to begin with, one that is graphically interesting. It has to be constructed in an intuitive way, because people don't want to read manuals to figure out how to work it. If you really want to make an interesting product, you have to anticipate how someone will want to use it and build in shortcuts for them. Planning ahead is extremely important, and at the same time, you have to be willing to make adjustments all the way down the line. The attention to detail on an undertaking such as this is enormous. Entering into such a project should not be taken lightly.

Judson Rosebush: *The worst part about being a developer is when you don't have enough budget and worry about money. Also, it's when you're working for people who don't know what they're doing, so you spend a lot of time making a product that ends up a mess. Working with better people, both as employees as well as clients, is a superior way to make a better product. And working with people who are insensitive, arrogant, self-aggrandizing, insecure, and overbearing is a way to make an inferior product. You can't make great stuff with second-rate people, no matter how great your "tech."*

I think that the qualities that make a good multimedia developer include extremely good scheduling discipline, truthfulness, courage, very good interpersonal skills, good judgment, and the ability to deliver on time, on budget, and with quality. And you need modesty, which is the ability to abdicate credit to those above and below you for work you might have done. At the same time, you need to know when to toot your own horn!

The best parts of being a developer are closing the deal, making something you can be proud of, seeing your name on a product, and knowing you're making things that others are enjoying or finding useful.

Afterword: Writing for Games

Some developers are able to create multimedia titles either alone or together with their programmers and interface designers without formal scripts, but in the case of complex titles and games with a lot of depth and breadth, freelance professional interactive scriptwriters are called upon. When Judson was asked by Byron Preiss Multimedia to develop a CD-ROM edutainment game based on the drawings of Gahan Wilson, he turned to game designers Barbara Lanza and Walter Freitag, whom he had met at a Computer Game Developers Conference.

It is unusual for small or mid-sized developers to keep writers on staff full-time since the work of script development is periodic in nature—there are only so many projects a developer can produce in a year. In any case, writers require more intense concentration than can often be found in a bustling office with phones to be answered and meetings to attend. Interactive scriptwriting is typically outsourced in all but the largest publishing companies.

In the case of writing *Gahan Wilson's The Ultimate Haunted House*, the writing team of Lanza and Freitag did not even live in New York City, where Judson Rosebush Company is located. For the first few months of intensive design and writing, they were in daily electronic mail and phone contact from their home in Massachusetts. "It was mostly to clarify little things," Barbara explains, "like changes to the design to fit the kind of programming they were using." Once a month over the course of a year they flew from their studio for face-to-face meetings. She says she appreciated the competence of the staff at Judson Rosebush to handle such issues as the speed of the animation, the color balancing, the matching of sound duration to action, and so forth, leaving the game designers with the job of pacing and paying attention to the entertainment value of the game as a whole.

It took Lanza and Freitag six weeks to come up the core mechanism, the actual "guts of the game," which were "items" (animate or inanimate), each with their own variables and behaviors. Barbara says this is what makes this title more game-like than most CD-ROM games, which are often simply on the model of click-and-branch. Barb and Walt wanted something different to happen all the time. This six-week design stage, during which new versions were written and faxed back and forth, might take less time for games with fewer novel and unorthodox elements.

Over a period of four to five months, they worked out the game design: the characters and inventory items, the processes and functionality of game play, the dialog, animation directions, and the unified design of all the pieces. There were periods of intense work to meet deadlines for creating specific phases of the designs, and other times they were called upon only to resolve problems, answer questions, or provide additional details or documentation. They became heavily involved again toward the end of the year-long development/production cycle, after the beta phase, when they needed to "play-test" the design to see if the game was well-paced, entertaining, and balanced. When the process was finished, they had a 400-page script that had been written half in English (describing how the game mechanics work) and half in a "pseudocode" format similar to HyperCard's HyperTalk scripting language (containing the detail level of game functionality). A sample of Barb and Walt's "pseudocode" scripting language can be found at the end of this chapter.

Game / Story Designers

Barbara Lanza and Walter Freitag

Game designers, *Gahan Wilson's The Ultimate Haunted House*
Somerville, Massachusetts

Walt started programming in FORTRAN and BASIC in grade school in Pennsylvania in the 1970s, using the computers of a nearby university. In the early 1980s he became fascinated with role-playing games such as Dungeons & Dragons, particularly the aspect of interactive storytelling. He was also playing a precursor to the LucasArts and Sierra On-Line games of today—a text-only game on mainframes called Adventure. *By his early twenties he was writing scenarios for live-action games in which friends were given a character description and played their roles in someone's basement or at a sci fi convention. ("Spaceships supplied by your imagination.") He knew that someday the technology would exist to create artificial worlds and that people would want to tell interactive stories. He majored in computer science at Harvard but left before completing his degree. He took a day job at a medical research lab programming and maintaining electronic equipment, but in his off hours focused on of interactive storytelling. With the publication in 1988 of* Star Saga One: Beyond the Boundary *(Master Play Publishing), his hobby moved into a livelihood.*

Barb decided to try her hand at writing "at the advanced age of 33," went through "all the usual nonsense of beginning novels and short stories and getting rejected," and ultimately found she preferred creating live games to writing. She had attended the University of Miami in biology but quit before graduating. Working as an accountant for a corporation "to keep a roof over my head as a single parent," she met Walt at a writers' group, among whose members were some table-top game players. She discovered the creative satisfaction of creating live role-playing games, where in addition to being the writer, she could be the director and producer as well.

You prefer to call yourselves designers rather than writers.

BL: "Writer" implies that we were hired to do the audio portion of the game, all the witty dialogue. That's not the half of it. We come up with what the product is going to do and how it's going to do it. We are primarily game designers. We write the dialogue because for the sake of smoothness it's good to have the writer and the designer be the same person. We could have been just writers, or just programmers, but we're not. What are we? This other thing—designer— that combines the two so the audience has a better time.

WF: The relationship between the function of the game designer and writer is close in interactive storytelling. In traditional screenwriting, when writing a scene the writer has control over what has happened to the character up to that point. In an interactive story line, there are many ways of arriving at a scene. The writer must write different versions of that scene depending on what has happened before. Or maybe it's a scene where several plot lines have converged, which means that certain things in the scene have to be written in such a way that they make sense regardless of which path the player used to get there.

So the more the writer knows about how the pieces fit together, the more likely the writer is going to be able to write each scene so that it works. And the person who knows the most about how the pieces fit together is the designer. I'm using "designer" as in game designer, which is a title from the game industry, not the multimedia industry. In multimedia, "designer" tends to have a graphic implication. In the game world, it's the person who designs the functionality, the rules of the game. As CD-ROM companies become increasingly interested in game play as a feature of their products, they'll need to pay more attention to game design as an aspect of production.

BL: We function as designers and as writers because in interactive design, it takes more time to explain to a writer how to be an interactive writer than it takes a designer to just do it. We design the game; we decide what kind of interface we want.

WF: We design what the buttons do. Some CD-ROM entertainment products are primarily made of hyperlinks, so in that case we create those, too.

WF: In film, a director is a director whether it's a western or a sci fi movie. In electronic entertainment, the type of product does affect the function. In the game industry, the game designer is the ultimate director, because everything that happens in the game is the design. The designer is essentially making the major decisions. In a product that has no game component, such as a CD-ROM coffee-table book, the only design issues are user interface design and other aspects of graphic design. In this case there's more likely to be a director managing everything, including the creation of the content. The graphic design and user interface designer are separate from the content in those cases.

In between, we have the hypermedia story—the strongly story-oriented game—where the writing is important and the player's decision-making is important. The problem with this type of project in the middle ground is that the role of the game designer has not been well defined. There is no standard hierarchy. And that's why we have some of the confusion of terminology. There are people making games without involving a game designer. And where a game designer is involved, he or she is not necessarily involved with the process.

We produce a lot of design documents that describe what the game actually does. That includes not only what the player sees, but what happens behind the scenes—anytime the computer makes a decision or anytime the player picks an option, the process has to be described.

How did you know how to make interactive games that work?

BL: All the give and take between player and computer program is a balancing act that requires a knowledge of game mechanics. If you want your player to experience a heroic adventure wherein they might experience some great personal tragedy, you might have to make some excruciating decision. How do you know it's time for a character to suffer dire consequences? That's design! Those are game mechanisms—if you know how to do that, you're golden.

And how do you know? You like games to begin with. If you have a closet full of games, you're on the right track. When you play games . . . some you like and some you don't. You notice while playing one you thought would be great that you're not having a consistently entertaining time, and you know why. Anybody can know they're not having fun, but a designer knows why. It may be poorly designed because the person with the first turn gets too high an advantage over other players. Or perhaps the game might be poorly balanced to the point where if a player started losing, they should cash in their chips, go into kitchen, and make a pot of coffee.

If you play games and find yourself reinventing rules to make it better, you're a designer. If people come to your house and play your games with "house rules" you've written, you're a designer.

What is the time frame for completing a complex multimedia game?

BL: Often, the designer begins a project with a three-to-four-month period to come up with design documents. At the bare minimum, this is a 30-page functional spec that tells how the game works, how it will be controlled, how it will run, what the mechanisms behind it are.

WF: After that initial period, we typically continue to be involved over the course of a year, but there are other projects we work on during that time.

BL: A designer can be involved with getting Product No. 1 to market and during the "middle period" be designing something else. If you design a product, you need to be available all the time to the rest of the team to clarify anything. However if you are the designer but not the director, you're not needed on site every hour of every day.

WF: We have periods of intense exclusive work to meet deadlines for creating specific phases of the design. These are times you're on call to resolve problems, answer questions, provide additional details or documentation, redesign things as they become necessary. Entertainment products are particularly complex. There are other kinds of multimedia, such as training programs, where the designer can hand off the design to the programmer and then never be consulted again. Entertainment products tend to push the limits, and therefore result in more changes and more decision making during the development phase (when programming is actually being done).

How much time do you typically spend on a daily basis?

BL: It goes in fits and starts but usually averages eight hours a day, five days a week. But sometimes it can be a matter of working twelve hours a day for three days, taking off an afternoon to read a book, then getting back to twelve-hour days.

Is the designer involved very much after the initial creation/writing phase is finished?

BL: The designer is back in the thick of things again after the beta phase. You're on call all through the testing period, when you're fine-tuning this thing, making sure it works. The best person to play-test a design, especially a complicated one, is the designer. Because designers know what they're looking for and what they're trying to balance.

WF: Again, this is specific to games, because there is not only testing to remove bugs, but there is play-testing, to determine, for example, whether the game is too easy. And that's becoming truer in multimedia, as more game play is put into the products.

BL: In something like an animated product—where how often characters appear, how easy or difficult it is to find keys, how hard it is to get the house angry at you are based on mathematical formulas—at the beginning we have a pretty good idea of what we think those mathematical formulas should be in order to keep the pacing correct.

WF: But we can't actually test if they're right until all the machinery that runs those formulas and plays the game is working.

BL: You can't notice playability issues unless you're playing the entire game from beginning to end, unless that whole game is there to test, and unless you know what to look for.

Describe the process of creating an interactive script.

BL: You have an idea of your own about what kind of game you want to develop fully. The first thing you do is to write it up in proposal or treatment form. (The East Coast calls it proposal, the West coast calls it treatment, but they're analogous.) It runs about three to four pages. You can't bore them, because these people—publishers or producers—are busy and trying to find someone to invest their money with.

You explain in a few paragraphs two things: one, here is a game that would be fun, interesting, and is doable; here's what it offers the players. Two, this is how I'm going to do it, the mechanisms I'm going to use.

Here's something people trying to break into the business should know: sometimes designers and writers are afraid to offer a good idea to a publisher. Beginners are afraid that if they put their idea on paper, someone will run away with it. But this doesn't happen because it takes so much work to actually execute that idea. There are very few people who understand enough to see a few sentences about the mechanism and be able to copy it or execute it. My advice to new writers is this: don't hide your light under a bushel, don't play your cards so close to the vest that you won't tell anyone how you're going to get things done.

What is your intent when you design a game?

WF: In our case, we emphasize giving players choices about what to do with inventory items. We want the inexperienced player to have the same enjoyment as the experienced adventure game player. And once a player becomes more experienced, we want the game to still hold their interest.

You put this into the treatment that's submitted to the publisher?

WF: Yes, we describe how at outset the player will be learning things, but doesn't need to know everything to win. That helps replayability. First-time players can approach the game for its explorability, and after that, they can start playing strategically. If hypothetically they knew everything, it would still be a fun game to play, because they'd still have decisions to make. Also, some elements of the game are randomized—some items difficult to find in one game will be easy to find in another.

BL: All this finds its way into an accepted treatment. On the first go-round it may not get accepted; there is something the publisher might object to. I keep bringing publishers up, because they don't write you a blank check and say, "I like your ideas and I don't know where you're going with them, but I'll give you lots of money." Since marketing is their problem, they need to have some input.

Is this when you create the design document?

BL: Yes, after the treatment, and after everyone has agreed on the product they want us to make, the next step is the design document, also called the functionality specification. Depending on how complicated a project is, this could run from thirty pages for a rather simple coffee-table book CD-ROM to upwards of hundreds of pages—500 or 600 pages—for something that is very complicated and really interactive.

WF: The reason there is such a wide variation is because in a conventional multimedia product that isn't a game, you can usually separate out the interface design and the content. For example, if you're making a multimedia dictionary, your design document doesn't need to include all the vocabulary words. But if you're making a game, you do need to describe all the monsters.

BL: We just said the design document could run hundreds of pages, but they always start with a thirty-page overview section. It's the short version of what the product is going to do, how the user will use it, how it will respond to the user, and why it will be fun. The design document lays out the groundwork for everybody. It tells the graphic artists what kind of artwork will be needed; it tells the audio people what kinds of voices and sound effects will be needed. That's their field of expertise; I don't have to tell them what kind of car noise they need.

This is where it helps if the designer is also a writer, because the design document has to be clear and understandable. If they also have a streak of advertising or marketing in their blood, that's good, too. Although by the time you reach the design document stage you know the project is definitely going to happen, in some ways you're always selling your project. If something happens—if things are stalling, animations are behind schedule or over budget—and you know that the publisher is thinking about whether to put your project on the back burner or not, the design document should always be giving it a little push. You spend a year of your life designing these products: they've got to be great!

WF: The project benefits by having everyone involved understand its goals, know how it's going to achieve those goals, and believe that it will be a good product.

BL: The design document is a way of making your enthusiasm contagious. That document will oftentimes be presented to a programming team, an animation studio, or even a prospective publisher without your being there. It has to represent itself, without you on the sideline going "rah, rah."

Once you're past the first thirty pages, you finally get down to the nitty-gritty. It's incredibly detailed. You write down what the interface will be like, what it controls, what it doesn't control, and perhaps how it will look graphically. In some cases we want nothing on the screen to come between player and the game: no bars, no pull-down menus—just point and click. In other instances we might say we want the player to communicate with a character on screen, to give him or her a choice of sentences to say or make up. That might mean you need pull-down menus and that some part of the screen will have to show sentence choices.

WF: We would not specify the color of an object, unless color were a part of the game. If it were a matter of matching green to green objects, we would, but if that's not the case, we'll let people who know and work with color deal with those issues.

BL: I'll happily tell animators what kinds of characters I want in the product: "I want a kid no older than six, and a vampire," and beyond that I don't say much except describing the personalities, because that helps the graphic artist to draw it. But the character sketch is short; the artists know what they're doing. They trust that the design I came up with will run. I trust that their sense of line and the programmer's sense of timing, will make the product look good.

What happens after the design documents are done?

BL: They are presented to the production team: programmers, graphic artists, sometimes the interface designer (if the interface is elaborate), and the project manager. You've been talking to the project manager all along, because the production team needs to be brought together: How many programmers will be needed? Are there any special team members required? Will it require a director? (Sometimes the designer will be the director; other times the roles are separated.) Now it's their turn. They look at it, and say whether it's doable. Now the production team starts building visuals.

WF: Programmers create a document called the technical specification. Where the design document says something is going to happen, the technical spec describes how the programming will make it happen.

BL: The technical specification is actually very important, especially in multimedia, because we get to see the techniques they intend to use to implement things. And sometimes they say they can't do something we've asked them to do.

WF: So the design has to be changed if necessary to meet technical, budget, and platform limitations.

BL: The design document is not written in stone.

WF: This is where game design differs from other kind of multimedia design. In corporate multimedia design or interactive books for entertainment, the design document is usually very firm once it's written, to the point where in some cases the designer may not even meet the programmer. Most multimedia products are done within known tools, such as HyperCard. In computer games, especially disk-based games, we're always trying to push the limits of the technology, and therefore there is a research phase where programmers are experimenting. And as the programmer gets results, he might show the designer what he was able to get the game to do. At the same time, something you wanted won't work.

What is your advice to someone trying to get into this kind of work?

BL: Any writer can come up with a story, but only a designer can come up with that very special thing called an interactive experience. I would like to tell people, if you're a designer, design something, even if it's a running HyperCard stack. Practice a lot. And once you have a spiffy game to show a developer or a publisher, dare to present yourself as a designer or a designer-in-progress. Maybe you took a choose-your-own-ending book and programmed it to make it run beyond its normal capacity. Or you have a board game that you designed for Halloween. Being a designer is like being a musician: it's talent. People who are designers normally do these things for fun, anyway. Designers are very playful people; we never quite grew up.

So the designer shouldn't have the attitude "I have a project I've created, and I don't want to do anything else. I want to do my precious idea." It's going to take a long time before somebody thinks your idea is as precious as you think it is. But if you have talent as a designer, then hire yourself out to design somebody else's project.

Tell me about the collaborative process.

BF: Either one of us could create a product from scratch, but because there's the two of us, we reinforce each other's goals. We have heights we want the product to hit. We encourage each other when one of us thinks something can't be done. We hold out for each other. If the developer is not pleased with a great idea that one of us came up with and both of us support, the originator might back off, but the other partner might stand up for it.

The most fun we ever have as designers is thinking this stuff up. You don't think it's fun writing it down, do you? Even when it turns into a program and it puts on its suit of graphics, and it has all its audio, and everything is in place, and it's actually being run—yes, it's fun to see that. I'm not saying I don't want to see my own product "in the flesh," but it's a long development process. Way in the beginning you go through this creative burst, and it's awesome! And a lot of times the only person who understands is Walt. It will take a while for other people to figure out what we've just done. They're going to have to see it in its final form and be able to play it as a game before they honestly understand what it was we did. Because they can't see it the way we see it.

It's like having a seed grow into a tree right before your very eyes, and you see it bearing fruit; we know exactly what it's going to be like when it's finished. In the year it takes for the tree to really grow, everybody is saying, "Isn't that a great tree?" and we say, "Yeah, we know, but we're on another project now."

You've obviously thought a lot about interactive storytelling.

WF: One failing of interactive stories is that they're not really interactive. They pretend to give you a choice, but if you make the wrong choice, you reach a dead-end or your character dies and you can't go any further. Really you don't have any choice at all, because only one choice continues the story. In a good interactive story, any choice should allow the player to continue.

The basic rule in the computer game world is that in order to play in an interactive story, you have to solve puzzles. But the multimedia industry, which is not the same as the computer game industry, has had an awareness that there is something beyond puzzles. We don't know yet exactly what it is, but the struggle seems to be interactive versus story quality. Artificial intelligence researchers are trying to generate more sophisticated character behavior—the idea being that the more the computer character acts like people, the better.

BL: Just to have two people talking to each other doesn't mean you'll have a story or an adventure. It isn't enough just to have characters who are like people; in the end you need the storyteller more than you did the characters (which are basically an extension of the storyteller). In this case, the storyteller is a computer instead of a person. Before you can design that thing called "a storyteller," you must know what makes stories work in first place: suspense, tension, anticipation.

WF: We're looking into how the traditional story structure of literature—the Icelandic sagas, the Homeric epics, or *The Thousand and One Arabian Nights*—can be applied in computer storytelling. These stories are simple and have fewer elements than other kinds of literature, so they're well-suited for interactive storytelling research.

Early in this century, research was done concerning how the bards would tell those stories. The theory is that they didn't memorize those stories; they memorized the structure and pieces of the stories, and would then spin the story to different lengths on demand, in real time, in the proper rhythm. They did that in what a computer scientist would call an algorithm. So we're trying to capture in a computer program the tale-spinning ability of the ancient bards.

Computer Games: What Does a Script Look Like?
(Courtesy of Lanza and Freitag)

The following design document is a design script that governs the actions of a CD-ROM character called Mikey. In the imaginary game "Go for the Gold" the player finds himself trapped in a dangerous bureaucracy composed of fifteen offices. To win the game the player must obtain ten gold coins by trading items with characters he meets in the bureaucracy. Each character likes and dislikes items depending on what properties they have. Every time the character takes an item from the player, he gives the player a new item. And there's a chance that a new item will be a coin.

ON GAME START:
    select Mikey's special item from the list of trinkets
    yucky counter set to zero

ON CLICK ON MIKEY (NORMAL OR ANNOYED STATE)
    50% chance he'll EXPRESS PRESENCE if normal, ANGER if annoyed
    50% change - random saying from list 1
    Move slider: activity +.01, max: .5
    He remains in the room.

ON DRAG INVENTORY ITEM TO MIKEY (when not fainted)

IF item is Mikey's "special Item" THEN
    MIKEY ACCEPTS SPECIAL ITEM (see below)
ELSE
    IF item is firecracker OR hornet THEN:
        FIRECRACKER BLOWS UP MIKEY (see below)
    ELSE (item is hornet)
        MIKEY WITH HORNET (See below)
    ENDIF
ELSE
    IF the special item is in the player's inventory THEN:
        MIKEY TAKES YUCKY ITEM (see below)
    ELSE
        IF item has property TOY, MUSICAL, or EDIBLE THEN
            MIKEY TAKES ITEM
            MIKEY MAY PRODUCE ITEM (see below)
            MIKEY LEAVES ROOM
        ELSE
            item is rejected (default rejection sound)
                ENDIF
              ENDIF
            ENDIF
        ENDIF
    ENDIF
MIKEY ACCEPTS SPECIAL ITEM:

Mikey TAKES ITEM.
EXPRESS HAPPINESS
SPEAKS: "Gee, thanks-a-roni. I really wanted that. I hope you win." (sound MikeyB07)
He then produces a coin if possible. It he's already produced a coin, then attempt MIKEY PRODUCES ITEM at order equal to special item order +3.

Move slider activity -.25 min: .3; opposition -.1 min: .3
IF Mikey was in ANNOYED state, becomes NORMAL state
Mikey leaves room.

FIRECRACKER BLOWS UP MIKEY
    MIKEY TAKES ITEM
    MIKEY TALKS: MikeyB05, "Uh-oh."
    EXPRESS FEAR
    Animation: firecracker explosion; Mikey disappears in the process
    SOUND: firecracker explosion
    IF Mikey is NORMAL THEN
        SOUND: Mikey's voice off camera, "That wasn't very nice" (MikeyB01)
        Mikey's state becomes ANNOYED
    IF Mikey is ANNOYED THEN
        SOUND: Mikey's voice off camera, "You'll be sorry" (MikeyB10)
        Mikey's state becomes ATTACK
    increase opposition +.3
    (Mikey leaves room)

MIKEY WITH HORNET
    ANIM ATION: Hornet stings Mikey and is consumed
    MIKEY TALKS: MikeyB05, "Uh-oh."
    IF Mikey is NORMAL THEN
        EXPRESS FEAR
        EXPRESS ANGER
        Change state to ANNOYED
    IF Mikey is ANNOYED THEN
        EXPRESS ANGER
        EXPRESS ANGER
        MIKEY SPEAKS: "Now you've done it" (MikeyB14)
        Change state to ATTACK
    Mikey leaves room

MIKEY WHINES
    Mikey consumes the item (regardless of item)
    IF Mikey is NORMAL THEN
        EXPRESS FEAR
        MIKEY SPEAKS: "You never share anything good with me" (Mikey B09)
    IF Mikey is ANNOYED THEN
        EXPRESS ANGER
        SPEAKS: "That's not what I really want" (MikeyB13)
    Mikey remains in room

move slider +.01 darkness

MIKEY TAKES YUCKY ITEM
    IF Mikey is in NORMAL state THEN
        increase opposition +.01 max: .95
        increment yucky counter by 1
        MIKEY SPEAKS (Sound MikeyB04, "Yecch!" followed
                by swoon)

        MIKEY FAINTS
        IF yucky counter >2 THEN
           reset yucky counter by 1
           change state to ANNOYED
           (Mikey doesn't leave room because he's fainted)
        ELSE
           nothing
        ENDIF
    ELSE (Mikey is in ANNOYED state)
        increment yucky counter by 1
        increase opposition +.02 max: .95
        IF yucky counter=1 THEN
    MIKEY SPEAKS; "Not again" followed by swoon (Sound Mikey B12)
        MIKEY FAINTS
        ELSE
           IF yucky counter=2 THEN
    MIKEY SPEAKS; "You're not my friend anymore" (Sound Mikey B15)
        MIKEY FAINTS (Sound MikeyB30)
        ELSE (yucky counter 3)
           MIKEY SPEAKS: "Now you've done it"(MikeyB14)
           MIKEY FAINTS (Sound MikeyB03)
        ENDIF
    ENDIF
ENDIF

MIKEY MAY PRODUCE ITEM:
    IF Mikey is in NORMAL state THEN
        PRODUCE ITEM, order is order of item taken +1, eligible for coin;
           produces list is ALIVE, FRAGILE, CONTAINER, and item
BOOK
        IF an item cannot be produced, EXPRESS HAPPINESS. IF
        an item is produced, MIKEY TALKS: "Thank you, this is
        for you now" (Sound MikeyB11)
        Mikey leaves room
    ELSE (Mikey is in ANNOYED state)
        MIKEY TALKS: "You're not nice and I won't be your friend
         anymore" (MikeyB15)
        (no item is produced)
        MIKEY leaves the room
    ENDIF

Titles Developed by the Judson Rosebush Company

Area 51. New York: Judson Rosebush Company. Distributor: Novell WordPerfect, 1995.

CBS Fall Preview. New York: CBS Marketing Interactive, CBS, Inc., 1994 (promotional marketing disk, not for retail sale).

CBS Photography & Press Guide. New York: CBS Marketing Interactive, CBS, Inc., 1994 (press photography disk for the press, not for retail sale).

Gahan Wilson's The Ultimate Haunted House. New York: Byron Preiss Multimedia. Distributor: Microsoft, 1993.

HBO Winter/Spring '95 Programming. New York: HBO Media Relations, 1995 (promotional marketing and press photography disk, not for retail sale).

Isaac Asimov's The Ultimate Robot. New York: Byron Preiss Multimedia. Distributor: Microsoft, 1993.

Nineteenth-Century Steel Engravings. New York: Wild Side Press. Distributor: Judson Rosebush Co., 1995.

Ocean Voyager. New York: Times Mirror Magazine Group; Washington D.C.: Smithsonian Institution. Distributor: Times Mirror, Inc., 1995.

The War in Vietnam. New York: CBS News and The New York Times. Distributor: Apple Computer, 1995.

Epilogue

This book has examined career opportunities in multimedia from various perspectives. First we identified the types of jobs that exist in the creation of a CD-ROM title and met the people behind those role designations, getting a look at their backgrounds, how they got into the field, what excites them about it, and what advice they have for those wishing to pursue a similar career path. Then we met people from various professions that are being impacted by multimedia: advertising, marketing, the record industry, film, publishing, corporate training, the legal profession, and the museum world. We heard from executive recruiters and learned about the issues regarding multimedia distribution.

The last section of the book integrated the information contained in the interviews and focused on the process of CD-ROM development using, by way of example, two titles developed at the Judson Rosebush Company in New York City. The remainder of the book consists of a resource guide: a glossary and lists of books, magazines, professional societies, and conferences recommended by the experts who have been interviewed in these pages. Finally, there is a list of educational institutions that offer courses in multimedia around the world.

The primary focus of this book is multimedia development for the CD-ROM delivery platform, but the information can as easily be applied to such evolving forms of multimedia as the Internet. The technology is changing so fast that some may feel hesitant to invest the time and effort to learn today's multimedia skills for fear they will be outmoded. This will not be the case. Much of the knowledge gained in one area will be transferable to whatever developments tomorrow brings.

This rapid change highlights a truism of this emerging field: Anyone who enters multimedia should be aware that it will require lifelong learning. That could mean taking classes at the local community college on Hypertext Mark-up Language (HTML) in order to create a "home page" on the World Wide Web, teaching oneself new computer applications, attending marketing conferences to stay abreast of advertising trends in the digital age, or learning the technologies to make interactive television successful. Even for those with skills within a specialty, the convergence of industries driving multimedia means there will always be something new to learn, especially for those aspiring to such management or supervisory roles as project manager, director, producer, or company president.

Can a revolution be launched on the back of a technology as slow and cumbersome as CD-ROMs—one which, for all its megabytes compared to floppies, is ultimately limited in carrying capacity? The distribution and marketing paradigms for CD-ROMs are still in their infancy. Ease of use is not a phrase that comes to mind for some users. But CD-ROMs will probably not be totally superseded because they are physical objects that can be saved, collected, and stored for those who like to save, collect, and store. Even if CD-ROM storage in the long run ends up being used for nothing more than archiving, in the short run developing CD-ROMs represents a source of paying jobs that are available now. In that sense, the information contained in this book will remain relevant for some time to come even as technology continues to improve upon what we have.

Though multimedia is attracting a lot of talent quickly, it is heartening to realize that no one has a lifetime of career experience under his or her belt, yet. There is no established elite in multimedia; indeed, some of the early players have already bitten the dust. This means that there is less of a long-term power structure to buck. Creative artists and communicators who have traditionally found their offerings poorly valued may discover the tables turned in an era where content is king and power shifts to those who can feed the great information maw. In multimedia, as in Hollywood, the emphasis is not so much on what one has done before or what school one attended, but rather on whether one can pull a magic product—the next *Myst*—out of the hat.

Multimedia is also changing the rules of the media game. More than simply being an advance in technology or another new form of media, multimedia has profound social and cultural implications as well. Electronic publishing on the Internet fundamentally changes the traditional structure of media delivery. Couch potato-style television is not likely to disappear, but no longer will the only option be the one-to-many model of today's broadcasting paradigm.

No longer will those with a message need to make an enormous capital investment in purchasing equipment, such as that required by television and radio stations and printers, or in setting up costly distribution channels to get magazines and newspapers on the newsstand. For a relatively low capital investment, and the sweat equity to learn the skills required, one can have one's own Web site for poetry, photographs, résumés, or what has been dubbed, "way new journalism" by *Time* magazine's Josh Quittner (for the information superhigh*way*, and a play on the slang, "way cool").

In this more decentralized, democratic environment companies or individuals can market products without big budgets. Hyperlinked text can align one's message with other's, creating a new type of community that is more up to date, potentially organic, and always changing. For the first time since Gutenberg, the individual is able to communicate at a level that has been traditionally reserved for the entrenched powers. Small companies can put up a Web site as easily as multinational global corporations. In fact the most creative efforts seem to be coming from the younger generation and their nascent startup companies. Some of the larger traditional media corporations are stumbling in their efforts to rush headlong into an area they only vaguely comprehend.

The implications of digital media are profound. When media become digital, all media become unified. Something fundamental changes when the creation, production, storage, and distribution of information is transmuted into a common denominator. We know already that this allows media to move more quickly, to be revised and rebroadcast more efficiently. But beyond that, the implications are harder to fathom. Scenarios cover the gamut from the dark-side Orwellian Big Brother vision of a state of chaos and control by a digital elite to a brighter vision of a postindustrial, postmodern society where information and its nonpolluting manipulation become the dominant force in the economy.

However it evolves, those who decide to learn the skills of the information age know they won't be locked out of the future.

animation
A sequence of images that produces the illusion of movement when shown in rapid succession. Traditional cell animation was hand-drawn; animation created digitally is called computer animation. Sometimes computer animation is still hand-drawn and then scanned into the computer to be integrated with other elements.

application program
The program used by a computer user to accomplish a task, whether word processing, spreadsheet calculations, or to play a multimedia game. This is in contrast to programming, which is the set of instructions created to run the application and which is transparent to the user.

assets
In the context of multimedia production, assets are the components that go into making a multimedia title: scanned photographs, digitized video or audio, music or sound effects, text, computer animation, or software programming. Assets may be generated by the multimedia developer as original creations or purchased or licensed from third parties, such as movie scores.

authoring tool, authoring language
A plain-English computer program used to develop multimedia or hypertext applications. Generally, authoring languages are easier to program than traditional computer languages because logic and content are combined.

bandwidth
The frequencies at which information can be transmitted without distortion. Used conversationally, bandwidth refers to the size of the "pipe" through which information flows expressed as a unit of time (bits per second). The national goal for an information infrastructure—the so-called "information highway"—will be realized as its bandwidth increases to permit rapid transmission of large files, such as video or music, without loss of quality. The greater the information-carrying capacity of the medium of transmission, the greater the bandwidth.

branching
One of the basic structures of information flow in multimedia, whereby the user selects a path among choices, is taken to another screen, and from there selects yet another branch, and so on. Unfortunately, limitation in disk storage makes branching choices finite, but in a well-conceived, well-constructed title users have the illusion of directing the experience. In a reference title, the branching might simply be a matter of learning more and more about a particular fact, in greater and greater detail. In hyperfiction, branching would refer to the various story alternatives selected by the "reader."

button
In a multimedia interface, a button is a text or graphic component, such as an image or an icon, in which functionality is embedded. As programs become more creative and users become accustomed to the conventions of multimedia, buttons are increasingly assuming metaphoric and nonrepresentational shapes.

CBT
Computer-based training. Even before digital multimedia, educators and trainers taught workers how to run complex equipment, or explained their company's personnel policies, by using computers running simple text programs.

CD-i

Compact Disk Interactive. Developed by Philips and the Sony Corporation, CD-i is a mass-market entertainment and information system that plays digital data (visual, audio, graphic) stored on a compact disk. Unlike CD-ROMs, which play on a computer, CD-i plays in a box connected to a television set. Philips believes multimedia titles are easier to use. CD-i disks are used in the home, in education, and in business. The CD-i format in the home has proven more popular in Europe than in the United States, so far.

CD-ROM

Compact Disk—Read Only Memory. A CD-ROM is a delivery medium for digital information. Its key feature—as compared to analog video- or audiotape, for example—is allowing for random access, creating the technological underpinning for interactivity. CD-ROMs are the primary delivery mechanism for multimedia games, programs, and services today. This technology could be said to have kicked off the multimedia revolution in the 1990s by inexpensively providing enough storage capacity for the large files of multiple media—such as video, audio, and 3-D animation. CD-ROMs store about 650 megabytes, about 450 times the amount of data contained on a high-density floppy disk. Since CD-ROMs are built around the same basic technology as the audio CD, they are very cheap to manufacture. The limitations of CD-ROMs are that they cannot be "recorded to" without specialty equipment, and they are slow.

clearances

The use of existing media in a multimedia production must be legally cleared with the copyright or trademark holder. "Clearances" are to multimedia as "rights and permissions" are to video production. Rights to assets can be cleared with the help of lawyers or specialty clearance houses, and need to be handled at the earliest part of the planning phase of multimedia production.

code

Slang for programming code, the information that instructs programs how to run.

compression

The translation of massive amounts of video, audio, or other digital data into a manageable size and data rate for storage or transmission. "Codec" refers to a compression/decompression scheme.

convergence

As used in multimedia, refers to the coming together into one business arena of disparate and traditionally distinct industries, such as the telephone companies ("telcos"), the computer hardware/software industries, the entertainment business, and the cable/broadcast television industries.

cross-platform

Refers to the capability of a program to run on more than one type of computer platform. A computer or game "platform" refers to its operating system—for example, Macintosh or Microsoft Windows, Nintendo or SEGA. Early multimedia producers often only developed titles for one platform, but technology increasingly permits simultaneous development for multiple platforms. A hybrid disk is a single CD-ROM that contains a title capable of being played on both MPC and Macintosh operating systems.

desktop video or digital video

Video that has been digitized into a computer for editing, manipulating, and outputting. By bringing video into the computer, images can be altered using graphic and "paint" programs, and sequences can be edited using random-access techniques (thus allowing for changes at any time during the editing process, which is not easy in traditional videotape editing). The finished product can either be presented on the computer display—for example, for a sales presentation—or output to tape for playback using analog videocassette players and TV monitors.

digitize

To transfer analog video and audio into digital information for storage in or manipulation on the computer. (When still images or photographs are brought into the digital domain, they are typically said to be "scanned" in.) The ability to digitize video and audio is an essential component in the evolution of text-only computers to multimedia-capable computers.

Director

The proprietary name of a commonly used authoring program for multimedia development (both in Macintosh and Windows), originally created by Marc Canter and now owned by Macromedia. It allows developers to combine text, graphics, animation, sound, digital video, and interactivity to create multimedia productions. Director is used to create entertainment and education titles, corporate demonstrations, interactive multimedia presentations, visualizations and simulations, and kiosk presentations.

edutainment

Portmanteau word drawn from "education" and "entertainment." Refers to a category of multimedia titles intended for use in the home, as compared to education titles to be used at school.

engine, multimedia engine

Slang for custom-designed, proprietary programming that creates a software program to run a multimedia application. Multimedia can be created from off-the-shelf authoring programs, but developers often want to develop something with their own programming to accomplish certain tasks or effects. If the product that results is elegant, compelling, and easy to use, someone might attempt to buy that developer's "engine" to create and run another multimedia program.

full-screen, full-motion video

Early video on the computer was thumbnail sized and herky-jerky, typically running at less than the 30 frames per second required by the human eye to see movement as natural in video. Although computer experts were initially thrilled simply to bring video to the computer environment, video professionals saw only unacceptable, slow-moving blurred images. As technology improved, video digitizing boards were able to bring desktop video up to fill the screen, at rates of 60 fields/30 frames per second. Computerized video images continue to improve, challenging the meaning of "broadcast quality." When manufacturers talk about the products that allow better digital video quality, or multimedia developers describe how a video clip appears in a program, they might use the phrase "full-screen, full-motion video" to indicate the improvements in video representation in the desktop environment.

functional specification

A document used in the creation of a multimedia program that communicates to the programmers what is supposed to happen on the screen at any given moment. Game designers prepare a "functional spec." to explain what various possibilities they want available when the player clicks on a certain image on the screen, and the programmer writes the program that allows that to happen.

gold master

After the development process of a CD-ROM is complete, a gold master is created—the physical disk used as the starting point of the manufacturing process. The "dupes" or "duplicates" of the CD-ROM are made from the gold master.

HTML

Hypertext markup language, the "style sheet" standardization protocol for creating documents for the Internet's World Wide Web.

hot spots

Places on the screen that have been programmed for interactivity, so that when a user clicks the cursor on them (or runs a mouse or some other input device over them), an event occurs: the screen changes, a voice gives an answer, a sound is emitted, the button flashes, etc.

HyperCard

A high-level programming language that organizes information randomly. Though one of the earliest multimedia scripting languages, it continues to be widely used and is considered accessible even to nonprogrammers. ("High-level" denotes programming that uses more English commands than traditional programming.) HyperCard permits users to hyperlink—or connect—from information in one area to information in another. HyperCard was originally created for the Macintosh but now also runs on Windows and other operating systems.

hypertext

Hypertext functionality links information through various pathways, allowing users to move between related documents along thematic or idiosyncratic lines. The word *hypertext* appears in a phrase familiar to Internet users: HyperText Markup Language (HTML), an authoring tool for documents on the World Wide Web.

installed base

In multimedia, the number of computers with CD-ROM drives either built in or attached. The success of the multimedia business in its early days rested on a large-enough installed base of multimedia-capable machines to justify a wide variety of titles, including ones for niche markets. The installed base of CD-ROM drives is increasing exponentially.

interactivity

In the context of multimedia, interactivity is the degree to which a program responds to actions by a user. The quality of interactivity is determined by the speed at which the computer program responds, as well as the usefulness, cleverness, aesthetics, humor, or intuitiveness of the response. Boring interactivity is referred to as "point and click," or as being a "slide show," because the interactivity is repetitive and predictable. Not all multimedia is interactive (for example, archival CD-ROMs used simply for clean and safe storage).

interface

The place where computers and human perception meet and interact. In multimedia, an interface is the set of screens in which the user makes choices. The interface hides some of the mechanics at work in interactivity. A good interface is one that is intuitive, unobtrusive, appropriate to the purpose of the program, and hopefully, pleasing to the user. Aesthetic color choice and attractive presentation represent only one aspect of interface design. The interface designer is part artist, part information designer. Interface designers can be graphic designers, writers, or programmers.

Internet

Sometimes called "the network of networks," the Internet is a web of computer networks linking many millions of computers worldwide. The Internet is the child of the computer links originally set up by the U.S. Defense Department to connect its military research and testing facilities and, eventually, certain universities. The Internet blossomed when this basic networking backbone was built upon by the general public, libraries, private bulletin board services, and commercial on-line services, such as America Online. Primarily used initially as a conduit for electronic mail (e-mail), the Internet grew into a gargantuan interconnected information source of data and databases, eventually allowing people to see and talk to each other across the globe using video-conferencing software. The Internet is still in its infancy in terms of easy-to-use interfaces, indexing, and search programs, and the issues of privacy and intellectual property rights and recompense for retrieved material have yet to be successfully addressed. (See World Wide Web.)

JPEG

JPEG is an international standard for compressing and decompressing digital still images or a series of still images (for example, video) to be used in a computer. JPEG is named after the international group attempting to define such standards, the Joint Photographers Expert Group.

kiosk

A freestanding pedestal containing a monitor and computer device to run a multimedia program. Kiosks are often used in public spaces for information, or at trade shows for marketing purposes. Multimedia programs running in public spaces tend to use touchscreen monitors rather than using such easily damaged input devices as keyboards or mice.

MIDI

Musical Instrument Digital Interface, an industry standard connection for computer control of musical instruments and devices. MIDI-compatible sound cards permit music composition and manipulation of sound in the computer. (In Appendix IV, see International MIDI Association.)

MPEG

The name of the committee that is defining international standards for the digital compression and decompression of video and audio when used in computers. The name of the committee has become the name of the standard. JPEG compresses frame by frame; MPEG does interframe compression, allowing it to compress video into a smaller bandwidth.

on-line

Connecting to other computers through electronic mail systems, commercial network services, the Internet, or through BBSs (bulletin board services). In the context of multimedia, on-line is a delivery mechanism for content and can in that sense be considered a method of publication. As a many-to-many medium (as opposed to television broadcasting, for example, which is one-to-many, or telephone conversations, which are one-to-one), access to the on-line world promises to be as radical a technology as was Gutenberg's printing press. For the first time in history, the power of publishing to the entire world at a single stroke is in the hands of the ordinary individual at a relatively low cost.

Photo CD

Eastman-Kodak's method for storing images digitally while maintaining photographic quality. Kodak's compression technology permits high-quality images to be stored (with text and branching capability) on a single disk. Disks store hundreds to thousands of images, depending on the image quality sought by the user.

pixel

"A 'picture element' of a viewing screen. A rectangular screen is composed of thousands of pixels, each representing the color of an image at a given point on the screen" (definition courtesy of Pixar). The term is commonly used in computer graphics and animation to identify intensity or color level. Determining the number of pixels used to create images is one way to measure resolution.

QuickTime®

A multimedia software standard that allows viewers to view and edit video and still pictures, music, and animations on the computer, extending paste/cut functions originally available only with text. Originally an extension to the Macintosh operating system, it is now used on various computer platforms. QuickTime® VR (Virtual Reality) permits a user to rotate 360-degrees within an image, creating the verisimilitude of turning one's head around a room. QuickTime® Conferencing is a cross-platform multimedia and communications technology permitting "video conferencing" at the desktop, allowing participants at various locations to hear and see each other and to mark up a common "whiteboard" document.

RBOCs

Regional Bell Operating Companies, formerly known as the Baby Bells. These aggressive companies, formerly part of AT&T, are major players in the convergence of media and technology companies. The Internet and commercial on-line services were built on the backbone of existing phone service.

set-top box

Generic term for a piece of equipment that attaches to a television and is used to play games, to watch multimedia titles, or in the long run, to covert the set into an interactive television. The term *set-top box* is a bit of a misnomer because in some interactive television trials it rests under or next to the television set.

SME

Subject-matter expert. When creating multimedia titles, experts in a particular field may be consulted or brought onto the production team to help develop content and to ensure its accuracy.

storyboard

The stage of the creation process for a multimedia title in which the text, screen instructions, and images all appear in hard-copy document form before being created digitally. In a typical storyboard format, the text, dialogue, and programmer's notes appear on the left-hand side of a page, with the corresponding images, animations and video appearing on the right-hand side.

storybook

As in the world of literature, where "storybook" refers to books with stories for children, "storybook" as used in multimedia designates reading products as compared to "edutainment" products, which tend to be more information-based.

World Wide Web

The multimedia portion of the Internet, where hypertext documents are created and "browsed." The media-rich interface of the Web's "home pages" has made searching out information, some of it containing video and graphics, easier for the general public than other systems, such as Gopher.

Works Cited and

Selected Bibliography

Advertising Age. (Published weekly by Crain Communications, 220 East 42nd St., New York, NY 10017. Tel: 800/678-9595. Fax: 313/446-6777) "Provides information on marketing, advertising, and media in a variety of formats." Weekly section: Interactive Media and Marketing. Interactive Advertising and Media Awards available in video (Tel: 212/210-0287). Advertising Age/Creativity Online available on Prodigy and E-World, with articles and information on conferences, services, and subscriptions updated daily.

Animation Magazine. (Published eight times a year by Thoren Publications, 5889 Kanan Rd., Agoura Hills, CA 91301. Tel: 800/996-TOON or 818/991-2884. Fax: 818/991-3773. E-mail: Anniemag@AOL.com) Covers the entire animation industry from the traditional (cell animation) to the technical (computer graphics). Expanded multimedia column covering companies and trends, along with regular columns on animator news, computer graphic images (CGI), commercial breaks, feature films, festivals and markets, historical perspective, licensing, post-production, and television production. Also reviews of software/hardware/animation tools.

Aston, Robert, S. Swaminathan, and Joanna Tamer. *Emerging Distribution Models for Consumer Interactive Media.* Ed. Dana De Puy Morgan and Vicki Vance. Cupertino, CA: Multimedia Business Development Group, New Media Division for the Apple Multimedia Program, 1994.

Axcess. (Axcess Ventures, P.O. Box 9309, San Diego, CA 92169. Tel: 619/270-2054. Fax: 619/270-2159. E-mail: Editor@axcess.com; AOL/Axcess) Founded in 1994, "Axcess Magazine's unique view of music, technology and style has exposed today's counterculture arts to the mainstream audience. It is a key source for information on the role of technology in the arts and everyday life." Runs column on the Internet; World Wide Web site presents articles in interlinked hypertext format, complete with graphics. (Internet World Wide Web: http://www.internex.net/axcess)

Bergman, Robert E., and Thomas V. Moore. *Managing Interactive Video/Multimedia Projects.* Englewood Cliffs, NJ: Educational Technology Publications, 1990.

Boorstyn, Neil. *Boorstyn on Copyright*, 2nd ed. Ed. by Dvora Parker. Deerfield, IL: Clark Boardman Callaghan, Thomson Legal Publishing, 1994.

Brand, Stewart. *The Media Lab: Inventing the Future at MIT*, 2nd ed. New York: Viking Penguin, 1988.

Brinson, J. Dianne, and Mark F. Radcliffe. *Multimedia Law Handbook: A Practical Guide for Developers and Publishers.* Menlo Park, CA: Ladera Press, 1994. Tel: 800/523-3721. A comprehensive guide to legal issues on multimedia, containing numerous examples to illustrate legal issues. It also provides sample contracts (for example, a music license) and appendices with lists of stock houses, multimedia organizations, and books.

Bunzel, Mark J., and Sandra K. Morris. *Multimedia Applications Development: Using Indeo Video and DVI Technology*, 2nd ed. New York: McGraw-Hill, 1994.

Byte. (Published monthly by McGraw-Hill Publications, One Phoenix Mill Lane, Peterborough, NH 03458-0809. Tel: 800/232-BYTE. E-mail: editors@bix.com) "Founded in 1975, *Byte* is the oldest continuously published microcomputer magazine in the world. Content includes technical features, news and reviews concerning all aspects of microcomputing—DOS/Windows, Mac, UNIX and emerging platforms—with a readership of advanced computer users, engineering managers, technical executives and MIS." Sample articles: review of the DCI (display control interface) layer; lab report on graphics accelerators for Windows and Mac; "How to Do Digital Video in a Networked Environment."

Caffarelli, Fabrizio, and Deirdré Straughan. *Publish Yourself on CD-ROM: Mastering CDs for Multimedia*. New York: Random House Electronic Publishing, 1992. Note: includes CD-ROM.

CD-ROM Professional. (Magazine published bi-monthly by Pemberton Press, 462 Danbury Rd., Wilton, CT 06897-2126. Tel: 800/248-8466) "The magazine for CD-ROM publishers and users."

CD-ROM World: The Magazine for CD-ROM Users. (Magazine published eleven times a year by Mecklermedia, 11 Ferry Lane, Westport, CT 06880. Tel: 203/226-6967. Fax: 203/454-5840. Internet: meckler@jvnc.net. Link: Meckler. CompuServe: 70373,616) Consumer magazine for users of CD-ROMs, so bulk of magazine is devoted to reviews. Feature articles look at technology issues (hardware technology, compression, drives) and trends (language disks, rock n' roll CD-ROMs). Sample articles: "Moving Pictures—Video Clips on CD-ROM"; "A Mighty Amiga—Commodore's CD32 Player"; and "The Lay of the LAN—A Special Guide to CD-ROM Networking Options."

Child. (Magazine published ten times a year by Gruner & Jahr USA Publishing, 110 Fifth Ave., New York, NY 10011. Subscription tel: 800/777-0222. Tel: 212/463-1000) Family magazine containing research and analysis about parenting. Sample articles: "How Are Children Really Doing Today?"; "Full Esteem Ahead." Among regular columns are Learning ("Mad about science: fun ways to inspire your kids' curiosity"); Stages (focusing on development at different ages); and Media Kids (rating of TV shows and video, cartoon characters, etc.).

Communication Arts. (Magazine published eight times a year by Coyne & Blanchard, 410 Sherman Ave., Palo Alto, CA 94306. Tel: 415/326-6040. Fax: 415/326-1648. E-mail: camag@AOL.com) "Professional journal for designers, art directors, design firms, corporate design departments, agencies and everyone involved in visual communications . . . Everything is reproduced with attention to detail unmatched by any trade publication, utilizing the most sophisticated printing technology." Four annual issues are multidisciplined regular issues; four are single-discipline juried annuals. A "dedicated technology section" contains software reviews, resources, and book reviews. Bi-monthly columns on technology ("Great PhotoShop Techniques," "Cyberspace Lexicon"), as well as on design issues, freelancing, advertising, legal issues, and new materials. Annual interactive multimedia competition; selected entries available on CD-ROM.

Computer Gaming World. (Magazine monthly published by Ziff-Davis Publishing, P.O. Box 57167, Boulder, CO 80322. Subscription Tel: 800/827-4450. Editorial online: CompuServe/76703,622; Genie and AOL/CGW; Prodigy/ EXPT40B). Founded in 1981, the oldest computer game magazine has the "mature audience" niche (reader average age: 28) and contains reviews, sneak preview coverage, and in-depth strategy articles. Regular columns: strategy games, high-end flight simulators, and role-playing games. Sample articles: "Where No PC Has Gone Before: Star Trek Games"; "Doom Two" (about Doom games clones).

Computer Law Association Bulletin, The (incorporating The CLA International Update). (Quarterly newsletter published by the Computer Law Association, 3028 Javier Rd., Suite 402, Fairfax, VA 22031. Tel: 703/560-7747. Fax: 703/207-7028) This newsletter comes as a benefit of membership in the Computer Law Association, whose focus is to educate the legal community about issues arising from computer/communications technology. The newsletter covers the latest developments in computer law and provides an employment listing service. Recent articles: "Microsoft Consent Decrees"; "Employment Opportunities for Computer Lawyers—Membership Survey"; "Multimedia Works and Moral Rights: An EC Perspective."

Computer Lawyer, The. (Monthly newsletter published by Prentice Hall Law & Business, 270 Sylvan Ave., Englewood Cliffs, NJ 07632. Tel: 201/894-5222)

The Computer Paper. (Periodical published monthly by Canada Computer Paper, 3661 West 4th Ave. #8, Vancouver, BC V6R 1P2. Tel: 604/733-5596. Fax: 604/732-4280) Hefty general-purpose newspaper with news, features, and reviews about computer industry throughout Canada and North America, including coverage of the multimedia industry. Sample articles: "Reinventing Hollywood—Tinseltown Meets Siliconia"; "Conversation with Forest Baskett, VP of Silicon Graphics"; "Show Report—Multimedia Trade Show and Conference."

Computer Retail Week. (Tabloid-sized newspaper published weekly by CMP Publishing, 1 Jericho Plaza, Wing A, Jericho, NY 11753. Tel: 516/733-6700. Fax: 516/733-6960. Stories posted weekly on Internet: http://techweb.cmp.com/techweb/crw/current/default.html) Focuses on computer retailing, but in addition to retailers the magazine is read by software publishers, distributors, hardware vendors, and the financial community. Sample article: "Microsoft to Debut Surround Video." Regular section covering multimedia: Entertainment Extra.

Cotton, Bob, and Richard Oliver. *The Cyberspace Lexicon: An Illustrated Dictionary of Terms from Multimedia to Virtual Reality.* London: Phaidon Press, distributed by Chronicle Books, San Francisco, 1994.

___. *Understanding Hypermedia.* London: Phaidon Press, distributed by Chronicle Books, San Francisco, 1993.

Design Graphics. (The Journal of the Australian Graphic Design Association, sold in the USA, printed six times a year by Design Editorial, A.C.N. 0055 763 744, 11 School Road, Ferny Creek, Victoria 3786 Australia. USA subscription: 800/688-6247. E-mail: 100241.2657@compuserve.com; AppleLink/Design.Edit) Highly visual, bi-monthly journal devoted to all aspects of digital publishing. Information on hardware/software, plus reviews, interviews, and instructional section called Studio Skills. Sample articles: "CD-ROM Gallery"; "CorelDraw5: Henry Thomas Looks at the Latest Version of This Graphics, Multimedia and Publishing Solution." Regular columns: application program and book reviews, new production information, and "digital design update" column.

Digital Imaging: The Magazine for Users of Graphic Services. (Bi-monthly magazine published by Micro Publishing Press, 21150 Hawthorne Blvd. #104, Torrance, CA 90503. Tel: 310/371-5787. E-mail: mpn@designlink.com) Each issue features in-depth articles devoted to the graphic imaging process, including product roundups, key software and hardware overviews, practical techniques for users of graphic design applications, and technology assessments. Complimentary subscriptions available to qualified graphics professionals.

Digital Media: A Seybold Report. (Newsletter published monthly by Seybold Publications, P.O. Box 644, Media, PA 19063. Tel: 610/565-6864 or 800/325-3830. Fax: 610/565-1858. Editorial E-mail: dmedia@sbexpos.com) "Reporting on the emerging digital world," with articles about multimedia, interactive TV, the cable industry convergence with the telcos, etc.

Dondis, Donis A. *A Primer of Visual Literacy.* Cambridge: MIT Press, 1973.

Electronic Entertainment. (Magazine published monthly by Infotainment World, 951 Mariner's Island Blvd. #700, San Mateo, CA 94404. Fax: 415/349-7781. E-mail: CompuServe: 73361,265)

Electronic Musician. (Magazine published monthly by ACT III Publishing, P.O. Box 41525, Nashville, TN 37204. Tel: 800/888-5139 or 615/377-3322) A poll of readers indicated that 13% produced multimedia projects in 1993 and that 40% plan to in the future. In addition to equipment reviews and technical features about electronic music, articles have included "Computer-based Mixers Promise Total Control of Audio Spectrum"; "Turn Your Computer into a Monster Signal Processor"; and "Electronic Kiosks Offer New Outlets for Your Music."

Electronic Publishing. (Published monthly by PennWell Publishing, 10 Tara Blvd., 5th Floor, Nashua, NH 03062-2801. Tel: 918/831-9537. Fax: 918/831-9497) Publication focusing on new products for digital publishers, prepress professionals, and graphic designers. Sample articles: "NEC Unveils MultiSync X Series"; "Ikegami Attacks Monitor Market"; "Apple Unleashes Fastest Ever."

Entertainment Law and Finance. (Newsletter published monthly by Leader Publications, a division of New York Law Publishing, 345 Park Avenue South, New York, NY 10010. Tel: 212/545-6170. Fax: 212/696-1848) "Newsletter focusing on the legal and business side of the entertainment industry, featuring practical articles for practitioners." Sample news articles: "Negotiating Exec. Producer Agreements for TV"; "Different Methods to Distribute Independent Film Productions."

Eye—The International Review of Graphic Design. (English magazine published quarterly by Wordsearch Ltd., 26 Cramer St., London W1M 3HE. Tel: 011-44-71-486-7419. Fax: 011-44-71-486-1451) Established in 1990, the magazine has an audience of graphic designers, art directors, creative directors, and exeuctives with client companies who commission design.

Gibson, William. *Neuromancer.* New York: Ace Books, 1994.

Graphis. (Swiss magazine published bi-monthly by Graphis US, Inc., 141 Lexington Ave., New York, NY 10016. Tel: 212/532-9387. Fax: 212/213-3229) Magazine for graphic designers, art directors, advertising agencies, illustrators, and photographers: "In-depth profiles on creative leaders . . . as well as interviews with CEOs of design-directed corporations."

Hall, Brandon, *Getting Started in Multimedia Training: A Resource Guide.* Sunnyvale, CA: Multimedia Training Newsletter, 1995. (Tel: 408/736-2335. Fax: 408/736-9425)

Haykin, Randy, senior ed., *Multimedia Demystified.* New York: Random House, 1994. Note: formerly *Demystifying Multimedia.* Published by Apple Computers, Cupertino, CA; produced by Vivid Publishing, San Francisco, 1993.

Holsinger, Erik. *How Multimedia Works.* Emeryville, CA: Ziff-Davis, 1994.

Hone, Bob. *QuickTime: Making Movies with Your Macintosh*, 2nd ed. Rocklin, CA: Prima Publishing, 1993.

Hone, Bob, and Margy Kuntz. *Making Movies with Your PC.* Rocklin, CA: Prima Publishing, 1994.

I.D. (Magazine published bi-monthly by Magazine Publications, 440 Park Ave. South, 14th Floor, New York, NY 10016. Tel: 212/447-1400. Fax 212/447-5231) International design magazine, covering product, graphic, furniture, and environment design; packaging; and new technology. Sample articles: "Multimedia Roundtable"; "Muriel Cooper's Visible Wisdom" (about Visible Language Workshop at M.I.T.); "Paul Saffo's Rules of the Digital Game."

IICS Reporter. (Monthly newsletter of the International Interactive Communications Society. See listing in Appendix IV.)

Interactive Content: Consumer Online Services Monthly. (Monthly newsletter published by Jupiter Communications, 594 Broadway, #1003, New York, NY 10012. Tel: 800/488-4345 or 212/941-9252. Fax: 212/941-7376) "A source for breaking news and analysis on the rapidly evolving world of the consumer on-line services." Sample articles: "Can Women's Mags Change Cyberspace?"; "America Online on the Internet Attack."

InterActivity: The How-To Multimedia Magazine. (Magazine published bi-monthly by GPI Publications, 411 Borel Ave., #100, San Mateo, CA 94402. Tel: 415/358-9500. Fax: 415/358-9527. Internet: interactivity@mfi.com. CompuServe: 72662,136) Stated goal is to provide "developers and enthusiasts with practical hands-on, how-to information about interactive multimedia," covering "all manner of interactive delivery systems from CD-ROM to online, from location-based entertainment systems to whatever else comes along."

Internet World: The Magazine for Internet Users. (Magazine published eleven times a year by Mecklermedia, 11 Ferry Lane West, Westport, CT 06880. Tel: 203/226-6967. Internet: meckler@jvnc.net. CompuServe: 70373,616. AppleLink: meckler) Emphasis on articles about doing business on the Net and on legal issues.

Iris Universe: The Magazine of Visual Computing. (Quarterly magazine by Silicon Graphics, 2001 No. Shoreline Blvd., Mail Stop 415, Mountain View, CA 94039-7311. Tel: 415/390-1278. Fax: 415/960-1737) A magazine for users of Silicon Graphics computers. Subscriptions available upon request to qualified users.

Jerram, Peter, Michael Gosney, et al. *Multimedia Power Tools*®. Cardiff, CA:Verbum, Inc., and The Gosney Company; distributed in the U.S. by Random House and in Canada by Random House of Canada, 1993.

Journal of Interactive Instruction Development. (Journal published quarterly by the Society for Applied Learning Technology [SALT], 50 Culpeper St., Warrenton, VA 22186. Tel: 703/347-0055. Fax: 703/349-3169) Professional journal for instructional system developers and designers, providing perspectives on emerging technologies and design methodologies.

Kennedy, Joyce Lain. *Hook Up, Get Hired: The Internet Job Search Revolution.* New York: Wiley, 1995.

Kerlow, Isaac Victor, and Judson Rosebush. *Computer Graphics for Designers & Artists*, 2nd. ed. New York: Van Nostrand Reinhold, 1994.

Kernighan, Brian W., and Dennis M. Ritchie. *The C Programming Language*, 2nd ed. Englewood Cliffs, NJ: Prentice Hall, 1988.

Laurel, Brenda, ed. *The Art of Human-Computer Interface Design.* Reading, MA: Addison-Wesley, 1990.

Macworld. (Magazine published by Macworld Communications, IDG Communications, P.O. Box 54529, Boulder, CO 80322-4529. Tel: 800/288-6848 or 303/604-1465. E-mail: AppleLink/Macworld1. CompuServe/70370,702. MCI Mail/294-8078. Internet e-mail: macworld@macworld.com. Internet page: http://www.macworld.com) Feature articles on latest Macintosh technology plus numerous product reviews, with special sections on graphics, networks, buyers' tools, and "at work."

McCarthy, J. Thomas. *McCarthy on Trademarks and Unfair Competition*, 3rd ed. Vol. 1. Intellectual Property Library. Deerfield, IL: Clark Boardman Callaghan, Thomson Legal Publishing, 1994.

Mix. (Magazine published monthly by Cardinal Music Entertainment Group, 6400 Hollis St., #12, Emeryville, CA 94608. Tel: 800/888-5139. Fax: 510/653-5142) Technical sound production magazine for audio professionals (engineers, producers, and musicians), dealing with recording, audio for film, and audio for video. Sample articles: "Digital Multitrack Recorder Buyers Guide"; "In the Studio with the Rolling Stones"; "Sound for Terminator II."

Mondo 2000. (Magazine published quarterly by Fun City MegaMedia, P.O. Box 10171, Berkeley, CA 94709-0171. Tel: 510/845-9018. Fax: 510/649-9630. E-mail: subscriptions@mondo2000.com) Highly designed, image-rich, glossy "cyberzine" for the edge-crowd. Article samples: "Getting Gutenberg: Scott McCloud"; "Arguments for the Redemption of TV: An Interview with Video Pioneer Stephen Beck"; "William Latham's Computer Graphic Images" and "Hyperwebs: VR Update."

Morrison, Mike. *The Magic of Interactive Entertainment*. Indianapolis, IN.: Sams Publishing, a division of Prentice Hall Computer Publishing, 1994. Note: includes CD-ROM.

Multimedia and Technology Licensing Law Report. (Monthly 8-page newsletter published by Warren Gorham Lamont, 31 St. James Ave., Boston, MA 02116. Tel: 800/950-1205 or 617/423-2020. Fax: 617/451-0908) "Covers business and legal developments, and provides analysis on topics relevant to multimedia and technology licensing. Audience includes intellectual property attorneys and business professionals involved in media and technology transfer and licensing." Recent articles: "Licensing Patents and Know-How in the European Community"; "Avoiding Intellectual Property Misuse Problems and Antitrust Violations in Multimedia Licensing."

Multimedia Monitor. (Monthly 32-page newsletter published by Future Systems, Inc., P.O. Box 26, Falls Church, VA 22040-0026. Tel: 800/323-3472 or 703/241-1799. Fax: 703/532-0529. E-mail: CompuServe/71333,2753) "Since 1983, the newsletter of record for the interactive multimedia industry. Comprehensive source for worldwide news and analysis of interactive multimedia companies, technologies, applications and market trends." Future Systems also publishes the Multimedia Resources Catalog, with information on how to order specialty directories and reference books.

Multimedia Producer. (Magazine published monthly by Knowledge Industry Publications, 701 Westchester Ave., White Plains, NY 10604. Tel: 914/328-9157. Fax: 914/328-9093. Subscription E-mail: CompuServe/72123.353. Editorial E-mail: AppleLink/KIPII;AOL/CompPict) Magazine directed towards "creators and developers of multimedia productions." Its stated mission is to provide readers with "useful, up-to-date information and expert opinions on the use and capabilities of multimedia production tools." Each issue spotlights an important technology: digital signal compression, recordable media, RISC processors, etc. Sample articles: "Video Capture Boards: A Resource Directory"; "A Quick Take on QuickTime"; "Kiosk Design: Information Access for All."

Multimedia Strategist. (Newsletter published monthly by Leader Publications, a division of the New York Law Publishing Co., 345 Park Avenue South, New York, NY 10010. Tel: 212/545-6170. Fax: 212/696-1848) A new publication (since November 1994) featuring practical articles that focus on the law as it applies to multimedia. Sample articles: "Reuse of Magazines in Interactive Electronic Media"; "On-Line Services: Mechanics for Subscriber Agreements." Regular column: Technology Tips (vocabulary, etc.).

Multimedia Training Newsletter: Multimedia, Computer-Based Training and Performance Support. (Newsletter published bi-monthly by Multimedia Training Newsletter, 1623 Edmonton Ave., Sunnyvale, CA 94087-5202. Tel: 408/736-2335. Fax: 408/736-9425. E-mail: brandon_hall@cup.portal.com) Articles with success stories of best training programs in the country, getting started in multimedia training, hardware and software reviews, professional development, and interviews with industry experts. Upcoming events calendar.

NewMedia Magazine. (Magazine published monthly by HyperMedia Communications. Subscriptions through JCI Customer Service, P.O. Box 1771, Riverton, NJ 08077-7371. Tel: 609/786-4430) "Sent without charge for new media professionals in the United States, with subscriptions available for those who don't qualify." Read industry-wide for news and articles that cover recent developments in technology. Sponsor of annual NewMedia INVISION Awards for multimedia applications in the categories of entertainment, business, government, consumer, education, and community service. (Invision Awards Tel: 415/573-5170. Fax: 415/573-5131)

New York Times. (Daily newspaper with nationwide circulation. Tel: 800/631-2500) Coverage—especially on Monday—of converging industries of computers, telecommunications, entertainment, and telephony; multimedia business news.

Nimmer, Melville B., and David Nimmer. *Nimmer on Copyright: A Treatise on the Law of Literary, Musical and Artistic Property, and the Protection of Ideas.* Vol. 1. New York: Matthew Bender, Times Mirror Books, 1994.

NowMedia 1: An Interactive Guide to the Players, Politics and Production Issues of CD-ROM. (CD-ROM available through Millimeter magazine, New York. Tel: 800/326-4146. Fax: 216/696-6023. Produced by Millimeter, authored by SuperMac Interactive Systems, and designed by Marks Communications, 1994)

OnLine Design, California's Monthly for Electronic Design & Graphics. (Magazine published monthly by OnLine Design Publications, 2261 Market St. #331, San Francisco, CA 94114. Tel: 415/334-3800. Fax: 415/621-6760) Newsprint, oversized magazine for graphic designers.

Passman, Donald. *All You Need to Know About the Music Business.* New York: Simon and Schuster, 1994.

PC/Computing: How Multimedia Computers Work. (CD-ROM by Mindscape, Inc.; distributed by Ziff-Davis Press, 1994)

PC Magazine. (Magazine published monthly by Ziff-Davis Publishing, 1 Park Avenue, New York, NY 10016. Tel: 800/289-0429). General purpose trade magazine for users of DOS and Windows operating systems.

PC World. (Newspaper published monthly by IDG, 501 Second St., #600, San Francisco, CA 94107. Tel: 415/243-0500. Fax: 415/442-1891. E-mail: customer_service@pcworld.com) "The largest monthly computer publication written for business managers who buy and use personal computer products, to help them in hardware and software purchases, and to offer strategies to improve productivity." Sample articles: "Cover Story/Multimedia—Best CDs of '94, Best CD-ROM Drives and Sound Boards"; "Special Report: Multimedia—Beating the Multimedia Blues."

Peppers, Don, and Martha Rogers. *The One-to-One Future: Building Relationships One at a Time*. New York: Currency/Doubleday, 1993.

Post. (Magazine published monthly by Testa Communications, 25 Willowdale Ave., Port Washington, NY 11050. Tel: 516/767-2500. Fax: 516/767-9335) An "applications" magazine focusing on people and projects, covering all aspects of post-production, audio, video, animation, and film. Sample articles: "Posting for Interactive Media—Post Pros Lend Their Expertise to the World of CD-ROM Audio for Multimedia."

Print. (Magazine published bi-monthly by RC Publications, 3200 Tower Oaks Blvd., Rockville, MD 20852. Tel: 800/222-2654. Fax: 301/984-3203) "America's graphic design magazine," devoted to graphic design, illustration, commercial photography, and advertising art. Quarterly feature column with color illustrations: Digital Soup.

Publishers Weekly. (Magazine published weekly by Cahners Publishing, 249 W. 17th St., New York, NY 10011. Subscription Tel: 800/278-2991. Fax: 310/978-6901) The magazine of the book publishing business, with reviews and regular columns on technology and new media.

Rand, Paul. *Design, Form, and Chaos*. New Haven, CT: Yale University Press, 1993.

___ . *A Designer's Art*. New Haven, CT: Yale University Press, 1985.

Raysman, Richard, et al. *Multimedia Law*. New York: Law Journal Seminars Press, 1994.

Red Herring: The Technology Strategic & Financial Monthly. (Magazine published monthly by Flipside Communications, 550 Bryant St., Suite 950, San Francisco, CA 94103. Editorial telephone: 415/865-2277. Subscriptions: x 212 or x 202. Fax: 415/865-2280) Financial and business publication aimed at venture capitalists that covers high-tech communications and entertainment. Each issue focuses on a different subject: networking, education, client server industry, digital Hollywood.

Rheingold, Howard. *The Virtual Community: Homesteading on the Electronic Frontier*. Reading, MA: Addison-Wesley, 1993.

Rose, Lance, and Jonathan Wallace. *Syslaw*, 2nd ed. Winona, MN: LOL Productions, 1992. Distributed by PC Information Group, 1126 East Broadway, Winona, MN 55987.

Rosenberg, Peter D., *Patent Law Fundamentals*. Vol. 1. Deerfield, IL: Clark Boardman Callaghan, Thomson Legal Publishing, 1994.

Scott, Michael E. *Multimedia Law and Practice*. New York: Prentice Hall, 1994.

Sheff, David. *Game Over, How Nintendo Conquered the World*. New York: Vintage Books, 1994.

Shemel, Sidney, and M. William Krasilovsky. *The Business of Music*. New York: Watson-Guptill, Billboard Books, 1990.

SMPTE Journal. (Professional journal published monthly by the Society of Motion Picture and Television Engineers, 595 West Hartsdale Ave., White Plains, NY 10607. Tel: 916/761-1100. Fax: 914/761-3115) Technical journal covering standards in traditional as well as digital video and audio. Recent articles on optical disc solution for digital video storage, multistandard image sequence storage, displays and colorimetry for future television, and digital television system scalability and interoperability.

Tufte, Edward. *Envisioning Information*. Cheshire, CT: Graphics Press, 1990.

___. *The Visual Display of Quantitative Information*. Cheshire, CT: Graphics Press, 1983.

Videography. (Magazine published by P.S.N. Publications, 2 Park Ave., #1820, New York, NY Tel: 212/799-1919. Fax: 212/213-3484) Monthly technical journal for video production professionals, with features, news, commentary, and reviews. Sample articles: "Annual Special Report: Video and the Mac"; "Shooting the Chief: The Dos and Don'ts of Interviewing Corporate Leaders."

Wall Street Journal. (Newspaper, five days a week. Tel: 800/568-7625) Regular coverage of the converging computer/telco/cable/interactive TV/entertainment industries from a business perspective.

White, Ron. *PC/Computing: How Computers Work*. Emeryville, CA: Ziff-Davis, 1994. Note: includes CD-ROM.

Wired. (Magazine published monthly by Wired Ventures, 544 Second St., San Francisco, CA 94107-1427. Tel: 415/904-0660. Fax: 415/904-0669. E-mail: info@wired.com) Day-Glo–designed magazine that focuses on the cultural and social implications of digital technology, with a regular column by MIT's Nicholas Negroponte, news section whose layout attempts to echo interactivity, and thought-piece features by futurists and pundits. Sample articles: "Triumph of the Plastic People," by Bruce Sterling (Czech hippies with cultural authority); "Ziff Happens," by David Armstrong (about publishing magnate Bill Ziff); "Designer as Engineer," by Rochelle Garner (focus on David Kelley).

Wurman, Richard Saul. "Hats." *Design Quarterly* 145 (1989).

___. *Information Anxiety: What to Do When Information Doesn't Tell You What You Need to Know*. New York: Doubleday, 1989. New York: Bantam Books, 1990.

APPENDIX III

Conferences

ACM Multimedia Conference and Exposition
(Produced by Danieli & O'Keefe Associates, Sudbury, MA. Annually in the fall, alternating between the east and west coasts. Tel: 800/524-1851. Fax: 508/443-4715. E-mail: Reg.DOK@Notes.compuserve.com) Multimedia component of the annual meeting of the Association for Computing Machines: "Conference features both the media content and the technical side of multimedia, through panels, papers, courses, workshops, videos and exhibits. . . . Offers information about research, emerging programming technologies, engineering methodologies, and an exhibit of the latest in interactive multimedia." Arts Night celebration. (See also ACM SIGGRAPH.)

ACM SIGGRAPH
(ACM, Special Interest Group on Graphics. Annually in July/Aug., alternating between Orlando and Los Angeles. Recorded conference information: 312/321-6830. To speak with someone in New York, Tel: 212/869-7440. Fax: 312/231-6876) Premier gathering in the computer graphics industry, with a large exhibition of new products, plus technical papers and general conference sessions. Best of computer graphics of the previous year featured in an annual film and video show, available on video. (See also ACM Multimedia.)

CD-ROM Expo & Conference
(Mitch Hall Associates, Dedham, MA. Annually in September in Boston. Tel: 617/361-0817. Fax: 617/361-9074) "Conference sessions and exhibits on the latest in CD-ROM and digital publishing technology. Hands-on, how-to track for CD-ROM creators and producers."

CES®—Consumer Electronics Show
(Sponsored by the Electronic Industries Association, Arlington, VA. CES is held each January in Las Vegas. Tel: 703/907-7600. Fax: 703/907-7601) "Enormous international trade show (more than one million square feet of exhibits and more than 100,000 attendees), featuring product categories covering all consumer electronics: audio, video, mobile, computers, electronic gaming, telephones and wireless personal communications." Special exhibit: Multimedia Pavilion.

CGDC—Computer Game Developers Conference™
(Computer Game Developers Conference, 555 Bryant St., Suite 330, Palo Alto, CA 94301. Annually in spring in Santa Clara, CA. Tel: 415/948-2432. Fax: 415/948-2744) "Academic-style conference with associated trade show and job fair, aimed at designers, programmers, artists and animators, composers and producers and anyone who creates electronic entertainment." It bills itself as "THE premier conference for interactive entertainment."

Convergence™: Interactive Television Conference
(Produced by Multichannel CommPerspectives, Denver. Annually in the fall in California (with an exposition) and in the winter on the East Coast. Tel: 303/393-7449. Fax: 303/329-3453) "Covers all aspects of the development and delivery of interactive television, including technology, competition to be the service provider, trials, shopping services, interactive advertising, games and navigation systems." Audience: people from cable television, telephone, computer hardware or software, multimedia, program production, new media, publishing, advertising, and retailing businesses.

Digital Hollywood: The Media Marketplace
(American Expositions, New York City. Annually in February in Beverly Hills. Tel: 212/226-4141. Fax: 212/226-4983) Conference brings together "producers, distributors

and title developers, tools and technology providers, production houses, and the communications, technology and financial communities." Sponsors Digital Hollywood Awards and Digital Hollywood Awards for Technical Excellence.

Digital World

(Seybold Seminars, SOFTBANK Expositions. Annually in June in Los Angeles. Tel: 800/488-2883 or 415/578-6900. Fax: 415/525-0199) "Gathering for leaders in digital media and communications industries," covering industry trends from the Internet to the cable industry, interactive TV to CD-ROMs. Attended by executives, artists, and production professionals from the publishing, advertising, video, film, computer, and interactive media industries. Free mini-conference on the exhibit floor: the Creative Cafe, co-sponsored by the Writers Guild of America.

E3—Electronic Entertainment Expo

(Co-produced by Infotainment World, San Mateo, CA, and Mitch Hall Associates, Dedham, MA. Annually in May in Los Angeles. Tel: 8617-361-8000). Large buying event for vendors and retailers of interactive media and games. "E3 showcases a full spectrum of applications, including multimedia, edutainment, reference, special interest and virtual reality."

Hollywood 2000: The Future of Home Entertainment

(Advanstar Associates, Santa Ana, CA. Annually in October in Los Angeles. Tel: 800/854-3112, ext. 422. Tel: 714/513-8400. Fax: 714/513-8481) Addresses business opportunities from the perspective of the film and television community.

intermedia: The International Conference & Exposition on Multimedia and CD-ROM™

(Reed Exhibition Co., Norwalk, CT. Annually in late winter / early spring in San Francisco. Tel: 203/840-5634. Fax: 203/840-9634) Since 1985, show for interactive product designers, hardware and software developers, producers and integrators, and distributors from the publishing, entertainment, communications and computing industries. Seminar tracks for technology, creative development, business and multimedia markets (including education, games and entertainment).

Internet World

(Mecklermedia, Westport, CT. Multiple international venues. Tel: 800/632-5537 or 203/226-9676. E-mail: iwconf@mecklermedia.com. Internet: http://www.mecklerweb.com/shows) Internet publishing, legal, finance, technical and industry/commerce tricks; plus sessions on how to create your own home page with HTML.

Macromedia International Users Conference

(Sponsored by Macromedia, San Francisco, produced by Reed Expositions, Norwalk, CT. Annually in the fall in San Francisco. Tel: 800/287-7141 or 203/840-5660. Fax: 203/840-9860) Highlights multimedia product development, technology, publishing, marketing, and business strategies for developers, graphic designers, publishers, and other Macromedia software customers. Seminars, plus hands-on training sessions at various skill levels in how to use Macromedia products—Director, Authorware Professional, FreeHand, Action!, SoundEdit16, and 3-D products. People's Choice awards based on multimedia productions featured in kiosks in a multimedia gallery.

MacWorld Exposition

(Mitch Hall Associates, Dedham, MA. January in San Francisco; August in Boston; October in Toronto. Tel: 617/361-8000) "An international exposition and conference featuring hundreds of the latest Macintosh products and services for home and business use. Conference sessions and exhibit floor vendors discuss products for multimedia, PowerMac, business education, entertainment, networking and CAD/CAM."

MultiComm: The Conference & Exposition on Multimedia Solutions for Business and Education

(University of British Columbia, Vancouver, British Columbia, Canada. Annually in November in Vancouver. Tel: 604/822-0692. Fax: 604/822-9826. E-mail: multicomm@cce.ubc.ca) "Conference designed to bring business, education and the arts together in a more generalist environment through plenary, concurrent, panel presentations and a small technology exposition. Each year a specific theme is chosen." Cascadia Awards are given in separate categories to professionals, amateurs, and students for multimedia production excellence.

Multimedia Expo East/Digital New York and Multimedia Expo West/Digital San Francisco

(Produced by American Expositions, New York, NY. Sponsored by the Multimedia Development Group and the International Interactive Communications Society. Annually in the fall in the San Francisco Bay Area and in the spring in New York City. Tel: 212/226-4141. Fax: 212/226-4983) Three-day conference with 300 speakers, focusing on the convergence of the communications, technology, and entertainment industries, and the corporate use of multimedia.

Multimedia for Publishers

(AIC Conferences, New York, NY. Annually in January in New York City. Tel: 212/952-1899. Fax: 212/248-7374) Focuses on business components of multimedia, interactive television, and the information superhighway: "Presentations by and for top-level executives in publishing, software development, and multimedia production."

NAB MultiMedia World

(National Association of Broadcasters, Washington, DC. Annually in March or April in Las Vegas. Tel: 202/429-5300. Fax: 202/775-3520) "Conference presents workable business models for interactive television and compares the leading operating systems that will deliver interactive multimedia." Seminars from sales/marketing, engineering, legal, and management perspectives. Exhibits of multimedia developers and manufacturers. Technical panels on digital TV production.

NATPE—National Association of Television Program Executives

(2425 Olympic Blvd. #550E, Santa Monica, CA 90404. Show held annually in January in Las Vegas. Tel: 310/453-4440. Fax: 310/453-5258) International conference and exposition—"programming and software marketplace"—for television professionals. Presentations on Hollywood, cable, "the new media revolution," "on-line meets prime time," and "making money with interactive advertising."

NetWorld+Interop

(SOFTBANK Expos & Conference Co., Foster City, CA. Annually in Las Vegas, Atlanta, Tokyo, and European cities. Tel: 800/488-2883. Fax: 415/525-0194) A conference focusing on interoperability and connectivity, "providing an educational source for networking challenges in LAN, WAN and enterprise networking."

New Media Expo
(The Interface Group, Needham, MA. Annually in February/March in Los Angeles, CA. Tel: 800/325-8850 or 617/449-6600. Fax: 617/449-2674) Focusing on "the business of interactive information," the conference addresses a wide range of industries: "content providers, technology enablers and information transporters," with program tracks for advertising and sales, education, production, information highway, new media communications, and business applications, among others. Showcases the Interactive Advertising and Media Awards (sponsored by *Advertising Age* magazine), with consumer and business-to-business categories from on-line to kiosk to interactive television. (Awards tel: 800/378-7450)

Online Developers Conference
(Jupiter Communications, New York. Annually in September in San Francisco. Tel: 800/650-7272 or 212/941-9252. Fax: 212/941-7376) "Brings together players from the online industry—content providers, executives from the commercial online services, investment bankers, publishers and teleco managers—who know how to build and promote efficient, compelling and profitable online applications."

Seybold San Francisco/Seybold Boston
(Seybold Seminars, SOFTBANK Exposition, Foster City, CA. Annually in September in San Francisco and in March in Boston. Tel: 800/488-2883. Fax: 415/525-0199) "The world's largest and most comprehensive publishing and graphics event." Attendees include electronic communicators, printers, photographers, graphic designers, publishers, and software developers. Topics include publishing on the Internet, multimedia design tools, workflow automation, and color management.

SIGGRAPH. See ACM SIGGRAPH

TEDSELL
(TED Conferences, Newport, RI. First conference to be held in February 1996 in Monterey, CA. Tel: 401/848-2299. Fax: 401/848-2599. E-mail: Wurman@media.mit.edu) Sponsored by Richard Saul Wurman of the TED conferences (Technology, Education and Design), this new conference focuses on high-tech approaches to marketing and addresses "the way that goods, services, and information can be brought together and how the the process of purchasing and repurchasing will be affected and understood." Focus is on these industry tracks: auto and electronics, real estate and finance, consumer goods and food, travel and leisure, entertainment and sports, healthcare and insurance, and learning and information. Audience is described as "need-to-know" corporate leaders.

Video Expo/Image World
(Knowledge Industry Publications, White Plains, NY, with *AV Video* magazine. Annually in Sept./Oct. in New York City and periodically in other U.S. cities. Tel: 800/800-5474 or 914/328-9157. Fax: 914/328-0649) For video professionals, art/creative directors, graphic designers, production engineers, C.G. artists, sound and lighting personnel, producers, directors, and scriptwriters; advertising managers; corporate communications directors; CATV and broadcast studio production specialists; AV managers; marketing professionals; trainers; directors of photography; imaging center professionals; service bureau professionals; videographers.

Western Cable Show: The Global Telecommunications Expo

(California Cable TV Association, Oakland, CA. Annually in Nov./Dec. in Anaheim, CA. Tel: 510/428-2225. Fax: 510/428-0151) Exhibits and panels showcasing the latest in technology, regulatory issues, and new programming services. While traditionally a cable show, it is also attended by people from computer and telephone companies. Sponsors technology demonstrations at shows stressing the interoperability of the various systems— for example, between television and on-line.

W.R.I.T.E.—Writers' Retreat on Interactive Technology & Equipment

(University of British Columbia Continuing Studies, Vancouver, British Columbia. Annually in June in Vancouver. Tel: 604/822-0692. Fax: 604/822-9826. E-mail: write@cce.ubc.ca) Three-day conference for writers, focusing on the products and content of the emerging electronic publishing industry and multimedia: "The spirit of WRITE is to search for ideas and opportunities for writers to create literature and information-based products for CD-ROM, multimedia programs, interactive TV, the Internet and other 'information highways.' WRITE addresses the special needs of all writers . . . who will be the creators of content for interactive digital products and services."

APPENDIX IV

Professional Associations

ACM SIGGRAPH—Association for Computing Machinery, Special Interest Group on Computer Graphics

(Contact national office for local chapters: 1515 Broadway, New York, NY 10036. Tel: 212/626-0500. Fax: 212/944-1316. E-mail: acmhelp@acm.org) "An interdisciplinary community interested in research, technology, and applications in computer graphics and interactive techniques. Members include developers and users from the technical/academic, business, and art communities." Annual conference alternates between Anaheim, CA, and Orlando, FL. SIGGRAPH Video Review series available of state-of-the-art computer graphics.

AECT—Association for Educational Communications and Technology

(Contact national office for local chapters: 1025 Vermont Ave., N.W., #820 Washington, DC 20005. Tel: 202/347-7834. Fax: 202/347-7839) "The only national and international organization dedicated to the improvement of instruction through the full range of media and technology."

American Association of Advertising Agencies

(666 Third Ave., 13th Floor, New York, NY 10017. Tel: 212/682-2500. Fax: 212/682-8391) Also known as "The 4As," the association "fosters professional development among advertising agencies, and encourages the highest creative and business standards." It also serves as "an advocate of advertising, studying the ways in which it contributes to the economy and society. . . ."

American Association of Museums

(1225 Eye Street, N.W.,Washington, DC 20005. Tel: 202/289-1818) Publishes bi-monthly journal, *Museum News.*

ASIFA—Association Internationale du Film d'Animation

(General correspondence: ASIFA Central, c/o Stay Tooned! Gallery, 220 South. Cook St., Barrington, IL 60010; Membership: c/o Marie Cenkner, 1463 Glencoe Ave., Highland Park, IL 60035) International volunteer-based association, chartered in France, with six regional U.S. chapters "devoted to the encouragement and dissemination of film animation as an art and communication form." Maintains an employment database and annually publishes the School List, describing animation programs in schools around the world. Chapters in New York City (212/258-7727), Hollywood (818/842-8330), San Francisco (415/386-1004), Washington, DC (301/593-9178), and Portland, OR (503/280-5840, ext. 203).

ASTD—American Society for Training and Development

(Contact national office for local chapters: 1640 King St., Box 1443, Alexandria, VA 22313-2043. Tel: 703/683-8100. Fax: 703/683-8103) "The world's largest professional association in the field of employer-based training . . . representing professionals such as managers, human resource specialists, designers, technical trainers, instructors, evaluators, consultants, researchers and educators." Sponsor of two annual conferences, plus, for a supplemental fee, an on-line service called ASTD Online. It has electronic bulletin boards under various headings (for example, instructional technology, total quality management), where comments can be posted, as well as an on-line literature database, in which keyword searches call up abstracts for subscribers. Internet access is available. (E-mail for Information Center: ASTDIC@capcon.net)

Austin Area Multimedia Alliance

(13809-B Panorama Dr., Austin, TX 78732. E-Mail: Subscription information aama@bga.com—type "aama info" in text of message. Internet: http://www.sig.net/~aama/aamahome.html)

Austin Software Council & Austin Technology Incubator

(8920 Business Park Dr., Suite 150, Austin, TX 78759-7405. Tel: 512/794-9994)

Computer Law Association

(3028 Javier Rd., #402, Fairfax, VA 22031. Tel: 703/560-7747) Has programs about multimedia and also a newsletter with relevant articles.

IICS—International Interactive Communications Society

(Contact national office for local chapters: IICS Executive Office, 14657 SW Teal Blvd., Suite 119, Beaverton, OR 97007. Tel: 503/579-4427. Fax: 503/579-6272. Internet: For more information and membership benefits, contact iics@netcom.com—enter subject: Send brochure. E-mail: 70274,1075@compuserve.com and mltimedia@AOL.com) IICS's emphasis is on the people who create multimedia and who provide the services to support the emerging industry. Membership is drawn from the allied fields of training, education, computer science, animation, graphic arts, instructional design, multimedia production, music, video, and communications. According to its mission statement, IICS aims to "promote the use of interactive communications . . . encourage the development of standards . . . and pool information and research on the use of interactive communications." With monthly meetings, it provides a forum for the presentation of new products, systems, and ideas, with the intent of increasing the skills, knowledge, and professional standards of its members.

IMA—International Multimedia Association

(48 Maryland Ave. #202, Annapolis, MD 21401-8011. Tel: 410/626-1380. Fax: 410/263-0590) The mission statement notes that the IMA "has become the key provider of forums advancing the development of multimedia technologies and applications in order to establish a strong and profitable marketplace." The emphasis is on "reducing barriers to widespread use," such as cross-platform incompatibility, and unresolved issues about intellectual property law. Membership is drawn from multimedia companies, not from individuals. (Job bank: 410/268-2100, document #1410; Multimedia Recruiters, Tel: 214/ 490-9171 or E-mail: multim_usa@aol.com)

International MIDI Association

(23634 Emelita St., Woodland Hills, CA 91367. Tel: 818/598-0088. Fax: 818/346-8578) Association for electronic musicians. Provides MIDI "spec" documents to members.

MDG —Multimedia Development Group

(2601 Mariposa St., San Francisco, CA 94110. Tel: 415/553-2300. Fax: 415/553-2403. Internet: info@mdg.org) "A market development association that serves the business and professional needs of the multimedia community." Membership is made up of individuals and approximately 500 companies, half of which are multimedia developers, the remainder of which are technology companies and professional service providers. The mission statement emphasizes "fostering the growth of multimedia creative developers, because we recognize the market growth for the industry will be driven by the availability of content-rich, easy-to-use, interactive software that they will create." Seminars, workshops, library, electronic bulletin board service.

Museum Computer Network

(8720 Georgia Ave., #501, Silver Spring, MD 20912. E-mail: mdevine@cni.org) Publishes *Spectra*, c/o Suzanne Quigley, Detroit Institute of Arts, 5200 Woodward Ave., Detroit, MI 48202. E-mail: Squigle@cms.cc.wayne.edu.

NSPI—The National Society for Performance and Instruction

(1300 L St., #1250, N.W., Washington, DC 20005. Tel: 202-408-7969. Fax: 202-408-7972) Organization for corporate trainers that tracks developments in multimedia and computer-based training.

New York New Media Association

(Tel: 212-459-4644. Fax 212-682-5869. E-mail: nynma@AOL.com) Organization to promote the development of multimedia within the greater metropolitan area, its monthly Cybersuds meeting is "a chance to meet other people in the New York media community in a casual atmosphere to exchange ideas, business opportunities and gossip."

Software Publishers Association

(1730 M St., N.W., Suite 700, Washington, DC 20036. Tel: 202-452-1600. Fax: 202-223-8756) Founded in 1984 to promote the interests of the personal computer software industry. Membership includes publishers and developers of business, education, productivity, and leisure microcomputer software. Tracks quarterly CD-ROM sales numbers, provides on-line services, and undertakes other research.

Multimedia Educational Resources

New programs are being announced regularly as many traditional schools and private companies begin to offer resources to meet the marketplace demand for multimedia training and education. This list represents a sampling of what is currently available. If you have additions, please E-mail to: <MMwriter@AOL.com>

North America / West

Academy of Art College, Computer Education Center
(79 New Montgomery St., San Francisco, CA 94105. Tel: 800/544-ARTS or 415/274-2200) Degree programs in computer arts and digital media. B.F.A., M.F.A., or certificate programs in graphic design, illustration, computer arts.

American Film Institute, Professional Development Division
(2021 Western Avenue, Los Angeles, CA 90027. Tel: 213/856-7690) AFI offers a certificate of completion in imaging, digital video, and multimedia. Courses include 2-D and 3-D production, Photoshop, desktop editing, and nonlinear storytelling. In addition, AFI regularly offers a series of Computer Media Salons.

BAVC—Bay Area Video Coalition
(1111 17th St., San Francisco, CA 94107. Tel: 415/861-3282. Fax: 415/861-4316) In addition to hands-on courses in off-line and on-line, traditional tape editing, and digital video editing, BAVC offers workshops in Internet, multimedia, and digitizing video for CD-ROM.

CCAC—California College of Arts and Crafts
(5212 Broadway, Oakland, CA 94618-1487. Tel: 510/653-8118. Fax: 415/621-2396 [attention David Bolt]. E-mail: ccac@AOL.com) An ISDN line allows video conferencing into "image shop" labs that teach multimedia and graphic design software applications. CCAC is in the midst of creating a curriculum that integrates new media technology within the schools of Fine Art, Design, and Architecture. By the end of the decade, CCAC hopes to have this new media interdisciplinary program as a matriculating degree.

Center for Electronic Art
(950 Battery Street, Suite 3D, San Francisco, CA 94111. Tel. 415/956-6500. E-mail: info@cea.edu) Classes offered include Director, HyperCard, production tools, and 10-day intensive workshops. Labs with PowerMacs and PCs.

College of Marin, Digital Village
(835 College Ave., Kentfield, CA 94904. Tel: 415/382-7700) Over a dozen courses are offered, ranging from Internet to Macromedia Director.

Computer Arts Institute
(310 Townsend St. #230, San Francisco, CA 94107. Tel: 415/546-5242. Fax: 415/546-5237) Founded in 1987, with courses in multimedia, video game animation, and computer painting.

Media Alliance
(814 Mission St., Suite 805, San Francisco, CA 94103. Tel: 415/546-6491. Fax: 415/546-6218. E-mail: ma@igc.org) Nonprofit center formed to "change the way media does business" offers media (writing) and computer skill classes (hands-on Mac basics, Internet, Photoshop, Illustrator, Director). Jobsfile and MacLab.

Pacific Imaging Center

(535 Lipoa Parkway, Suite #201, Kihei, Maui 96753 Hawaii. Tel: 800/280-MAUI. Fax: 808/875-6899. E-Mail: pacimage@maui.com) Courses in multimedia graphic and design software programs, networking for graphic design and production. Also, programs for children to learn basic computer graphics. Annual imaging conference and hands-on training seminars. Supercomputer available for animation.

San Francisco Digital Media Center

(3435 Army St., suite 222, San Francisco, CA 94110. Tel: 415/824-9394. Fax: 415/824-9396. E-mail: sfmdg@well.com) Nonprofit community arts production center offers production and World Wide Web courses and special events at Joe's Digital Diner. The center focuses on teaching nontechnical people how to use multimedia to tell personal histories and family stories.

SFSU—San Francisco State University, Multimedia Studies Center

(Downtown campus, 2nd Floor, 425 Market St., San Francisco, CA 94105. Tel: 415/904-7700. Fax: 415/904-7760) Offers the most extensive lineup of multimedia courses in Northern California, including an associate's degree in multimedia. Classes range from introductory courses to advanced technical training.

UCLA—University of California, Los Angeles Extension, Entertainment Studies

(10995 LeConte Avenue, Los Angeles, CA 90024. Tel: 310/825-9971) Program offers a variety of classes for both beginners and advanced learners. The Department of Engineering Information Systems and Technical Management offers workshops in CD-ROM development and user-oriented interface design, among others. (Tel: 310/825-1047. Fax: 310/206-2815. E-mail mhenness@unex.ucla.edu)

UCSC—University of California Extension, Santa Cruz

(courses also in Santa Clara, Monterey, and San Benito). (740 Front St., Suite 155, Santa Cruz, CA 95060. Tel: 800/660-8639 inside California; 408/472-6600 outside state) Certificate programs in graphics and video arts. Courses in multimedia authoring, graphics, and writing courses; video and graphics; and video engineering. Technology Education Certificate program in the "use and integration of technology into instructional programs."

University of Southern California, School of Cinema-Television

(University Park, Los Angeles, CA 90089-2211. Tel: 213/740-2911. Fax: 213/740-7682, Attention Student Affairs) Two undergraduate multimedia classes are offered: interactive entertainment and multimedia, and writing and designing for interactive entertainment. Also, graduate program in Film, Video, and Computer Animation (M.F.A.). Interactive lab facility available.

North America / Northwest

911 Media Arts Center

(117 Yale Avenue North, Seattle, WA 98109. Tel: 206/682-6552. Fax: 206/682-7422) Nonprofit, year-round, full-service media arts center that holds workshops on how to make film, video, and multimedia. Sample offerings: a survey course on how to make a multimedia title; series on how to create a Web page. They often hold screenings of artists' work and provide low-cost access to film and video editing equipment.

North America / Midwest

Art Institute of Chicago
(37 Wabash Ave., Chicago, IL 60603. Tel: 312/443-3600. Fax: 312/899-1840) Offers courses in computer animation and graphic arts.

Columbia College
(600 S. Michigan, Chicago, IL 60605. Tel: 312/663-1600. Fax: 312/663-1568) Offers a BA in multimedia and 30 different courses including computer programming, interactive programming, and authoring production as well as design.

North America / East

Fashion Institute of Technology, Division of Continuing Education, State University of New York
(Seventh Ave. at 27th St., New York, NY 10001-5992. Tel: 212/760-7650) courses in computer graphics and animation, multimedia computing for advertising and communications.

NYU—New York University Center for Digital Multimedia
(719 Broadway, 12th Floor, New York, NY 10003. Tel: 212/998-3374. Fax: 212/995-4122. URL: http://found.cs.nyu.edu/) Founded in 1993, the center offers seminar series, hands-on lab courses, research activities, and custom corporate courses. Staff is drawn from NYU's compute, arts, business, and education schools.

NYU—New York University Interactive Telecommunications Program, Titsch School of the Arts
(721 Broadway, 4th Floor, New York, NY 10003-6807. Tel: 212/998-1888) Offers a master's degree program and a wide variety of postgraduate interactive media courses.

NYU—New York University School for Continuing Education, Information Technologies Institute
(48 Cooper Square, Room 104, New York, NY 10003. Tel: 212/998-7190. Fax: 212/995-3550) Offers certificate in multimedia and courses in graphic design, desktop tools, presentation software, and marketing applications.

Pratt Institute
(200 Willoughby Ave., Brooklyn, NY 11205. Tel: 800/331-0834 or 718/636-3669) Bachelor of Fine arts program in computer graphics includes courses in animation, video production, electronic and interactive databases, and interface design.

Rhode Island School of Design Continuing Education
(2 College Ave., Providence, RI 02903-2787. Tel: 401/454-6200. Fax: 401/454-6218) Director programming and animation classes, plus workshops on planning and production.

School of Visual Arts
(209 E. 23rd St., New York, NY 01110-3994. Tel: 212/679-7350) Multimedia courses offered in the Computer Art Department, along with animation and fine arts. Courses in M.F.A. program include 3-D modeling and animation, electronic imaging, designing interfaces, graphics programming, interactivity, HyperCard, and Lingo scripting.

North America / South

Florida Atlantic University, College of Engineering, Department of Computer Science and Engineering
(777 Glades Rd., Boca Raton, FL 33431. Tel: 407/367-2766. Fax: 407/367-2800. E-mail: helene@cse.fau.edu) M.Sc. and Ph.D. in computer science and engineering that include

courses in introduction to multimedia systems, multimedia system design, and video processing in multimedia systems. New Multimedia Laboratory opened in 1995 to support research and development.

FIT—Florida Institute of Technology.

(150 West University Blvd., Melbourne, FL 32901. Tel: 407/768-8000, ext. 8020) Multimedia courseware under development in the science education and computer science departments (programming, software engineering, etc.)

Georgia State University Dept. of Communications

(One Park Place South, Office 1040, University Plaza, Atlanta, GA 30303. Tel: 404/651-3200. Fax: 404/651-1409)

Georgia Tech

(225 North Ave. Northwest, Atlanta, GA 30332. Tel: 404/894-2547. Fax: 404/853-0117) Offers over twenty continuing education courses, including multimedia production basics and Director, Photoshop, and Premiere, as well as marketing and legal issues.

Canada

UBC—University of British Columbia, Continuing Studies

(5997 Iona Dr., Vancouver, BC V6T 1Z1. Fax: 604/222-5249. E-mail: compureg@cce.ubc.edu) Multimedia studies certificate program with courses in design, audio, authoring, and digital video editing, plus multimedia in education and training. Also courses in Internet tools and marketing.

INTERNATIONAL EDUCATIONAL RESOURCES

(The plus symbol before a telephone country code indicates the need for an international calling code. Calling from the United States, the international code is 011.) Thanks to Peter R. Cook, Grolier Electronic Publishing, U.K., for Europe listings.

United Kingdom

ARThouse

(5 Aston Quay, Temple Bar, Dublin 2, Ireland. Tel: (+353-1) 67-77-81. Fax: (+353-1) 67-77-857. E-mail: user@arthouse.internet-eireann.ie) Innovative media center for the arts providing training and education programs for artists and the wider cultural community.

Dublin Institute of Technology

(14 Upper Mount St., Dublin 2, Ireland. Tel: (+353-1) 611-133. Fax: (+353-1) 762-608) Courses in interactive multimedia taught in a new center with a specially designed communications department and computer laboratory linked by high-speed digital networks.

The London Institute—London College of Printing

(Elephant and Castle, London, SE1 6SB. Tel: (+44-10-71) 735-8484. Fax: (+44-1-71) 735-0759) The largest university-level institution of art and design in Europe. The institute's School of Media teaches in the European master of arts program in interactive media, and has launched a degree program for European master of arts in media technology administration.

Middlesex University

(White Heart Lane, London, N17 8HR. Tel: (+44-1-81) 362-5000. Fax: (+44-1-81) 365-1772) Has been conducting pioneering work in image synthesis and computer animation for over twenty years. The university's Centre for Advanced Studies in Computer-Aided Art and Design is a national center carrying out research, education, and training. The university validates the European M.A. in image synthesis and computer animation.

The Royal College of Art

(Kensington Gore, London SW7 2EU. Tel: (+44-1-71) 584-5020. Fax: (+44-1-71) 225-1487) Unique in the world as a postgraduate university of art and design, the college is a leader in inter-active media design and computing, and validates the European M.A. in interactive multimedia.

University of Wolverhampton, Interactive Media Education

(Stafford St., Wolverhampton VW1 1SB, United Kingdom. Tel: (+44-0902) 322471/321000. Fax: (+44-0902) 322739. E-mail: LE1812@WLV.AC.UK) Multimedia coursework.

Continental Europe

Ensci—Les Ateliers

(Ecole Nationale Supérieure Création Industrielle, Les Ateliers, 48 Rue St. Sabin, 75011 Paris, France. Tel: (+33-1) 49-23-12-12. Fax: (+33-1) 43-38-51-36) The French national school of industrial design, with long experience in computer-aided design. It is in the forefront of the development of interactive information products using CD technology, and one of the centers teaching the master of arts in interactive multimedia.

Hogeschool voor de Kunsten Utrecht

(Centrum voor Kunst & Media Management, Maliebaan 81-87, Postbus 1520, 3500 BM Utrecht, The Netherlands. Tel: (+31-30) 332501. Fax: (+31-30) 367313) The largest art and design "monotechnic" in the Netherlands. Its faculty of Art, Media and Technology specializes in digital video production and postproduction, digital sound and music, image syntheses and animation, interaction design, and multimedia. The faculty teaches all of CITE's European master's degrees.

Universidad de las Isles Baleares, Spain

(Son Lledo. Campus Universitari, Ctra. de Valldemossa, Km. 7'5, 07071 Palma, Spain. Tel: (+34-71) 17-30-00 or 01. Fax: (+34-71) 17-28-52 or 17-30-69) An established European leader in computer image-making and interactive multimedia. The Department of Mathematics and Computer Science has major research and development projects and teaches interactive multimedia and image synthesis/computer animation at the master's level. Many students are festival prize-winners.

Asia

National Institute of Multimedia Education

(6-201, 3-53 Takinogawa, Kita-ku, Tokyo 114, Japan. Tel: (+81-43) 276-1111. Fax: (+81-43) 275-5117)

Australia

University of New South Wales, College of fine Arts, Multimedia Centre

(PO Box 259, Paddington, New South Wales, 2021 Australia. Tel: (+61-2) 385-0888. Fax: (+61-2) 385-0706. E-mail: e.gidney@unsw.edu.au) The college offers courses at the under-graduate and postgraduate levels in art and design, and has been a test site for "broadband multimedia applications development." It also runs intensive short training courses in mul-timedia and imaging to fulfill the need for "more visually literate content creators."

Other

Club d'Investissement Media and The Minister de la Culture et de la Francophonie pro-duces a guide to European Training Programs for 16 countries. (Club d'Investissement Media, 45, Avenue de Europe 94360, Bry-sur-Marne, France. Tel: (+33-1) 49 83 28 63. Fax: (+33-1) 49-83-26-26)

INDEX

ABC-TV, 7
Access, 57, 192
Actors, 8, 46, 144–145, 147
ADDIE model, 202
Adobe Illustrator, 6, 35, 208
Adobe Photoshop, 6, 35, 45,
    57, 60, 93, 94, 96, 208,
    224
Adobe Premiere, 6, 35, 45,
    93, 96, 208
Advertising, 124–132
Advertising Age, 132
Affinity advertising, 126
AimTech CBT Express, 201
AimTech IconAuthor, 201
Alias Upfront, 45
Allen Communication Quest,
    192, 201
Allison, Graham, 196
*All You Need to Know About
    the Music Business*
    (Passman), 180
American Association of
    Advertising Agencies,
    132
American Association of
    Museums, 187
American Society for Training
    and Development
    (ASTD), 12, 92, 204
America Online, 11, 175
Ameritech, 171
Animation, 50
Animation Magazine, 62
Animator Pro, 6
Animators, 8, 30, 59–62,
    215–216
Apple Hypercard, 6, 24, 208,
    212
    game design, 232, 240

picture editing, 94
programming, 225
scriptwriting, 117, 119–120
Art directors, 7, 44–51, 63–70,
    192
*Art of Human-Computer
    Interface Design, The*
    (Laurel), 78
Art technicians, 47
ASIFA (Association
    Internationale du Film
    d'Animation), 12, 62
Association for Educational
    Communication and
    Technology, 92
ASTD (American Society for
    Training and
    Development), 12, 92,
    204
Astound, 122
Asymetrix Multimedia
ToolBook, 6, 100, 117, 201
Austin Area Multimedia
    Alliance, 109
Austin Software Council, 110
Authorware, 57, 192, 201
Autodesk Animator Pro, 6
Autodesk 3D Studio, 6, 45,
    115
AVID, 11
Axcess, 110

Backes, Michael, 139–149
Baker and Taylor, 7, 134
Basic, 100, 192, 208
BBSs (Bulletin board services),
    10–11
Benton, Randi, 170–172
Bergman, Robert E., 92
Bertelsmann Music Group, 6

Beta testers, 38, 41
Big Top Productions, 37–42
Blaine, David, 175–180
Blank, Deborah, 79–92
Boorstyn, Neil, 161
Boorstyn on Copyright
    (Boorstyn), 161
Brand, Stewart, 132, 174
Brinson, J. Dianne, 138, 161
Brøderbund, 135, 170–171
Bulletin board services
    (BBSs), 10–11
Business uses. *See* Employee
    training; Marketing;
    specific topics
Byron Preiss Multimedia,
    229, 231
Byte, 13, 99

C, 101, 192, 225
C++, 192, 225
Cable companies, 27
Cakewalk, 107
California School for the
    Arts, 62
Canter, Marc, 22–27
Career preparation, 10–20.
    See also Professional
    associations; Professional
    reading; Skills;
    *specific people and
    topics*
computer expertise, 10
content expertise, 14
education, 14, 62, 89
internships, 13–14, 47
on-line access, 10–12
press coverage, 13
product study, 10, 48
prototype creation, 15

Riley Guide, 15–20
trade shows, 12, 36, 61, 99, 138
writing, 14
Case study
  participants, 207–216
  planning, 217–220
  product integration, 227
  production, 222–223
  programming, 225–227
  quality assurance, 228, 230
  visuals, 223–225
  writing, 220–222
CBT. *See* Computer-based training
CBT Express, 201
CD Plus, 179
CD-ROM Producer, 13
CD-ROM Professional, 138
CD-ROM World, 51
CD Today, 51
Chapter Notes (IICS), 57
Child, 42
Cognitive psychology, 89
Color, 70
Commercial on-line services, 11, 175
Communication Arts, 36, 105
Compel, 122
Composers, 106–110
Compton's New Media, 7, 135
CompuServe, 11, 175
Computer animators, 8, 59–62
Computer-based training (CBT), 81-82, 192, 199. *See also* Employee training
Computer expertise, 10, 48
Computer Game Developers Conference, 12, 36
Computer Gaming World, 51, 62
Computer graphic artists, 8
Computer Law Association, 162
Computer Law Association Bulletin, The, 162
Computer Lawyer, The, 162
Computer Retail Week, 42
Computer Weekly, 42
Computing, 180
Conferences. *See* Trade shows
Consumer Electronics Show, 12

Content experts, 8, 14, 82–83
Content outline, 54
Convergence, 12
Copyright law, 154
CorelDraw, 57
Corkboard, 119
Courchesne, Luc, 184
C Programming Language, The (Kernighan & Ritchie), 101
Creative directors, 62
Credit issues, 50
Cyberclubs, 22
Cyberspace Lexicon, The: An Illustrated Dictionary of Terms (Cotton & Oliver), 122

Davidson, 39
De-Babelizer, 60
Debugging, 104, 228, 230
Deluxe Paint, 45
Demystifying Multimedia (Haykin), 138
Design Mirage, 6–7
Desktop video editors, 8
Developers, 7, 8, 37–42
De Wulf, Frédéric, 102
Digital Hollywood, 138
Digital Imaging, 42
Digital Media, 138
Digital media artists, 46
Digital Voodoo, 106–110
Digital World, 138
Director (Macromedia), 6, 22, 24, 35, 57, 122, 192, 225
Director (Macromind), 60, 100, 208
Distribution, 133–138, 154, 228–229
Distributors, 7
Dondis, Donis A., 78
Doom, 139, 141, 142, 146

E3 (Electronic Entertainment Expo), 138
Eames, Charles, 77
Eames, Ray, 77
Educational multimedia, 5
Education for multimedia careers, 14, 62, 89, 99
Edutainment, 5, 37–42
Electronic Art Deluxe Paint, 45
Electronic Arts, 135
Electronic Entertainment Expo (E3), 138

Electronic Learning Factilitators (ELF), 79–92
Electronic mail, 11
Electronic Musician, 110
Electronic Performance Support Systems (EPSS), 202–203
Electronic Publishing, 42
ELF (Electronic Learning Factilitators), 79–92
E-mail, 11
Emerging Distribution Models for Consumer Interactive Media (Aston, Swaminathan, & Tamer), 138
Employee training, 5–6, 53–54, 69, 165–166, 199–204
  instructional designers, 8, 79–92, 192
Ensoniq SoundScape, 107
Entertainment Law and Finance, 162
Entertainment Law Reporter, The, 162
Entertainment software, 5
Envisioning Information (Tufte), 78
EPSS (Electronic Performance Support Systems), 202–203
Equilibrium De-Babelizer, 60
Equity-based compensation, 152
Erdmann, Bridget, 59–62
Essence of Decision (Allison), 196
Evaluation, 84
Evans, Bruce H., 186
Evans, Dave, 106–110
Evans, Jennifer, 106–110
Excel, 57
Executive producers, 22–36
Executive recruitment, 188–193
Eye, 183

Family Portrait (Courchesne), 184
Fathom Pictures, 43
Fedworld, 17
Filemaker Pro, 94
Film, 140–145, 149, 152–153, 219
Filmmaker Pro, 57
Flow charts, 54, 118

Focus groups, 38
Fodor's Travel Publications, 171
Foreign languages, 3
Fractal Design Painter, 6, 60
Freelancers, 11, 56, 88, 100
  animators, 215–216
  sound designers, 108, 109
Freitag, Walter, 231–245
Functional specification, 54
Furuhasi, Teiji, 185
Future of multimedia, 69, 115, 172, 248–250
  accessibility, 35, 43
  advertising, 131–132
  distribution, 136–137
  employee training, 203
  games, 51, 148–149
  industry control, 197–198
  marketing, 101
  recording industry, 179–180
  technological advances, 116

Gabriel, Peter, 178
Gadget, 148
Gahan Wilson's The Ultimate Haunted House, 206, 229, 231–232, 243–245
Game designers, 8, 98, 231–242
Game Developers Conference, 12, 36
Game Over: How Nintendo Conquered the World (Sheff), 51
Game theory, 196–197
Gender differences, 85, 146
Getting Started in Multimedia Training (Hall), 203
Gibson, William, 174
Gold Disk Astound, 122
Gopher, 18
Gould, Stephen J., 92
Graphic designers, 8, 63–70, 181–183, 192
Graphis, 36

Hall, Brandon, 199–204
Hare, Garry, 43
"Hats" (Wurman), 78
Hawkins, Trip, 194–198
Heller, Joel, 223, 227, 229
Herr, Laurin, 208
High Fidelity, 180
Hollywood. *See* Film

Home Studio, 107
Hone, Bob, 111–116
Hook Up, Get Hired: The Internet Job Search Revolution (Kennedy), 15
HotWired, 174
Hypercard. *See* Apple Hypercard

ICD Publishing, 203
IconAuthor, 201
I.D. (International Design), 183
IICS (International Interactive Communications Society), 12, 92, 110, 138, 162, 193, 204
IICS Reporter, 162
Illustrator, 6, 35, 208
Illustrators, 8. *See also* Animators; Graphic designers
IMA (Interactive Multimedia Association), 138, 162
Independent contractors, 40
Information Anxiety (Wurman), 78
Information designers, 8, 71–78
Information Superhighway, 27. *See also* Internet
Ingram Micro D, 7, 134
Inspiration, 54, 57, 119
Instructional designers, 8, 79–92, 192. *See also* Employee training
Intellectual property rights, 154–155, 156, 160–161
Interaction designers, 71–78
Interactive Content, 162
Interactive Multimedia Association (IMA), 138, 162
Interactive press kits (IPKs), 181–182
Interactive scriptwriters, 8, 54, 117–122
Interactivity, 4, 115, 195. *See also specific topics*
  and advertising, 125, 126–127, 128
  and game design, 241–242
  and instruction, 80–81
  interface design, 84–85
  museums, 184–185
  and music videos, 23, 25–26

  recording industry, 179
  and video, 114
Interactivity, 162
Interface design, 84–85, 227
*inter*media, 12
Intermedia, 138
International Interactive Communications Society (IICS), 12, 92, 110, 138, 162, 193, 204
International MIDI Association, 110
Internet, 5, 11, 27. *See also* On-line world; World Wide Web
  job resources on, 15–20
  recording industry, 175–176
Internships, 13–14, 47
IPKs (Interactive press kits), 181–182
Iris Universe, 13
Irwin, Terry, 63–70

Jewels of the Oracle, 168–169
Journal of Interactive Instruction Development, 92
Judson Rosebush Company, 206–246
Jurassic Park, 143–144
Just Grandma and Me, 33

Karam, David, 181–183
Karstedt, Lucinda, 38
Kelly, Kevin, 149
Kennedy, Joyce Lain, 15
Knowledge Adventure, 171
Knowledge engineers, 202–203
Koenig, Joel, 188–191
Konkle, Kathy, 215–216, 223–224
Krasilovsky, M. William, 180

Labels, 179
Language labs, 3
Lanza, Barbara, 231–245
Laser disks, 3
Laurel, Brenda, 78
Lead programmers, 97
Learning Company, 39, 50
Legend Entertainment, 171
Licensing, 39, 40
Linden, Steve, 28–36
Lingo, 6
Lip-synching, 61
Listservs, 19

Liu, Philip, 6
Living Books, 28–31, 59–62, 170–171
London, Barbara, 184–185
Los Angeles Times, The, 13
Lovers, The (Furuhasi), 185
LucasArts, 44–51

MacFlow, 119
Macintosh. *See* Platform differences
Macromedia, 22, 23–24
Macromedia Authorware, 57, 192, 201
Macromedia Director, 6, 22, 24, 35, 57, 122, 192, 225
Macromedia International Users Conference, 12
Macromedia SoundEdit Pro, 35
Macromind Director, 60, 100, 208
MacToolKit Corkboard, 119
MacUser, 13
MacWeek, 62, 99
Macworld, 12, 36, 61
Macworld, 62
Magic of Interactive Entertainment, The (Morrison), 110
Magic Pen, 6
Mainstay MacFlow, 119
Managing Interactive Video/Multimedia Projects (Bergman & Moore), 92
Mandala, David, 58
Manufacturing, 39
Marketing, 5, 12, 39, 53, 117–122, 163–169
case studies, 168–169, 213–215
McCarthy, J. Thomas, 161
McCarthy on Trademarks and Unfair Competition (McCarthy), 161
McConnell, Ericka, 93–96
McMillan, Sam, 117–122
MDG (Multimedia Development Group), 138
MechADeus, 100–101
MediaBand, 23, 25–26
Media Lab, The (Brand), 132, 174
Merisel, 7, 134
Metcalfe, Jane, 173–174

Michaud, Collette, 44–51
Microsoft, 6, 229
Microsoft Access, 57, 192
Microsoft Excel, 57
Microsoft Home, 7
Microsoft PowerPoint, 122
Microsoft Word, 57, 208
MIDI software, 24, 107, 108
Mint Museum of Art, 186–187
Mix, 110
Modernist design, 67–68
Moore, Thomas V., 92
Moore's Law, 116
Morph's Outpost, 138
Mosaic, 11
Moses, Jay, 206
MPEG standard, 115
Multimedia. *See also specific topics*
definitions of, 2–4, 27, 34, 82, 195
forms of, 4–6
Multimedia, 51
Multimedia and Technology Licensing Law Report, 162
Multimedia Applications Development: Using Indeo Video and DVI Technology (Bunzel & Morris), 138
Multimedia Demystified (Haykin), 138
Multimedia Developers Group, 162
Multimedia Development Group (MDG), 138
Multimedia law, 40, 150–162
clearance, 159–160
deal structures, 151–154
intellectual property rights, 154–155, 156, 160–161
professional reading, 161–162
Multimedia Law and Practice (Scott), 138
Multimedia Law Handbook (Brinson & Radcliffe), 138, 161
Multimedia Law Reporter, The, 162
Multimedia Producer, 13, 57, 92
Multimedia Recruiters, USA, 192–193
Multimedia ToolBook, 6, 100, 117, 201

Multimedia World, 138, 162
Museum Computer Network, 187
Museum News, 187
Museum of Modern Art (MOMA), 184–185
Museums, 184–187
Music
music videos, 23
recording industry, 175–180
sound designers, 8, 34, 106–110
Myrick, Jake, 37–42
Myst, 113

Nathan, Deb, 58
National Society for Performance and Instruction (NSPI), 204
NetWorld+Interop, 12
Neuromancer (Gibson), 174
New Media Expo, 138
NewMedia Magazine, 13, 36, 51, 57, 62, 92, 110, 138, 162, 193
Newsgroups, 11
New York Times, The, 13
Nimmer, David, 161
Nimmer, Melville B., 161
Nimmer on Copyright (Nimmer & Nimmer), 161
Nintendo, 26
Nonlinearity, 3–4
NSPI (National Society for Performance and Instruction), 204

Ocean Voyager, 206, 216, 218, 223–225, 228, 230
One-to-One Futures (Pepper), 174
On-Line Design, 183
On-line world, 4, 10–12, 129, 175–176
On-screen talent, 8
Out of Control (Kelly), 149
Owners of content, 7
Oziel, Sid, 168–169

Paik, June, 184
Painter, 6, 60
Paper materials, 87
Passman, Donald, 180
Patent law, 154–155
Patent Law Fundamentals (Rosenberg), 161

PC Week, 99, 180
PC World, 13, 99
Peddie, Britt, 97–101
Pepper, Don, 174
Performance, 77–78
Phone companies, 27
Photographers, 8
Photo researchers, 8, 93–96
Photoshop, 6, 35, 45, 57, 60, 93, 94, 96, 208, 224
Picture editors, 8, 93–96
Picture researchers, 8, 93–96
Pilot testing, 84
Platform differences, 25, 46, 140
PolyGram Records, 175–180
Post, 57
Post Tools, 181–183
PowerPoint, 122
Powers of Ten (Eames & Eames), 77
Premiere, 6, 35, 45, 93, 96, 208
Press, 13
Primer of Visual Literacy, A (Dondis), 78
Prince, 178
Print, 36
Prodigy, 11
Producers, 7, 8, 207–209
Production managers. *See* Project managers
Professional associations, 12, 36
    animators, 62
    distribution, 138
    employee training, 92, 204
    multimedia law, 162
    museums, 187
    programmers, 101
    sound designers, 109, 110
Professional reading, 27–28, 36, 197
    advertising, 132
    animators, 62
    distribution, 138
    edutainment, 42, 51
    employee training, 92, 203
    graphic designers, 70, 183
    multimedia law, 161–162
    programmers, 99, 101
    publishers, 174
    quality assurance, 105
    recording industry, 180, 183
    scriptwriters, 122
    sound designers, 110

Program designers, 97
Programmers, 97–101, 192, 209–213, 225–227
Project managers, 7, 8, 34, 47, 52–58, 62, 81
Prototypes, 15
Publishers, 7, 170–174
Publishers Weekly, 36

Quality assurance, 102–105, 228, 230
Quality hallmarks, 65, 116
    advertising, 125
    ease-of-use, 35, 196
    edutainment, 39
    employee training, 87–88
    interactivity, 4, 139
    video games, 145
Quark, 94
Quest, 192, 201
QuickTime, 96, 115
Quittner, Josh, 249

Radcliffe, Mark F., 138, 150–162
Rand, Paul, 70
Random House, 170–172
Rebel Assault, 49
Receptionists, 41
Recording industry, 175–183
Reingold, Howard, 174
Renewal rights, 157
Repertoire labels, 179
Reporter, The (IICS), 57
Researchers, 8
Retrospect, 94
Rhode Island School of Design, 62
Rights of personality, 151
Rights of publicity, 151
Riley, Margaret, 15–20
Ritchie, Kirsten, 8
Rogers, Ronn, 192-193
Rolling Stone, 180
Rosebush, Judson, 206, 207–209, 217–218, 219–220, 221, 222–223, 225–226, 246
Rose, Lance, 180
Rosenberg, Peter, 161
Rosetto, Louis, 173
Rundgren, Todd, 178, 179
RVAT, 225

Sabella, Frank, 163–167
SABROCO Interactive, 163–165

Satterlee, Mark, 52-57
Schelling, Tom, 196
Schlanger, Matthew, 209–211, 221, 224, 226–227
Schmitt, Dominic, 206, 216, 219
Scriptwriters, 8, 54, 117–122, 147–148. *See also* Game designers
Security issues, 5
SGI (Silicon Graphics). *See* Platform differences
Shedroff, Nathan, 71–78
Shemel, Sidney, 180
Sheridan, 62
Shono-san, 148
SIGGRAPH, 12, 36
Silicon Graphics (SGI). *See* Platform differences
Skills, 34, 45-46, 208
    advertising, 129, 130–131
    art directors, 48
    executive recruitment, 188–190
    information designers, 77–78
    instructional designers, 86, 89–90
    marketing, 163
    picture editors/researchers, 95
    producers, 31
    project managers, 55–56
    publishers, 172
Smethurst, Michael, 211–213, 221, 222
SMPTE, 57
SoftImage, 45
Software piracy, 40
Software Publishers Association, 36
S.O.S., 133–138
Sound designers, 8, 34, 106–110
Sound Edit, 208
Sound editors, 8
SoundEdit Pro, 35
SoundScape, 107
Spectra, 187
Stereo Review, 180
Storyboard, 54–55, 83
Streim, Sandy, 213–215
StudioGraphics, 52–57
Subject-matter experts (SMEs), 8, 14, 82–83
Superstores, 136–137

SysLaw (Rose & Wallace), 180

Tamer, Joanna, 133–138
Tech Data, 134
Technical specifications, 221–222
Technology licensing, 194–198
Telecommuting, 11
Television, 26–27, 116, 148, 150–151, 197
Telnet, 17
Testing, 102–105, 228, 230
Tetris, 146
Third Wave, The (Toffler), 71
This Business of Music (Shemel & Krasilovsky), 180
3D Studio, 6, 45, 115
Time, 42
Time-Warner, 7
Toffler, Alvin, 71
Tom Nicholson Associates, 93, 94–96
Trademark law, 155
Trade secrets, 155
Trade shows, 12, 36, 61, 99, 138
Treatments, 220–221, 237–238
Tufte, Edward, 78
Twelve Tone System Cakewalk, 107

Twelve Tone System Home Studio, 107
Typography, 8, 66, 68, 69

Understanding Hypermedia (Cotton & Oliver), 122
Upfront, 45
US Atlas (Wurman), 77
USA Today, 42
Usenet, 16–17

Viacom, 6, 7
Video games, 5, 145–148
Videographers, 8
Videography, 57
Video Installation: Eight Artists, 185
Video producers, 111–116
Video specialists, 46
Video technicians, 46
VideoWorks, 23. *See also* Macromedia
Viola, Bill, 185
Virtual Community: Homesteading on the Electric Frontier (Reingold), 174
Virtual companies, 88, 109
Virtual Fighter, 143
Visual Basic, 100, 192, 208
Visual Display of Quantitative Information, The (Tufte), 78

Vivid Publishing, 71–78
VizAbility: Experiences in Visual Thinking, 63, 66
Voice-over talent, 8, 106–110
Voyager, 93, 94, 95
Voyetra Technology WinDat, 107

Wallace, Jonathan, 180
Wall Street Journal, The, 13
War in Vietnam, The, 206, 218, 222, 223, 225–226, 227, 228, 229
Watson, Marcia, 102–105
White, Mike, 124–132
Wilson Learning Systems, 203
WinDat, 107
Windows. *See* Platform differences
Wired, 13, 36, 51, 62, 110, 138, 162, 173–174, 180
Word (Microsoft), 57, 208
Work orders, 224
World Wide Web, 5, 19–20, 176
Wurman, Richard Saul, 77, 78
Wu, Yee-Ping, 6